Multicultural education in colleges and universities: a
transdisciplinary approach.

MULTICULTURAL EDUCATION IN COLLEGES AND UNIVERSITIES

A TRANSDISCIPLINARY APPROACH

MULTICULTURAL EDUCATION IN COLLEGES AND UNIVERSITIES

A TRANSDISCIPLINARY APPROACH

Edited by

Howard Ball
University of Vermont

S. D. Berkowitz
University of Fort Hare
University of Vermont

Mbulelo Mzamane
University of Fort Hare
University of Vermont

 LAWRENCE ERLBAUM ASSOCIATES, PUBLISHERS
1998   Mahwah, New Jersey   London

Lawrence Erlbaum Associates, Inc., Publishers
10 Industrial Avenue
Mahwah, New Jersey 07430

Cover design by Kathryn Houghtaling Lacey

Library of Congress Cataloging-in-Publication Data

Multicultural education in colleges and universities : a
transdisciplinary approach / edited by Howard Ball, S. D.
Berkowitz, Mbulelo Mzamane.
    p.   cm.
Includes bibliographical references and index.
ISBN 0-8058-1693-3 (c : alk. paper). — ISBN 0-8058-1694-1
(pbk. : alk. paper)
    1. Multicultural education—United States. 2. Multicul-
turalism—Study and teaching (Higher)—United States. 3.
Pluralism (Social sciences)—Study and teaching
(Higher)—United States. 4. Education, Higher—United
States. I. Ball, Howard. II. Berkowitz, S. D. III. Mzamane,
Mbulelo.
    LC1099.3.M836   1998
    370.117'0973—dc21   97-31207
                                                            CIP

Books published by Lawrence Erlbaum Associates are printed
on acid-free paper, and their bindings are chosen for strength
and durability.

Printed in the United States of America
10 9 8 7 6 5 4 3 2 1

Contents

v

Preface

This volume provides readers with both an overview of the core dilemma in America—racism, and the deadly impact it has had on U.S. society—and an account of the ways in which we have attempted to deal with it in our own teaching practices. Two core chapters—by Berkowitz and Barrington and by Loewen—explore the theoretical and historical issues involved in defining "races" and "ethnic groups" in the West and issues of racial and ethnic inequality in U.S. society. It then examines a variety of strategies for "teaching the conflicts" in comparative literature and politics (Mzamane), African American literature (Dickerson), law, history, and political science (Ball), sociology (Danigelis), religion (Gussner), economics (McCrate), anthropology (Mahler), art (Rubin), and music (Ambrose). Mzamane advocates doing this by linking the study of comparative literature to the study of worldwide liberation struggles. These, he contends, can be linked back, in the minds of students, to the struggles of racial or ethnic minorities in the United States. Dickerson contends that the teaching of Africanism is inextricably bound up with teaching of Americanness in literature. She accomplishes this through a series of assignments that seek to engage the students in a series of encounters with "racialness." Ball argues that racism itself is the defining aspect of U.S. life. In addition to analyzing the role of racism in law and politics, he adds to this "analytic/historical component of [his] course" an "empathy paper" that seeks to move the student, through imagination, toward a more intuitive appreciation of the pains and disabilities brought about by racism. Danigelis describes his teaching practice in which he identifies three conceptual objectives: distinguishing theory from ideology, framing the key concepts, and applying ideas about race in the classroom. He carries out these objectives, in part, through the use of highly structured debates or conflicts that bring students' theoretical knowledge into articulation with their own environments. Gussner argues that we need to "recontextualize" the study of liberal and religious reform action in order to formulate new models of multiethnic education and understand minority religious movements. McCrate looks at inequality in America and argues that, in order to understand racism, we must find its roots in economic activities such as in the operation of labor markets. Mahler contends that ethnographic fieldwork provides an excellent way for students to explore other subcultures and to develop insights into differences among them. Rubin and Ambrose both find—Rubin in the area of visual art and Ambrose in the area of music—that the arts, as well as the humanities and social sciences, can be successfully used to involve students in concrete crosscultural comparison. Finally, Diouf and Berkowitz provide summaries of what we have learned both practically and theoretically about the pedagogy of a multicultural, transdisciplinary approach to education.

The approach we put forth here recognizes the fact that, in an ethnically plural society, specific subject matters and courses must reflect an amalgam of the cultures of the peoples who comprise that society. Multicultural education in America must address the structured inequality in our society, an inequality that preceded the formation of the Republic in 1787. Multicultural education contributes to the elevation of knowledge. It requires that our students know more about the world, not less, than we do.

This type of education, we feel, must be transdisciplinary, based on the perspectives offered by a multiplicity of interrelated disciplines. Clearly, scholars have a great deal to learn from one another about race and ethnicity in America and their implications for how individuals deal with one another in U.S. society. However, the current state of communication between scholars in the humanities, fine arts, social sciences, and natural science disciplines leads to a variety of anomalous situations. Another task of this book is to share knowledge about race and ethnicity with colleagues in order to provide them with relevant, correct information about these issues and their consequences for individuals living in America.

Furthermore, we cannot have a marginalization of the accomplishments of people of color in the effort to overcome racism in America. We must provide our students and ourselves with the knowledge gathered up and written about by W. E. B. DuBois, bell hooks, Malcolm X, Gandhi, Frantz Fanon, and others. There is a desperate need to combine knowledge about racism derived from the various liberal arts and science disciplines. In responding to this need, there must be a systematization of the products of research into questions of race, ethnicity, class, and gender in such a way that these data can be communicated and used by others in teaching the conflicts in college classrooms (Cain, 1994).

Multicultural education is exactly what America, with its ethnic pluralism, needs in order to spread the rights of citizenship to all persons and be competitive in a world that is changing at a rapid pace—a world that is truly a global village. This book is an effort to encourage university educators to understand the challenges we face as a society, and to be idealistic enough to want to draw upon the various strengths of our culture to assist in the remaking of U.S. democracy. *Not* overcoming racism, and *not* freeing up America's vigor, idealism, audacity, and vision is, we feel, a tremendous waste of natural and human resources.

Creating a program in multicultural transdisciplinary studies, of necessity, causes one to incur a range of intellectual debts. In addition to academic study, much of our thinking on race and ethnicity was shaped by participation in the movements for civil rights in each of three countries on two continents—Canada, the United States, and South Africa. Over the years we have benefited from advice and counsel from a number of people we have met in the course of these struggles. Ball would like to thank Ron Coleman, Bill Giles, Kate Green, Tom Lauth, Carl A. Lee, Charles and Suzie Lowery, and Sid Salter. Berkowitz feels indebted to David Barrington, Donald Black, Moustapha Diouf, Tom Hayden, Nancy Howell, Bal Jeffrey, Sharon Jeffrey, Helen Stone, and Don Wilkinson. Mzamane wishes to acknowledge his indebtedness to the late Steve Biko, Njabulo Ndebele, Mongane Serote, Sam Shakong, Houston Baker, Huck Gutman, and Rob Gordon. As usual, without the inspiration, support, and tolerance of our wives—Carol Ball, Terry Berkowitz, and Nthoana Mzamane—none of this could have been accomplished. How each of these wives turned out to be married to an insomniac workaholic diabetic is a mystery we may never solve.

—Howard Ball
—S. D. Berkowitz
—Mbulelo Mzamane

REFERENCE

Cain, W. (Ed.). (1994). *Teaching the conflicts: Gerald Graff, curricular reform, and the culture wars.* New York: Garland.

Introduction: Multicultural Transdisciplinary Education

Howard Ball
University of Vermont

S. D. Berkowitz
University of Fort Hare
University of Vermont

Mbulelo Mzamane
University of Fort Hare
University of Vermont

BACKGROUND

On April 18, 1988, a group of African, Latino, Asian, and Native American (ALANA) students occupied the offices of the president, the provost, and the other top executive officers of the University of Vermont (UVM).[1] This occupation followed months of frustrating and largely fruitless negotiations between the president's office and these students regarding not so much the goals but the specific "bread and butter issues" that needed to be addressed in order to bring about significant changes in both the composition of the student body at UVM and the sensitivity of all parts of the university community to issues of race and culture.

This occupation—and the negotiations that President Lattie Coor entered into with the ALANA students involved in an effort to resolve their differences—reached an impasse by Thursday, April 21. The unresolved issues included the mechanisms to be used in establishing goals for ALANA student enrollment at the university, recruitment of ALANA faculty to tenure-track positions, the creation of an effective program in ethnic studies, and—an especially complex issue—the

---

[1]The term "ALANA" is an acronym for "African, Latino, Asian, and Native American." The University of Vermont now has an ALANA Studies program.

establishment of a "program on race relations and ethnic diversity of approximately 3 weeks duration" to be "offered to all entering freshmen [*sic*] beginning with the Fall semester of 1988."

In order to resolve these issues, three faculty members—Professor H. Lawrence McCrorey of Allied Health Sciences, and Professors S. D. Berkowitz and Samuel F. Sampson of the Department of Sociology—were brought in to mediate the dispute. By the early hours of Friday morning, April 22, an agreement had been reached on particulars, and a series of activities were set in motion in order to carry out that agreement. In a very concrete and direct sense, both this book and the approach to multicultural studies it proposes are outgrowths of this agreement.

Of course, none of the changes outlined in the April 22 agreement happened in precisely the way envisioned by the university administrators, students, or faculty mediators who were directly involved in the original dispute. The process of generating social change within a university has, correctly we think, been likened to moving a cemetery: Old modes of thinking and ways of doing things make sudden shifts almost impossible. The structure of U.S. universities (and UVM is no exception) is a complex admixture of the forms taken by medieval guilds, early European trading companies, New England missionary churches, and modern conglomerate corporations; with a dash, in this region, of the New England town meeting thrown in for good measure. In a place where "freemen" (now "electors" or "freepersons") argue effortlessly and interminably about potholes and fixing the snowplow, it was a foregone conclusion that no such agreement would be implemented without considerable discussion.

Consequently, neither the April 22 agreement nor the process whereby it had been reached were universally acclaimed by UVM faculty. As faculty usually (but students seldom) understand, at most universities the creation of new curriculum is a faculty prerogative. Hence, university presidents can rarely commit their institutions to specific curriculum changes without the active concurrence and support of a substantial part of the faculty. This faculty prerogative is jealously guarded at UVM. Thus, it soon became clear that the most controversial part of the agreement—the mandatory one-credit, 3-week course in race and ethnic studies—was going to run into serious opposition within the university's largest unit: the College of Arts and Sciences.

By December 1989, three of the university's eight colleges required their students to take the one-credit course stipulated in the agreement. This course had been designed, in the interim, by a team of faculty drawn from across the campus. But the College of Arts and Sciences refused to follow this lead for a variety of reasons. Some faculty objected to any curricular change that had its origins in an "illegal act" (i.e., the occupation of the executive offices). Some felt that, under the best of circumstances, such a course would "have to be" superficial, and that this course would seem anomalous in a place where almost all courses carried three or four credits. Others (and this was the most substantial group) felt that if a majority of the faculty felt that a course in race and ethnic studies was an important component of a liberal education, it should be on the same footing as other courses.

In addition, the faculty of Arts and Sciences had practical and pedagogical objections to the one-credit course. As the largest college in the university, Arts and Sciences would have to devote considerable resources to teaching this one-credit course. These resources would have to take the form of additional academic appointments in, at most, two or three departments that had traditionally taught courses in the area. Because these departments—such as anthropology and sociology—are moderately small at UVM, by national standards, they would be seriously unbalanced by the addition of the three to four faculty members needed to staff this number of full-time equivalent enrollments (FTEs). No department wanted to become the "Department of Race and Ethnicity." Moreover, pedagogically, the faculty thought that a required course in this potentially volatile area would sit better with those students who might not have taken such a course in the past if it began "where they were at" (i.e., in their several fields and concentrations). Thus, the college began the process of identifying what human resources existed in each of a dozen or so fields who might be turned to the task of introducing students to the problems of race and ethnicity in America.

Thus, at this time a process was set in motion that resulted in the creation of a transdisciplinary approach to multicultural education. Although not unique to UVM, it was felt that this approach more adequately reflected how Arts and Science faculty, as scholars and teachers, thought multicultural education in general ought to go on in this country, rather than any single course or an unstructured set of such courses might.

As a result—and after much handwringing, philippic argument, proposals, counterproposals, and outside review—the faculty voted in February 1991 that each student in the college be required to complete one three-credit course on race and ethnic studies in partial fulfillment of his or her bachelor's degree. In contrast to the usual procedure, however, this course was to be selected from a broad list of courses in a wide range of fields.

With the passage of this motion, UVM began its experiment in transdisciplinary multicultural education. From the beginning, the self-identified faculty cohort involved in this experiment—assembled by Deans Howard Ball and James Lubker—felt it necessary to share ideas and develop a core of common materials and approaches to presenting this subject to students, albeit from the vantage point of each of several disciplines.

WHAT IS TRANSDISCIPLINARY MULTICULTURAL EDUCATION?

"We are kept prisoner by society," Berger (1963) said, "only to the extent to which we permit ourselves to remain ignorant of its influence over us. With knowledge and understanding of the way in which society operates, we can begin to free ourselves of its controls" (p. vii). Ironically, although so many are imprisoned by modes of thinking rooted in stratification based on race, ethnicity, religion, class, and gender, we are experiencing what Diouf (chap. 3, this volume) refers to as the "Browning of America." By the year 2020, Diouf notes, "white Americans will become a statistical minority in the United States." As Diouf further relates, according to the most recent population projections, by the end of the 20th century, "Asian Americans will increase by an estimated 22%, Hispanics by 21%, blacks by almost 12%, and whites by only a little more than 2%."

At the same time, these imprisoning modes of thinking have clearly diminished the lives of all people living in this country. As McCrorey (1994) argued:

> By severely limiting our views, by keeping us from knowing each other, and by teaching us to react to images and inventions rather than seeking truths, [racism] has distorted our perceptions and forced us into a "we" and "they" mentality. The great [educational] institutions of the country have the responsibility to lead the way, to act as change agents, to undo this horrible web. This endeavor calls for an intellectual community of equals, with the right and responsibility to teach and to learn from each other. [Multiculturalism] in its fullest, most expansive form is essential for the creation of such a community.

To begin to think of accomplishing this task, educators must be, in John F. Kennedy's words, "idealists without illusions": They must combine academic knowledge with social responsibility. This view is, to some extent, a radical one in U.S. education. Educational traditionalists have not appreciated the linkage between universities' academic and social missions. The traditional assumption is that "legitimate academic work" should not be consciously tied to immediate political or social considerations—unless, of course, this work supports prevailing structural and ideological arrangements.

In order to build a nonracial community, however, we must devise an educational strategy that enables our students to effectively combat racism by looking at and understanding its effects from a number of different perspectives. The answers to the conundrum of racism, Cisneros (1994) maintained, "are not found in confrontation, obstruction, or denying access, but rather in inclusion, cooperation, providing facts, and trying to build a common stake in the future."

Educators, as a group, find overcoming an entrenched set of traditional cultural patterns a daunting task, because racism is part of society's institutional fabric. Thus, a strategy designed to overcome it must have, at its core, the notion of *pure democracy*: the absence of institutional hierarchies based on race, ethnicity, religion, class, gender, or anything other than a person's character or merit. In our classrooms, we face students who have, for the most part, been taught to become what Karenga called "vulgar careerists." They have been taught to fit into an institutional framework that incorporates racial-, ethnic-, religious-, class-, and gender-based hierarchies. Their education in multiculturalism is little more than a series of clichés, buzzwords, and enduring stereotypes. To overcome this, we must reorient their ways of thinking to accommodate to a new and/or prospective reality in which these traditional hierarchies will become less prevalent or significant.

West (cited in Gates, 1996) observed, correctly, that "so many white brothers and sisters are living in a state of denial in terms of how deep white supremacy is seated in their culture and society [that] we recognize that in a fundamental sense we really do live in different worlds" (p. 57). These two worlds are separate and unequal, as the Kerner Commission concluded in 1968. Whites live in a world, as novelist Reed (cited in Gates, 1996) noted, "where the police don't lie [and] don't plant evidence" (p. 57). It is a world in which, as white author Podhoretz (cited in Gates, 1996) noted, "Power is on my side, that the police are working for me and not for them" (p. 58). Podhoretz's "them" are the tens of millions of African Americans and other racial minorities who live in the other, unequal world. It is a world where, as older African Americans used to say, "When white folks say 'justice,' they mean 'just us'" (cited in Gates, 1996, p. 58).

Our task as educators is to pierce the veil of clichés and stereotypes held by our students by any means necessary, in order to overcome the consequences of racial and class discrimination in America. If we fail in this mission, then the two separate and unequal worlds will surely violently collide. We must not fail.

This book is an effort to address the significant pedagogical challenge we face as men and women who believe our merit, rather than our race, class, or religion, is what shall be used as the measure of quality and success. It is not an easy task to convince people of this—but it is well worth pursuing.

REFERENCES

Berger, P. (1963). *Invitation to sociology: A humanistic perspective.*
Gates, H. L., Jr. (1996, October 26). Annals of race: Thirteen ways of looking at a black man. *The New Yorker.*

I

The Core:
Race, Ethnicity,
and Their Consequences

1

Race and Ethnicity: Intergroup Relations in a Multi-Ethnic Society

S. D. Berkowitz
University of Fort Hare
University of Vermont

David Barrington
University of Vermont

The concept of race has been used since ancient times to refer to a wide variety of types of human groups: tribes (Celts, Sioux, Kikuyu), nations (the English, Germans, Spaniards), language groupings (Semitic, Slavic, Bantu), cultures ("Greeks" or "Romans"), religious minorities (Jews, Maronite Christians), and groups of similar-appearing people of mixed genetic backgrounds ("whites," "blacks," "yellows," "coloreds"). In fact, there is hardly a distinct category of men, women, and children anyplace in the world that has not, at some time or another, been referred to by either itself or by others as a "race."

Despite the persistent and widespread use of the concept, there is little agreement about how it ought to be employed, either among scientists or laypeople. This fact has to do, in part, with the methodological difficulties involved in trying to divide *any* human population up into a set of mutually exclusive and exhaustive categories and, in part, to a long history of the use of the idea of "race" to justify virtually any kind of evil practice—from exclusion to enslavement to expulsion and murder—that can be undertaken by one group against another.[1]

There are two general ways in which the concept of 'race' has been defined at

---

[1]In science, the less that categories of "things" overlap (be "mutually exclusive") and the more they include all such "things" (be "exhaustive"), the better able we are to draw straightforward conclusions about them.

different times and in different places by scientists: biologically, and socially or socioculturally. Those who use biological notions of 'race' maintain that racial groupings are homogeneous, or nearly homogeneous, with respect to important genetic traits; these genetic traits are reflected in things that are easily observed, such as similarities in appearance and behavior; these genetically carried traits can be associated with *cultural* capabilities, including the ability to form and use complex language; and even in multiracial societies, it is possible to detect the influence of these genetically carried traits in the cultural products of individuals.

To biologists who study human evolution, the term *race* has a clear and rather narrow meaning: 'races' are *subspecies* which vary from one another in ways which are biologically significant and systematic. Differences due to chance, or simple observable variation in the proportion of certain genes in a particular population (e.g., the frequency of the occurrence of genes for, say, blue eyes), is not enough to justify a division of a species into subspecies: Such differences must be sharp, geographically based, and must have clear consequences for the adaptability of the species as a whole. Thus, those who maintain that there is a biological basis for the division of our species, *Homo sapiens*, into races have traditionally proposed a series of relatively fixed and unchangeable 'ancestral races'—so-called "fixed types"—that reach back to the beginnings of humankind and from which contemporary racial divisions have evolved (Vander Zanden, 1983).[2] Many of those who have maintained this notion of fixed type racial variation have also been proponents of *polygenism*: the belief that there were multiple origins for our species. In evolutionary terms, polygenism corresponds to the belief that human beings independently evolved from a number of distinct individuals or separate groups of lower primates. As we see later in this chapter, historically there has been a close association between polygenism and a belief in the superiority or inferiority of various races.

After 1950, in the face of mounting biological evidence that it is impossible to separate human populations into these biologically based 'ancestral groups' in any rigorous way, those who maintained that there is a biological basis for racial categories among human beings devised a second, or 'breeding population' theory (Vander Zanden, 1983). Looked upon in this way, those biological 'types' that provide the basis for racial divisions are characteristic of the average tendencies of interbreeding groups within particular geographic areas, and are indicative of the

---

[2]The biologists and anthropologists who support this "fixed-type" model have not, of course, agreed on how many such "ancestral races" there are or were. Researchers have argued, in an equally authoritative tone, for as few as 3 and as many as 30 such races. Coon, Garn, and Birdsell (1950), in what was then considered to be the definitive summary of physical anthropology, argued for the existence of 30 contemporary races. Their typology included: "Murrayian, Ainu, Alpine, N. W. European, N. W. European Prototype, N. E. European, Lapp, Forest Negro, Melanesian, Negrito, Bushman, Bantu, Sudanese, Carpentarian, Dravidian, Hamite, Hindu, Mediterranean, Nordic, N. American Colored, S. African Colored, Classic Mongoloid, N. Chinese, S. E. Asiatic, Tibeto-Indonesian Mongoloid, Turkic, Am. Indian Marginal, Am. Indian Central, Latino, Polynesian, and Neo-Hawaiian" (Coon, Garn, & Birdsell, 1950, p. 117). This typology, obviously, not only violates the scientific rule of parsimony or simplicity, but flies in the face of what we know about human population migration.

commonness of certain phenotypic, or readily observable, traits among them (e.g., hair color). Thus, human "races" are *not* what biologists strictly refer to by the term '*race*,' but instead are closer to what biologists call "breeding populations."[3] This is significant, because "breeding populations" are neither as sharply defined, nor as biologically important, as subspecies.

Those who use the concept of race socioculturally maintain that "races" are significant social categories *because* social groups have attributed meaning to them, *not* because they are meaningful in and of themselves; racial categories vary from society to society and within societies as well; there is no easily observed and unchallengeable biological standard that may be used to sort human populations into racial categories; and there is no demonstrable one-to-one correspondence between racial categories, however defined, and sociocultural traits. Most of the scientists who view race in this fashion belong to what has been referred to as the "no-race" school (Vander Zanden, 1983). These researchers contend that biological differences among human beings are continuous, not discrete—that is to say, there is no sharp break that can be observed in these characteristics—and that there is no simple correspondence between those easily observed characteristics, such as body type, that have traditionally been used to sort human beings into biological races and the "marker genes" for things like blood type that reflect significant common genetic inheritance. Thus, these researchers view observable differences among human beings as the result of random variation and genetic drift (the tendency toward local variation within gene pools), *not* as the result of significant biological pressures. Consequently, most of these researchers have been proponents of *monogenism*: the idea that there was one origin for humankind. In evolutionary terms, monogenism corresponds to the belief that human beings have evolved from one individual or group of lower primates. Historically, monogenists have tended to reject the idea that "races" are important categories for interpreting human behavior.

Much of the debate about the viability of biological theories of race now centers around this question of the multiple or single (polygenic or monogenic) origins of humankind. If, as most scientists believe, *Homo sapiens* evolved from one population of lower primates, the likelihood that it diverged into several subspecies within, say, the last 100,000 years is quite small. If, by contrast, *Homo sapiens* is a by-product of the interbreeding of several distinct, independently evolved, populations of animals ("parallel evolution"), then the existence of distinct subspecies becomes much more plausible.

For those scientists who have viewed race in sociocultural terms, what are interesting and significant are the variations and changes that have occurred in the cultural patterns associated with different human groups. It is this tendency to evolve culturally, scientists contend, that is the single most characteristic aspect of our species. For this reason, those social scientists who study distinct groupings of people in this fashion prefer to use the term "*ethnic group*," rather than what they view as the somewhat old-fashioned and universally misleading term "*race*," to

---

[3]The technical term for these is "*demes*."

describe a group of people living with and marrying one another and sharing a common culture. It is these properties of common residence and culture—not some mythical common biological origin—that provide the true basis for the most striking differences we observe among different human groups.

BIOLOGICAL THEORIES OF RACE IN WESTERN CULTURES: DO THEY WORK?

Throughout history, "biological" notions of race have primarily been used by dominant groups to justify the subjugation of others. The "biological" concept of 'race' is comparatively new to Western Europe: Until the 15th century, 'race' was understood to be a social or cultural term (e.g., one was "Greek" or "Roman" if one was Greek or Roman in culture). Biological notions of 'race' came into being as part of the process of the formation of nation-states. They were used by ruling groups—what we call *dominant elites*—within these emerging modern states to justify the inclusion of some groups of people within a nation and the exclusion, from it, of others. Thus, the *social construction* of a given biologically defined 'race' and the *social construction* of a given 'nation' have, within the West, been part of the same process.[4]

There are several good reasons for this. As the early sociologist Ludwig Gumplowicz (1838–1909) observed, the "state" emerged in Western societies at the end of a long chain of events that began with small blood-kin hordes. These hordes established patterns of superordination and subordination among themselves through a constant process of conquest and accommodation. When, in a given case, this process became well established, it led to the amalgamation of the conquerors and conquered and the transformation of kin domination into class domination (Gumplowicz, 1885/1963). Thus, historically, there was a close association between notions of "peoplehood" and "nation," and it became the first task of the emergent state apparatus to distinguish between the "people of the nation" and others.

In Spain, for instance, the notion of *limpieza de sangre* or "purity of blood" was developed by the Spanish Catholic Church and monarchy for use against nonconforming Jews and Moors during the last phase of the so-called "Reconquest." By the latter part of the 15th century, Spain had been subject to invasion, conquest, and reconquest for more than 900 years. As a result, it had one of the most heterogeneous populations in Europe. Parts of this population—such as some Jews and Moors—had been forcibly converted to Christianity, but had retained an independent group identity. Thus, to distinguish between "old" and, presumably, "true" Christians and "new Christians," the Inquisition concocted a distinction between

---

[4]Note that one meaning of the word "nation" (Latin: *natio*) is "birth race." Nussbaum (1954) noted that the term originally referred, like the term *gens*, to a group sharing common ties. Indeed, in this sense, a "nation" *consisted* of a set of gens, or patrilineal clans. The idea of a *nation-state* that could include more than one nationality was a later development.

them based on ancestry. Since there had been widespread intermarriage between persons who had been of Jewish, Moorish, and Germanic ancestry, this notion of racial purity could be used by the Church in an arbitrary way to attack anyone suspected of less than absolute commitment to the Spanish state or whose wealth and property it coveted (Kamen, 1965). After the "discovery" of the New World, the Spaniards applied this distinction between racially "pure" and racially tainted ancestry to the indigenous population, with the consequence that it became justifiable to enslave or abuse or rob them since they were not of pure Spanish heritage.

During the 18th century, this notion of the division of humankind into biologically separate races was considered again as part of the general increase in interest in science. No less a naturalist than Carl von Linne (Linnaeus, 1707–1778), the Swedish botanist and father of modern biological classification, examined the division of the world's population into a series of racial groups in his *Systema Naturae*. But, even then, Linne contended that these different "varieties of mankind" had more of a cultural than biological basis. Georges Buffon (1707–1788), Linne's contemporary, attributed observable variations in human groups to climate and diet (Buffon, 1780). Johann Friedrich Blumenbach (1752–1840) went further to an almost radical environmentalism (Blumenbach, 1825). Indeed, as Harris (1968) suggested, the 18th-century naturalists in general were hostile to ideas that employed fixed and unchangeable categories that did not allow for the impact of environmental forces on human action. But the educated middle class generally accepted the idea that human populations could be divided into a series of biologically based races and, indeed, such a division was used, in a practical way, to justify the system of slavery in the United States (e.g., Jefferson) and the subjugation of the lower classes in Britain.

In many ways, it was during the 19th century that biologically based notions of race came into their own. One of the earliest writers to seek to make systematic use of a biologically based system of racial classification was Arthur de Gobineau (1816–1883) who, in his *Essai sur l'inégalité des races humaines* (*Essay on the Inequality of Human Races*), took a simple racial typology and systematized it into a theory of "superior" and "inferior" races. This simple schema, in various forms, was then associated with virtually every nationalist impulse down through the 20th century. For instance, Houston Stewart Chamberlain's (1855–1927) *Foundations of the Nineteenth Century* (1907), a simple extrapolation of de Gobineau, was translated into German and used as a virtual training manual for the Prussian officer corps. In this sense, the Nazis represented only an extreme point in a long ideological trend among dominant groups and classes.

More than anything else, Charles Darwin's work brought the issue of the biological basis of human races to the fore. Following the publication of *The Origin of Species* in 1859, there was an explosion of speculation about the relevance of the theory of natural selection to the origins and development of humankind. In the pre-Darwinian era, support for the notion of separate races had come from a *form* of polygenism that contended that each of the "ancestral races of mankind" had been separately created. Opposition to this doctrine came from the traditional, mono-genic Biblical creationists.

With the advent of Darwin's theories, the entire debate was moved into a secular and, specifically, social realm. From the outset, it was clear that Darwinism was incompatible with polygenism because of polygenists' belief in races as fixed types. No group of organisms, Darwinians contended, could remain unchanged in the face of the pressures generated by natural selection. At the same time, Darwinian theory gave comfort to monogenists in that it was extremely unlikely that more than one group of organisms could have evolved in precisely the same way from another group of similar organisms. In his own work specifically on the subject of human origins, *The Descent of Man* (1871), Darwin argued that the separation of human beings into visually observably different groups came about as a result of sexual attraction (e.g., small dark people were attracted to small dark people). Thus, while Darwin rejected the notion that human differentiation was a by-product of natural selection, he did not argue that all groups of human beings were alike or that they were equally capable of all things. Some groups, he contended, contained better admixtures of individuals with certain traits than others.

Even in their clearest and most simple form, then, it is obvious that speculations about the biological basis of humankind could not be divorced from larger social considerations. Moreover, the social thinking of the Victorian Era (1837–1901) was not burdened with self-doubt. As a result, Darwin's work came to be used to justify even the most barbarous examples of Western imperialism and racism. The notion of the "survival of the fittest"—itself an extrapolation of Darwin's ideas by Herbert Spencer[5]—came to be almost a moral principle in the hands of self-styled "Social Darwinists." Nature, they contended, favored those races of humankind that were best adapted through the process of natural selection. Conflicts between human groups—such as such dramatic contemporary events as the American Civil War and the Jamaican Revolt—could be seen as a simple extension of the principles of conflict within species. Alfred Russel Wallace (1823–1913), Francis Galton (1822–1911), John Elliot Cairnes (1823–1875), Charles Mackay (1814–1819), John William Jackson (1809–1871), and other writers of the era were vividly aware of the social, as opposed to biological or scientific, implications of Darwin's work, and its applicability to contemporary relations between and among social groups.

The Social Implications of Biological Theories of Race

While there are no consistent scientific indications of the existence and consequences of biological races, there is considerable evidence that biological notions of race have had important social consequences within Western societies. Those who accept the notion that there are biologically distinct races have, almost invariably, sought to find ways in which one race was superior or inferior to others. Since, according to

---

[5]Bannister (1979) gave an excellent account of the development of Social Darwinism and, moreover, showed how it is systematically related to other currents in Anglo-American social thought.

many in the Western tradition, the most important characteristic of our species is its ability to reason and to use complex language, many of these efforts to discover differences among races have centered on the notion of "intelligence."

Much of the 150-year history of the study of intelligence in the West is taken up with the search for innate differences between races. The basic structure of these inquiries, as well as the methods used, are suspect. Researchers have usually assumed that differences in intelligence between races are innate—that is, genetically based—and have developed the necessary evidence, however biased, to prove this empirically. Two cases provide especially powerful examples of this. Samuel George Morton was a practitioner of craniometry: the 19th-century practice of measuring cranial volume in order to determine mental abilities. This technique depended on the assumption that people with larger brains were smarter (Gould, 1981).

At the outset, it is important to understand that there is no evidence that "intelligence" varies with brain size in human beings. Brain size varies directly, of course, with body size. The idea that there was a relationship between brain size and intelligence had its origin in the comparison of various species of animals, and the observation that more intelligent animals often had proportionately larger and more complex brains. The idea that this observation could be extended to comparisons *within* a single species is tenuous.

Morton collected skulls. Early in his career, he began to compare the interior volumes of crania by filling them with white mustard seed. His particular interest was in demonstrating that different races had different cranial volumes—and, hence, different mental capacities. American Indians, he noted, had been conquered by European invaders. He proceeded to try to discover a cause for this in differences in brain capacity as measured by cranial volume. He had his answer; all he needed was the experiment to prove it (Gould, 1981).

Morton's case is instructive: He apparently was not aware of the biased nature of his experimental procedure. He first filled each skull with mustard seed, packing the seed down to make sure that the interior space was full. He then emptied the seed into a graduated cylinder to measure it. Later, he repeated these same measurements using lead shot—a much more uniform material, yielding more reliable results. Morton's lead-shot dataset showed larger and more uniform cranial volumes because shot packs more densely and more consistently than seeds. Gould (1981), in reviewing Morton's measurements with *the same* skulls, discovered that the increase in volume Morton found with lead shot was greatest for "blacks," less for American Indians, and least for "caucasians." Gould concluded that Morton had unconsciously (there is no evidence of conscious fraud) packed the mustard seeds more carefully into small "caucasian" skulls and less deliberately into the larger skulls of the races he presumed to be inferior. In any event, turn-of-the-century psychologists who attempted to find systematic relationships between cranial size and ability to perform tasks requiring reasoning discovered that differences in cranial measurements between "intelligent" and "unintelligent" individuals were insignificant.

The history of the use of intelligence tests is another example of bad science in the hands of individuals convinced that race and intelligence are related. Intelligence tests were first developed by a French psychologist, Alfred Binet, to identify children who might need special help in learning (Gould, 1981). Binet stressed that his tests could only be used as a rough guide for identifying those children with the most obvious difficulties. He also rejected the notion that whatever it was he was measuring ("intelligence") was somehow innate and unchangeable. In the hands of American researchers, however, his "IQ test" was turned into a way of making comparisons calculated to cause envy or discontent between adults drawn from different racial and ethnic groupings.[6]

Binet's IQ test was first brought to the United States by H. H. Goddard, who was persuaded (as Binet was not) that it was a good measure of a single, underlying, inheritable factor (i.e., "intelligence"). Goddard traced a good many of society's ills—such as poverty and crime—to "feeble-mindedness" in various subpopulations. It followed from this that the United States should attempt to prevent "morons" from immigrating to its shores and that states should undertake various social policies—including sterilization—intended to restrict the fertility of those with poor genetic inheritance. Goddard undertook research on immigrants at Ellis Island and on a family of supposed "mental defectives" (the "Kallikaks"), which led to restrictions on immigration and the sterilization of mental defectives a decade after he began his work (Gould, 1981).[7]

Lewis Terman transformed Binet's IQ test into its present form (the "Stanford-Binet"), but it was R. M. Yerkes who carried out the first mass testing program, using World War I recruits as subjects. As with other American proponents of intelligence testing of the era, Yerkes was convinced that intelligence, which is a single, identifiable and measurable attribute of mind, was inherited and largely uninfluenced by environment. Both Terman and Yerkes argued, without evidence, that IQ exams measured innate intelligence and not capability as constrained by such factors as nutrition and educational opportunity. Like Goddard's research, Yerkes' tests were used to determine the "educability" of different racial groups (Gould, 1981). Why, they argued, attempt to educate simple creatures beyond their capabilities? Isn't it a form of cruelty to attempt to do so? Wouldn't these simple creatures be happier if they were given an education better suited to their limited intellectual capabilities?

Yerkes' results were used to justify precisely the kind of differences in educational patterns that one would expect on the basis of these arguments. In the American South, they were used to justify segregation—despite the fact that Northern blacks scored higher on his tests than Southern whites. In the North, the

---

[6]The modern form of the IQ measurement was actually developed by Stern, who used Binet's scores to estimate a *relative* rather than absolute measure of differences in intellectual abilities. Thus, Binet calculated an individual's intellectual standing by subtracting his or her performance from the minimum performance of children his or her own age (e.g., chronological age minus mental age). Stern recognized that a relative measurement (e.g., mental age over chronological age) was needed (see Gould, 1981).

[7]As Gould (1981) noted, Goddard later dissociated himself from these policies.

results were used to justify special vocational (i.e., manual) education for blacks.

We can see the same assumptions at work, with the same consequences, in the research undertaken by Sir Cyril Burt. For many years Burt was a psychologist for the London County Council, and administered and interpreted IQ tests for London's schools. He appeared to be a careful experimenter, and often seemed to carefully consider alternative explanations for the data he gathered. However, he was so convinced that, due to heredity, "races" differed in their innate intellectual ability, that he would accept no alternative explanation. In fact, he gave little credence to evidence that did not support his theories and it is now widely accepted that he fabricated the evidence upon which his critical study of twins was based (Hearn-shaw, 1979).[8] His results were then used to justify providing vastly different educational opportunities to children drawn from different social classes.

This question of "educability" is, and has always been, the critical issue underlying discussions of the relationship between race and intelligence. Although he later recanted, Goddard originally argued that the United States should restrict the immigration of Southern Europeans and Eastern Europeans (e.g., Jews and Hungarians) because they were less educable than Northern Europeans. On the basis of Goddard's research and that of others, eugenicists[9] managed to obtain immigration quotas that had precisely this effect. Similarly, Goddard maintained that we should restrict the fertility of the "feebleminded." In response to this, a number of states enacted legislation permitting the forced sterilization of the "mentally incompetent."

As Gould (1981) clearly demonstrated, intelligence test results are still being used as part of a political program designed to restrict the educational opportunities of "inferior" groups. In 1969, Jensen published an article in the *Harvard Educational Review* entitled "How Much Can We Boost IQ and Scholastic Achievement?" This article purported to show that inherited "genetic" differences accounted for the differing performances of American "Negroes" and "whites" on standardized IQ tests.[10] It was roundly criticized for, as Gould (1981) showed, precisely the same *statistical* and *logical* errors that formed the basis of Cyril Burt's earlier work.[11] It was in Jensen's subsequent book, *Educability and Group Differ-*

---

[8]Hearnshaw maintained that there is considerable evidence that Burt, literally, fabricated two co-investigators ("researchers") whose names appeared with Burt's on later published versions of his studies of twins.

[9]The "eugenicists" advocated the use of "scientific breeding" to improve the human gene pool. In practical terms, this meant things like the forced sterilization of "defectives" and excluding "racially less educable human material"—other "racial groups"—from immigrating into an "enlightened" country (see Gould, 1981).

[10]No one can, of course, directly observe "genetic background." One of the major problems with Jensen's work is that the *socially defined* groups about whose performance on IQ tests he wished to draw inferences—American "Negroes" and "Caucasians"—are of *unknown* genotypic diversity. Thus, he took as given the main thing about which, and from which, he intended to draw conclusions.

[11]Flynn (1980) and Kamin (1974) summarized many of these issues. Note that Burt's studies, which Jensen cited favorably in his *Harvard Educational Review* article (1969), were *essential* to his argument: Jensen, to prove his case, had to show that the differences in performance he had observed were inherited and, hence, immutable. Jensen rejected Burt's evidence after the revelation, by others, that Burt's studies of identical twins were fabricated (Jensen, 1974). But this did not lead him to the obvious conclusion that there was an essential flaw in his own argument.

ences (1973),[12] that he made his *social and political* agenda clear: the undercutting of precisely those federal programs begun in the 1960s—Head Start and Follow Through—that were successful in raising the levels of educational attainment of *all* disadvantaged children of whatever "race." (See Brown, 1977; Harrell, 1983; Hubbell, 1983; Maccoby & Zellner, 1970; McCormick, 1975; Rhine, 1981; Rivlin & Timpane, 1975; Stallings, 1975; U.S. Dept. of Health and Human Services, 1981; Westinghouse Learning Corporation, 1969; Zigler & Valentine, 1979. Evaluating social experiments is not simple or direct; see Williams & Evans in Rossi & Williams, 1972.)

RACE, BIOLOGY, AND SCIENCE

Scientists work by constructing theories about orderly relationships between 'events' that can be observed in the 'real world' through the use of our five senses—sight, sound, smell, taste, and touch—alone or aided by instruments. Since the 'real world' is complicated, scientists construct simplified representations of it which have been reduced in both scale and detail. These simplified representations, or *models*, then act as analogs to complex observable physical, natural, or social phenomena. By comparing expectations derived from these models to information we can gather by observing the 'real world'—what are called *data*—we can then determine whether or not these models are consistent with our observations. If they are, we say our models are "confirmed." If they are not, we say they are "not confirmed."

This fundamental scientific act—the comparison of data to expectations derived from models—further requires that these models meet three criteria. First, models must be *parsimonious*: They must be as simple as possible. The more complicated a model, the greater the likelihood that it contains measurement error.[13] Thus, given two "equally good" explanations (i.e., the data conform to them equally well), we opt for the simpler on the grounds that it minimizes the risk of error. Second, models must be *consistent*: They must be logically coherent. They must "hang together," define their terms unambiguously, and clearly state the direction of cause they seek to imply. There must be a clear chain of reasoning between causes and effects in their explanations of events. Finally, models must be *falsifiable*: They must be capable, in principle, of being disproven. Not all parsimonious and logically consistent statements can be falsified. Only empirically verifiable statements (ones that can be associated with some clear set of observables) are capable of empirical

---

[12]His argument is so strongly rooted in Burt's that he *dedicated* this book "To the memory of Sir Cyril Burt."

[13]This idea of the importance of simplicity in explanations derives from the work of the English philosopher William of Occam (or Ockham; 1285–?1349) and, hence, is sometimes known as "Occam's Razor." It was systematized and applied in a precise way to the calculation of uncertainty in measurement by the German physicist Werner Karl Heisenberg (1901–1976) and is known, in this context, as "Heisenberg's Uncertainty Principle."

disproof. Thus, the principle of falsifiability demands that, both logically and empirically, it should be possible to accept evidence that runs counter to one's hypotheses.

Historically, biological theories of 'race' have not met these three criteria for scientific explanation. Fixed-type theories, for instance, fail the tests of consistency and falsifiability. If, indeed, there are (or were) a limited number of "ancestral races"—each, in effect, an independent evolutionary "start" for *Homo sapiens*—then there should be clear evidence of this in the fossil record. There is not. Each time there has been an attempt to establish some polygenic theory of the evolution of humankind, the fossil evidence has been scanty. This, in itself, has been suspicious since, to be successful, an evolutionary change must take hold among at least hundreds of interbreeding organisms. It follows from this that if we discover the remains of some organism that appears to demonstrate an important evolutionary change, we should find more than one. Each time someone has "found" the remains of such an organism, it has been found "alone." In the past, each of these "finds" has proven to be a hoax or a clear misreading of some fossil (Gould, 1981).

There are good theoretical reasons for this. Let us be exceedingly generous and assume that the chances of the evolution of *one* example of the species *Homo sapiens* is "one in a million."[14] The probability of the *independent* evolution of two morphologically compatible and interfertile organisms—as in the polygenic evolutionary model—would be one in a million million. The chances of three would be one in a million million million. The last polygenic model that gained any currency proposed four "independent evolutions": one in a million million million million, or 1/1,000,000,000,000,000,000,000,000. This is a very small number.

Beyond this, those scientists who have made *honest* attempts to establish polygenic theories of the evolution of humankind (*not* the hoaxers) seldom clearly state the conditions under which they would be willing to reject their hypotheses. This is because, like Morton, they have never seriously considered the possibility that their hypotheses were wrong. Therefore, they have not built models that are explicitly falsifiable, and have thus violated an important canon of the scientific world view: systematic skepticism. Scientists, like other people, like to be right. But, in order to guard against the natural tendency to simply gather evidence to support hypotheses, scientists are required to prove their case *in the face of rigorous tests of alternative explanations*. Those who support the fixed-type theory of race appear to have rejected this fundamental scientific idea.

The breeding population theory of human races flamboyantly fails the test of parsimony. If we took the breeding population theorists at their word, the 30 races put forward by Coon, Garn, and Birdsell would be a bare beginning for an enumeration of all the "interbreeding" groups in one country, let alone the world. When biologists use the term *deme,* they are referring to a highly localized group. Thus, in these terms, we would not be talking about, say, "whites"—nor even "white

[14]Actually, of course, it is much less.

Anglo-Saxons"—but instead "a large kinship group in northern New York state consisting of the descendants of eight nuclear families who migrated to the 13 colonies from the Midlands of England between 1630 and 1662 and who settled in this area." By these standards, a "race" is any interbreeding group with reasonable persistence in a particular geographic locale. Thus, for instance, most large universities—such as the University of Michigan—provide the basis for a race, in this sense, in that a large proportion of their graduates marry one another produce children, who then return to repeat the process. The best arguments against breeding population theories of race, then, are that "graduates of the University of Michigan" or "graduates of Ohio State" and "northern New York apple farmers" are not really what we have in mind as basic human race, and if we apply this definition in the way that biologists intended, we would have thousands—perhaps, tens of thousands—of "races" so-designated, in the United States.

Because of these flagrant violations of the most fundamental rules of scientific modeling, biological notions of race—and the arguments, such as Jensen's, based upon them—have, with rare exceptions, been in retreat since the late 1920s. Indeed, with the exception of Nazi Germany, racial explanations had virtually no *scientific* adherents by 1930 (Barkan, 1992).[15] This is part of the reason that Jensen's revival of racialist explanations of differences in IQ in the 1960s caused as much of a stir as it did: Serious biological and social scientists with an interest in human differences had abandoned the notion of biological races and had, instead, come to recognize that the notion of "race" was useful primarily because of what it tells us about social perceptions of group differences and intergroup dynamics.[16] Franz Boas (1858–1942) and other anthropologists were instrumental, in the interwar period, in convincing other scientists that races were best understood as 'social constructions'; that is, as things created as a result of social structural and cultural processes (Boas, 1940).

To truly understand the sources and effects of variations in human biology, we have to abandon the pseudo-science of biological racialism and seriously take up the study of what is called *population biology*: the study of reproductive biology, migration, and genetic variation in groups of living things belonging to a single

---

[15]One could argue that people like William Shockley, a Nobel-prize-winning chemist, are "scientists" who support the idea of the biological reality of "races." Note that Shockley, as a *chemist*, is not approaching the problem scientifically, but as a layman; and is well outside the area of his expertise. There were, of course, Nobel-prize-winning physicists who supported the idea of "Aryan physics."

[16]There has been, of course, a recent revival of the debate over the connection between "race" and intelligence or IQ in the form of Hernnstein and Murray's book *The Bell Curve: Intelligence and Class Structure in American Life* (1994). The definition of "*race*" used by Hernnstein and Murray was—as in most of the debate over the connection between "race" and "IQ"—a commonsensical one (i.e., race is that category people would list on a census form, and, as such, is not relevant to a scientific debate on the subject). It is tempting to critique this book at this juncture, but we resist it: Hernnstein and Murray, despite popular interest in their work, added nothing to the debate about the scientific meaning of race and repeated, in detail, the errors committed by their predecessors. (This includes those in Cyril Burt's demonstrably fraudulent work.) What is most interesting to social scientists about Hernnstein and Murray is not their work, but the social factors that lead to a periodic, if insubstantial, revival of this topic. But that examination is best left to later work.

species. Over the past sixty years, population biology has given us substantial insights into how populations work, largely through research into plants and nonhuman animals. Because it has not been based on research with humans, this work has had the advantage of being conducted largely without a racial agenda. But the techniques developed for dealing with these nonhuman species can be applied, perhaps with a bit less bias, to humans.

Why are scientists interested in human population biology? To begin with, people look different. In a whole-world view, as observers with a keen interest in people, we can see variation in skin color and facial construction, in hair color and development of facial hair (in males). Critically important, the variation in these features is apparently related to geography: It is difficult to find a blond in Japan, and it is difficult to find a male without facial hair in Northwestern Europe. Without the geographic dimension to this variation, it would probably not occur to us to ask how different we are from one another.

The idea that this geographically based variation provides evidence that there is more than one species of human being is no longer popular. Species definition is anything but a simple matter. But in some cases—such as with human beings—no modern student of species would argue for separate species status for two populations given the absence of true (absolute) discontinuities in physical features, a similar absence of fixed genetic differences, and the ability of all matings between human groups to yield fertile offspring. Population biologists have found variation within every species they have studied—hence, the human situation is by no means unique or unusual. Birdwatchers know that songs of their favorite species are different in different regions of the country. Botanists find observable differences between populations of the same species in different regions.

This variation within species is quantitative, not qualitative: There is gradual change in the organisms' appearance as one travels across a continent. For simplicity's sake, biologists will speak, for example, of a "Northern" and a "Southern" race, but it is understood that these "races" are part of a system of continuous variation. In some cases there are radically different populations in different regions, but a close look at the frontier between the two populations will reveal, at least in low frequency, individuals intermediate in easily observable traits who still yield fully fertile offspring.

Thus, none of the contentions of those who use the term "race" in a biological sense is supported by strong scientific evidence. First, we have no clear empirical basis for the existence of subspecies within *Homo sapiens*. There is, by contrast, considerable genetic variability within commonly used racial categories such as "black" or "white" or "yellow." If, for instance, we create a geographic map of predominant blood types in the world's population, we discover islands of like-typed populations that spread around the globe; that is, there is no simple mapping of blood types to those areas of the world we identify as the "homes" of various racial groupings.

Second, we cannot associate the genetic mix within morphologically similar populations with any complex traits. Our knowledge of how genes work, alone or in combination, is primitive. Except in the cases of a few genetically linked diseases, we cannot associate genes, directly, with even simple biologically based consequences. These traits are simple and do not include things that might affect a group's sociocultural characteristics.

Third, those adhering to biologically based notions of race maintain that we can discriminate between races on the basis of their appearance—or "phenotypic differences." But biological notions of 'race' have historically been applied to groups, such as the Irish or Jews, with considerable phenotypic variability in hair color, eye color, bone structure, or whatever, and without the genotypic[17] or physiological evidence we would need to classify them as a subspecies. It is clear that there is no simple mapping of phenotypes to the genetic background of groups.

Fourth, experimental studies show that, without other kinds of information, subjects are not even very good at sorting people into the major phenotypic categories (e.g., "white," "black") used in *other* societies. Americans, for instance, cannot sort pictures of people into the phenotypically based racial categories used in Brazil. So even this kind of elementary *racial sorting*, which most people take for granted, has to be learned (i.e., people must learn to *recognize*, say, differences in people's hair texture and *to associate these differences* with a particular socially defined racial category in order to perform these sortings). The process whereby one learns to do this varies considerably from society to society. Hence, people in different parts of the world are "aware" of some "racially specific" phenotypic traits and "unaware" of others.[18]

Fifth, no one has successfully found an independent association between biological 'race,' no matter how defined, and any sociocultural trait where they had also taken into account the effects of sociocultural transmission.

Finally, in multiracial societies, there are no associations between phenotypically defined races and sociocultural traits that cannot be *better* explained by processes of sociocultural transmission.

Although it is understandable that human beings would try to sort themselves into different categories, then, the genetic and morphological basis for arguing that there are separable, qualitatively different subgroups of the human species has never been found. Broad geographic zones in which populations intermediate between so-called human races exist, as between Asians and Europeans in Western Asia and Africans and Europeans in Central to Northern Africa. Fixed genetic markers have

---

[17]*"Genotypic"* means based on underlying genetic differences. Until the development of techniques of genetic fingerprinting, genotypes had to be inferred from observing actual crosses of genotypes (i.e., offspring). It is hard to do this in a way that is sufficiently controlled to make any sense out of human pairings.

[18]This can lead to a great deal of confusion when people leave one social environment for another. When one of the authors (Berkowitz) was teaching at the University of Toronto, he was forever encountering students who had moved to Toronto from the West Indies—and changed "race" in the process!

not been found that fingerprint any of the commonly suggested racial categories. On the contrary, the genetic traits investigated so far all vary in frequency in different populations in different regions. A particular allele (variant) of a particular gene may be common in New Guinea and rare in Mongolia, but the allele is present in populations throughout the world.

There are a number of straightforward historical reasons why biological notions of race such as those described here are so tenuous. First, as a species, *Homo sapiens* has evolved relatively recently. Since it takes many generations and strong environmental pressures for evolutionary change to occur in a species like ours, there simply has not been enough time for human beings to have diverged very much from one another. Second, the spread of *Homo sapiens* into what are often taken to be the characteristic niches of various races (e.g., Western Europe, Asia) is quite recent. This means that *Homo sapiens* has not, characteristically, had the kind of geographic isolation needed for the development of sharply different breeding groups. Third, massive population migrations, often associated with war and conquest (such as the Mongol invasions), have been common throughout recorded human history. These tend to spread around genetic material.[19]

Fourth, some parts of the world, such as what is referred to in the United States as the Middle East, have acted as highways for slow and less dramatic population migrations over a very long period of time. These movements, too, have tended to redistribute gene pools. Fifth, there have always been considerable areas of contact between the populations of Europe and those in the Middle East, Africa, and Asia. The Mediterranean rim—present-day France, Spain, Italy, Greece, Morocco, Tunisia, Libya, Israel, Lebanon, Turkey, and Egypt—has been a particularly fertile area for such contact. Middle Eastern peoples, moreover, have, at one time or another, moved down both coasts of Africa. Thus, there is a continuous network of near-to-distant kin connections between Europe and sub-Saharan Africa. Finally, no human population in the 20th century is truly genetically isolated from all others. Even populations such as Polynesians, Inuit, and Australian aborigines have, since the middle of the 18th century, been interbreeding with Western Europeans at some, largely unknown, rate. Thus, biological notions of race could not be consistently, falsifiably, and parsimoniously operationalized, even if they could be clearly defined.

It follows from this that much of what appears as striking differences between peoples in different geographic regions is not biological in any genetic sense, but instead is cultural. With the advent of language, people became able to transmit a cultural as well as a genetic inheritance between generations. The evolution of culture is reminiscent of organic evolution, but it happens much more quickly, so that in the past 100,000 years the world has seen the development of a diversity in customs of dress, of burying the dead, of speaking, of making music, and so on, at

---

[19]The best description of the both the social basis and social impact of the Mongol invasions is James Chambers' *The Devil's Horsemen: The Mongol Invasions of Europe* (Chambers, 1979). Henthorn (1963) showed the kind of biological impact such invasions must have had.

a rate that is far beyond the capacity for diversification of genetically transmitted information. It is this *cultural evolution* that has served as the basis for the idea that distinctive, qualitatively separable races of human beings exist. However, biologically, these "races" are no more different than the Southern and Northern "races" of forest birds.[20]

SOCIOCULTURAL THEORIES OF RACE AND ETHNICITY

Contemporary sociologists and anthropologists who use the concept of 'race' do so as part of the study of the sociocultural development of groups and/or of sociocultural relationships between them. Hence, to the extent that the term 'race' is still used, it is understood that it is really a special case of what we refer to as an *ethnic group:* a set of individuals within a larger population that intermarries; shares common national origins, language, religion, or other cultural traits; and is recognized by its members and others to do so.

This a useful way of looking at things, because it implicitly recognizes the dynamic and interactive processes underlying the formation and maintenance of group identity. Ethnic groups are networks of interrelated individuals sharing some form of common tie—such as language and/or religion and/or common geographic origin—that they use to define themselves *in relation to* the surrounding society, and that, in turn, is used in its broad outlines by the rest of that society to define them.

Note that there is a dual requirement here: Members of an ethnic group must see *themselves* as part of an ethnic group *and* they must be seen *by others* to be part of the same group. There are a number of important implications of this. First, since the definition of a given ethnic group depends on two structural processes—one internal and the other external to that group—the overall social definition of ethnicity in a society may be quite unstable. The ethnic divisions within a given society at one point in time will not necessarily correspond to the ethnic divisions in that same society at a later date. Second, since membership in an ethnic group may be based on one or another different social ties (e.g., religion or common national origin), ethnicity is always negotiated or "constructed" by groups of individuals within a specified context. The ways in which these negotiations take place determine, in some substantial measure, the *content* of ethnic group membership within a given society at a particular point in time. Finally, the particular ordered list of social attributes used by one group in defining another may not

---

[20]A new opportunity for racist interpretation of scientific inquiry is in the offing. With the advent of molecular fingerprinting, it is now possible to develop, with little trouble, a unique genetic profile for each person. Evolutionists are asking "Which profile is most advanced?" or "Which is most primitive?" with the idea of understanding something about human origins. The so-called "search for Eve" is on—using maternally inherited genetic markers as evidence. The theoretical understanding and experimental procedures are in place for doing this work, and it promises to be very interesting. However, there is no requirement that the person with the most primitive genetic fingerprint be the least intelligent—again, there is no relationship between this fingerprint and a person's intellectual capacity. Nevertheless, in the spirit of racism, which lives on, some people will choose to assume that this nonexistent relationship actually exists, and we will once again be required to go to the trouble of disproving some very bad science.

correspond to the ordered list of social attributes that members of that group use in defining themselves. This means that the identity of a given ethnic group may well emerge as a result of some kind of interactive and recursive process over time.

In Italy, for instance, most "Italians" identify with their regions (e.g., as Calabrian or Piedmontese or Sicilian). In their daily conversations, they usually speak one of several regional dialects. Unless they are born into the elite of educated families within a given region, they learn their "Italian" in school. Their diets vary a great deal from region to region, as does their cuisine (i.e., the way in which their food is prepared). Their marriage customs and patterns, sexual mores, and social attitudes have, historically, been quite different in different regions.

When members of these same regional "Italian" groups began migrating to the United States in large numbers around the turn of the century, however, the boundaries between these regional subcultures began to break down. Because the number of people from any given village or region was typically a small part of the total within any given locale, no group could dominate an entire area of settlement. Because each new wave of immigrants settled in areas adjacent to the others, they shared stores, churches, and funeral parlors. Their children attended the same schools. In time, they intermarried. Variations in their cuisines became "tastes" or "preferences." These immigrants from Italy were treated as members of one group by other American groups and by the U.S. authorities. In effect, "Italian" ethnicity emerged as a by-product of the process of immigration. It had to be socially constructed: The larger society had to come to treat "Italians" as part of one group, and "Italians" had, eventually, come to regard their regional cultural differences as relatively unimportant.

Similar dynamics seem to have been at work among American Jews. The earliest wave of Jewish immigrants to the United States were "Sephardim"; that is, they had come, via various intermediary points, from Spain and Portugal.[21] But the "Jewish Mayflower" disembarked only 23 people at New Amsterdam in 1654.[22] This was hardly enough to allow for the restriction of marriages within their religious group (within-religious-group endogamy), let alone among Sephardim. So even when more Sephardic Jews arrived a few years later, these original "pioneers" continued to intermarry with non-Sephardic Jews from Germany and elsewhere ("Ashkenazim"). Thus, what confronted the large mid-19th-century wave of German Jewish immigration was not a uniform group based in a Sephardic subculture, but a culturally mixed ethnic group that had, to some extent, intermarried with its non-Jewish neighbors. Because, initially at least, the German Jews chose to emphasize their common national origins and maintained German as the language of their homes, they did not immediately identify with the older Jewish group and, hence, maintained a separate ethnic group identity until the early 20th century.

---

[21] *"Sphard"* means "Spain" in Hebrew.

[22] Some argue that the "first Jewish community" in what is now the United States was established in what is now New Mexico around 1597. This, however, was a community of Marranos, or "crypto-Jews," and other such groups may have existed elsewhere.

This situation changed substantially with the massive numbers of Eastern European Ashkenazic Jews who began arriving in the United States in the 1880s. Both of the ethnic groups that had been formed by the earlier waves of immigration—the "Sephardic Jews" and the "German Jews"—had adapted to their surroundings by conforming to many of the customs of the other groups with which they had come in contact. These new Jewish immigrants were different. Many had lived in small isolated towns in rural areas. As a result, their religious practices and other customs had become far more different from those around them than those of the earlier immigrants. As a very large group, they were under less pressure to conform to external demands. Because they dressed in quite distinct ways, spoke a distinct language (Yiddish), and rejected integration into the older groups, these new immigrants forced the older groups to consolidate their communal institutions and to redefine themselves in relation to the newcomers. Hence, it was during this period that various institutions began to appear with the word "Hebrew" (and not "Jewish") in their titles (e.g., the Young Men's Hebrew Association), as the Sephardic/German Jews began to distinguish themselves from the Eastern Europeans.

As we can see in the cases of both Italian and Jewish American ethnic groups, then, ethnic group identity is not something that is simply given, but instead something that must be formed through a complex set of relational processes. These processes often involve patterns of dominance and subordination. This makes it extremely difficult to talk about ethnicity or ethnic groups over time, and to be confident that one is doing it in a rigorous way. For instance, the terms "negro," "black folk," "colored people," "black people," "Afro-American," and "African American" have all been used, at one time or another, to describe people belonging to particular groups whose boundaries, self-definition, and social position have varied throughout U.S. history. Given that these groups are *not* identical in relation to others, it becomes quite difficult to talk about, for instance, "the growth or decline in the size of the [blank] population of the United States."

DOMINANT VERSUS MINORITY GROUPS

There is nothing new about the existence of culturally distinct groups within a larger society. As H. Morris (1968) noted, the !Kung San of the Kalahari Desert have existed for millennia within the larger context of Tswana society. In fact, before the development of the nation-state and before the Industrial Revolution, there were weaker pressures toward ethnic consolidation in most societies than there are in many parts of the world today.

Historically, as in the United States, ethnic groups have often come about as a result of the immigration of one group into a geographic area occupied by another group or groups. This has been going on for millennia.[23] In many cases, these

---

[23]The word *"Hebrew,"* for instance, may well derive from *"Haibru"*: "people from across the river." Graetz (1891/1967) noted that, at the time of the return from Egypt, the "Hebrew" or "Israelite" tribes still thought of themselves as different from the aboriginal peoples of the Fertile Crescent (*"Anakim"*). These people were *not* the same as the "Canaanites," whom the Greeks called "Phoenicians" (Graetz, 1891/1967).

migrations have been a result of peaceful activities such as trade or labor force migration. In some cases—such as the Mongol invasions—migration has been a consequence of war and conquest, and has resulted in the establishment of the dominance of an invading group.

Migrations have led to the establishment of a variety of patterns of ethnic differentiation within given societies. In some cases, ethnic groups have simply established themselves side by side and are more or less institutionally complete and relatively equal to one another. In others, they have formed into *caste systems*: "a hierarchy of endogamous groups in which status is rigidly ascribed by birth and in which mobility from one group to another is not possible" (Morris, 1968, p. 169). In still others, they have formed the basis for a division of the society into *social classes*: groups with vastly different access to sources of wealth and privilege. Much depends on the extent to which, and in what ways, a given society is *stratified*, that is, divided up into subordinate and superordinate groups.[24]

The migration of ethnic groups into societies has led to patterns of geographic differentiation as well. In the case of groups trading around the Mediterranean rim, culturally distinct groups often occupied a special locale within a given city (e.g., the "Jewish Quarter," "the Syrian Quarter"). In some cases, these areas were established as result of formal negotiations between the inhabitants of a given country and the "visitor" group.[25] In others, they simply developed as a consequence of family ties, recruitment networks, and the ability of groups to use these networks to control resources. In most large American cities, we can identify portions of the urban landscape where a majority of the inhabitants are drawn from one particular ethnic group (e.g., African, Jewish, Greek, Italian, Cuban, or Chinese Americans). These "ethnic enclaves" usually contain specialized institutions—grocery stores, restaurants, bookstores, undertaking establishments, movie theaters, and so on—that reflect the cultural preferences and practices of the groups involved. Historically, these areas came about as a result of *primary* migration from some other part of the world, or *secondary* immigration within North America. San Francisco's "Chinatown," for instance, was originally established as a result of primary migration; Chicago's was established as a result of secondary migration from both coasts.[26]

Historically, the relationships between and among culturally distinct groups within given societies has varied from accommodation to conflict and rejection. We use the terms *dominant* and *minority groups* to refer to ethnic groups that can

---

[24]Note here the parallels between contemporary interpretations of "ethnicity" and Gumplowicz's formulation of the socially constructed notion of "race."

[25]For a discussion of the process involved, see Bonacich, 1973.

[26]In fact, the term *"ghetto"*—which we now use to refer to any social environment given over to the almost exclusive use of members of a culturally distinct group within a larger society—derives from the portion of the city of Venice, the *"ghetto vecchio,"* that was set aside, after protracted negotiations, as a place in which the Jews could continue to keep their own laws and customs (Curiel, 1990; Roth, 1946). A Jewish American sociologist, Louis Wirth, who had studied the "Jewish ghetto" in Chicago, first applied the term *"ghetto"* to a predominantly African American area (see Clark, 1965; Wirth, 1929, 1964).

be differentiated on the basis of their access to wealth, status, or power.[27] U.S. society today contains a sizable recognized minority population that includes African Americans, Chinese Americans, Japanese Americans, South and Southeast Asian Americans, Hispano-Americans, and Native Americans. It also includes a series of groups—such as Italian, Jewish, and Polish Americans—who, although they are not as limited in their access to wealth, status, or power as these other groups, are still not on the same footing as the dominant group, per se.

The term *dominant group*, as a residual term, is vague. We use it to refer to that culturally distinct group (or groups) that exercises disproportionate control over wealth, prestige, power, or other valued goods within a society. Laumann (1973) maintained that, in the United States today, this group consists of a series of ethnic groups with origins in the British Isles and Northern Europe that have amalgamated through intermarriage.

Intergroup Distance

One way of evaluating the current status of the relationships between groups in an ethnically plural society is to construct a set of measures of the distances between them. Since part of the definition of ethnicity is intermarriage, and since marriages between members of different ethnic groups imply a great deal of cultural similarity, we can use kin-distance—or actual marriage or descent distance—between two groups as a measure of their relative acceptability to one another.

Kin-distance is the actual number of ties, through marriage or descent, in a path linking a "source" and a "target" individual. The average number of such ties it takes to link together the members of two groups is a joint measure of kin-distance between them. Thus, if we were interested in determining the kin-distance between Protestants and Jews in a small town, we would, first, draw a map showing all the kinship connections for five or six generations of all members of both groups. We would find both within-group and between-group marriages. We would then trace, for each individual, the number of links it takes to get from that individual to the closest member of the other group ("shortest path distance between groups"; Berkowitz, 1982). The number we would obtain in this fashion would be a good measure of the degree of marriage assimilation between these groups. This is extremely important, because sociologists believe that marriage assimilation is the surest measure of cultural and social acceptability.

Kin-distance, of course, is difficult to calculate for any large population. We can, however, approximate it by looking at rates of intermarriage between groups. Since it only takes a few connections to create an extensive network of paths between groups, even modest rates of intermarriage over time will radically reduce the kin-distance between them. As a result, where we have high rates of intermarriage between two groups, we may well want to question the whole notion of treating groups as separate.

---

[27]Note here that the term *"minority group"* does not necessarily refer to a group that is a numerical minority within a given society. Thus, until recently, South African society contained a series of black ethnic minority groups that confronted a series of dominant white ethnic groups.

The evidence on U.S. religious intermarriage comes from three sources: census data, marriage records, and community studies. All are incomplete. The U.S. Bureau of the Census has not asked respondents for their religious background since the 1960s. Marriage records are incomplete because, despite the fact that the marriage license applications in all but two American states ask brides and grooms about their religion, in no state is it required that people actually fill in the space provided for this information. Thus, "none" is a growing religious category. Community studies only deal with some communities and imply that to be a member of a religious category one must be affiliated with a church, synagogue, temple, mosque, or some other religious institution; this excludes some individuals.

Given these facts, what evidence we do have about religious intermarriage probably underestimates it. Most groups in American society are getting closer to one another in terms of intermarriage, and therefore kin-distance. For instance, there has been a great increase in, and high sustained rates of, intermarriage among ethnic Catholics. But, in addition, there has been a striking reduction in kin-distance where cultural differences between groups have been primarily based on religion. Thus, for instance, Catholics and Protestants from the British Isles are now intermarrying at substantially higher rates than they did 30 years ago. Jews are marrying non-Jews at a high rate. In the period from 1900 to 1920, approximately 2% of U.S. Jews married someone who was not born Jewish. By the period 1966 to 1971, this number had risen to 31.7% (Mayer, 1985). Sociologists now calculate that marriage endogamy among Jews—the proportion of all Jewish brides marrying Jewish grooms—has decreased to just over or just below half, depending on which type of statistic you take seriously.

Racial intermarriage, and hence kin-distance between members of racial categories, is even more difficult to calculate in the United States than religious intermarriage, because in most of the 13 original colonies and, at one time or another, in 37 states, interracial marriages were prohibited or illegal and subject to penalties.[28] Thus, there has always been, until recently, a strong incentive for "passing": in this case, for brides and grooms to define themselves as members of the same racial category. In addition, as we noted earlier, because the definitions of racial categories change over time, comparing intermarriage rates in different time periods is difficult.

Our data on racial intermarriages are most complete for "blacks" and "whites." In the period from 1940 to 1949, it is estimated that there were 4,548 black–white marriages in the United States in which both partners were being married for the first time. In the period from 1960 to 1970, there were 23,771. The number of mixed

---

[28]Note the difference here: In most cases, states simply prohibited interracial marriages—usually between persons of African and European descent. This meant that a marriage, if performed, was not "countenanced," or recognized by the courts. But, as in other instances of violations of marriage laws, it is generally agreed that the state has a valid interest in maintaining high rates of the legitimacy of children. Hence, in other states interracial marriages, if performed and consummated, were valid but both the marriage partners and those officiating at these marriages were subject to fines or imprisonment, or both (see Porterfield, 1978; Spickard, 1989).

black–white marriages in 1970, irrespective of how many times the partners had been married, was 64,789 (Porterfield, 1978). In addition, it is estimated that there were approximately 100,000 persons of African ancestry who were reporting themselves as "white" in 1958 (Stuckert, 1958).

Another way of looking at intergroup distances is in terms of attitudes. We can use the term *ego-distance* to refer to how far one perceives oneself to be from a particular group. There are a variety of ways this can be measured. Since the 1930s, researchers have been administering a series of stereotyping tests to undergraduates ("Princeton Tests"). Over time, there have been changes in the negative (and positive) stereotypes that have been applied to various groups. The items used to measure these stereotypes can be constructed into scales that, in turn, can be used to construct a measure of the perceived distance between ego and a series of hypothetical alters. Similarly, the National Opinion Research Center of the University of Chicago has collected detailed data on the perceptions of blacks by whites and vice versa since the 1960s. These data can be arranged into a series of scales and a distance measure calculated over time.

The overall results of applying these measures of intergroup distance in the United States are quite interesting. Intermarriage between members of "white" ethnic groups—irrespective of religion—has increased dramatically in recent years (Johnson, 1980). Intermarriage between these groups and African Americans has increased slightly. However, although kin-distance in the United States has been decreasing, ego-distance has not changed nearly as much. In terms of both the Princeton and NORC measures, there has been almost no change in the ego distance between members of white ethnic groups and African Americans. Jews and White Anglo-Saxon Protestants (WASPS) are closer together, but Jews and Italians or Italians and WASPS are not.

THE STRUCTURE OF INTERGROUP RELATIONS
IN THE UNITED STATES

Once we have defined a series of dominant and minority groups within an ethnically plural society, and once we have defined a series of measures of their relationships to one another (e.g., intermarriage), we can then begin to talk in a dynamic way about how these relationships are differentially structured over time. Obviously, the terms "dominant group" and "minority group" are *relational*: A group cannot be dominant unless it has some other group to dominate. Similarly, minority groups cannot exist except in relation to some dominant group. Thus, the status of the relationship between any culturally distinct group and all other such groups determines its place within the larger pattern.

These relationships between groups may assume a variety of forms. The most common of these reflect cultural assimilation, cultural accommodation, and conflict or rejection.

Cultural Assimilation

"Cultural assimilation" occurs where a minority group begins to lose some of those elements of its culture that differentiated it from the dominant group and begins, in turn, to acquire the dominant group's characteristics. In the United States, because its original dominant groups were from the British Isles, this process is referred to as *Anglo-conformity*: conformity to the values, attitudes, and expectations of white Anglo-Saxon Protestants.

Cultural assimilation of this kind usually coincides with more tangible forms of structural integration, such as a breaking down of residential segregation between minority and dominant groups, intermarriage, and the shared use of common institutions, such as schools and churches. *Marital* assimilation is probably the most important of these: Because ethnic differentiation is based on culture, high rates of intermarriage indicate a great deal of cultural compatibility between the groups involved.

There is considerable evidence that in terms of the largest single non-British ethnic group in the United States—German Americans—this process of Anglo-assimilation has gone on to an astonishing degree. Although we retain the words "frankfurter" and "hamburger" as reminders of the large proportion of all Americans with some German ancestry, the number of people who report at least some German ancestry continues to decline rapidly. Some sociologists contend that the high degree of Anglo-conformity of German Americans was a by-product of initial similarities between them and white Anglo-Saxon Protestants (e.g., they were both Northern European, Christian, white, etc.). This argument alone is not sufficient because other, quite strikingly different groups have undergone a considerable degree of cultural and structural assimilation into American society. American Jews, for instance, have undergone considerable cultural assimilation despite the fact that they were primarily Southern and Eastern European and non-Christian.

Accommodation

Accommodation occurs where there is mutual acceptance of group differences on the part of minority and dominant groups. This is usually accompanied by at least some sharing and mutual influence in terms of culture. Because the relationship between dominant and minority groups is an unequal one, this usually means that the predominant pressure is toward the adoption by a minority group's members of important elements of the dominant group's culture. This is the process we refer to as *acculturation*. Although theoretically it is possible for dominant and minority groups to reach some measure of accommodation without the acculturation of the minority group, empirically it is rare. Those who support what is referred to as the "melting pot hypothesis," however, point to the fact that we have many examples of shared or exchanged cultural elements in the United States today. Spaghetti and pizza, for instance, are no longer considered simply "Italian" dishes, and bagels have become as American as apple pie. In cities such as Boston that have substantial

Irish and Jewish populations, one can find green bagels being sold on St. Patrick's Day. But how important are these kinds of "shared culture?" And to what extent does the mutual accommodation of Irish and Jewish Americans simply reflect the extent to which *both* are following the same trajectory toward Anglo-conformity and assimilation to the dominant group culture?

Conflict/Rejection

Here the relationships between minority and dominant group(s) are characterized by mutual suspicion or distrust, prejudice, rejection of group differences, discrimination, and physical conflict or violence. The reactions of the dominant group(s) to the presence of minority groups can include institutionalized discrimination, segregation, expulsion, and genocide.

Institutionalized discrimination occurs when social structural mechanisms or cultural patterns—laws, customs, values, tacit agreements, residential patterns, and so on—serve to limit or deny legal rights or opportunities to individuals based on their membership in a particular group. The pattern of legally sanctioned separation of "whites" and "coloreds" in the American South before the 1960s, and the pattern of Apartheid in South Africa, are clear and unambiguous examples of this mechanism. But subtler—and probably more deeply institutionalized—mechanisms can accomplish much the same thing. There has been broad concern, for instance, about the ways in which highly culturally biased standardized tests may serve to perpetuate discrimination vis-à-vis African and Hispanic Americans.[29] Lack of public transportation may make it impossible for those living in the inner city to apply for jobs in the suburbs. Cultural biases about what constitutes "appropriate work" may lead to biases against hiring members of certain groups as carpenters or welders. In principle, any social pattern might lead to discriminatory consequences—with or without people being directly aware of it.

Segregation (or *enforced isolation*) is a form of legally sanctioned discrimination in which members of minority groups are restricted in their social contacts with members of dominant groups, and vice versa. Good examples of the pattern were brought about as a result of the Nuremberg Laws passed by the Nazis to prohibit Jews from practicing their professions, attending certain schools, or employing non-Jewish female servants (Mendelson, 1982). In the United States, there have been, at one time or another, laws or legally sanctioned social practices that have prohibited serving alcohol to an American Indian; allowing an Irishman to buy a cigar in a store (Barron, 1957); Quakers, Jews, and Mormons from holding public office (Hallwas & Launius, 1995); sexual relations between "Negroes" and "members of other races"; the immigration of Chinese; Catholics from belonging to clubs at Harvard and Princeton (Wecter, 1937); and Jews or African Americans from teeing off at a public golf course. In cases where these patterns of segregation are based on laws, we refer to them as examples of *de jure* segregation. Where they are

---

[29]Note here that these tests are often used as part of the hiring process, where they clearly have no bearing on the work to be done.

a by-product of social practice but are not based on law, we refer to them as examples of *de facto* segregation.

Ethnic *expulsion* is the practice of forcibly removing members of an ethnic group from one place to another as a means of minimizing contact between minority and dominant groups. It has been a surprisingly common practice throughout American history. American Indians were expelled from parts of all of the original 13 colonies and most of the states from Tennessee south to Florida. They were then removed from parts of the Great Plains to other parts of the Great Plains.[30] Mormons were forcibly ejected from the Midwest and forced to move West (Hill, 1989; LeSueur, 1987). Jews were forbidden to live in Louisiana and were thrown out if caught (Kaganoff & Urofsky, 1979; Korn, 1969; Marcus, 1951–1953; Proctor & Schmier, 1984). Chinese were sent packing from some towns in the West, and Japanese Americans were placed in internment camps during World War II (Irons, 1989). In the period from about 1870 to 1920, there were so-called "sundown towns" in the Midwest, Plains, and South where blacks had been driven out and where they were expected to be "out of town by sundown." Even today, there are towns in the United States where, informally, the same rules apply.[31]

Genocide is the systematic destruction of the members of an ethnic group or "people." The term was coined after World War II to describe the Nazi program for the elimination of Europe's Jews (Hilberg, 1961). But the so-called "Final Solution" was *not* the first attempt to eliminate an entire people; the actions of the U.S. Cavalry in the last phases of the so-called "Indian Wars" were clearly just this. The Nazi Holocaust, moreover, was not confined to the Jews: Although there were many fewer Romany ("Gypsies") than Jews in Europe, the Nazis proceeded to carry out exactly the same program toward them as they had toward the Jews (Ramati, 1986).

We can find evidence for each of these patterns in the history of U.S. intergroup relations. Minority group reactions to attempts by dominant groups to impose one

---

[30]Written accounts of the "Indian Wars" tend to portray the cavalry as either the last best protection against marauding savages or as a group of thugs and murderers bent on eliminating all traces of the Native American population. Recent work—such as Churchill (1993), Jaimes (1992), and Reichlin (1987)—tends to adopt the latter view. Chalfant (1991), Svaldi (1989),and Norton (1979) presented detailed case studies, and Novack (1970) linked the extermination of the Indians to the requirements of an expanding American capitalism. In some sense, whether this view or the earlier tendency to lionize "the brave Indian fighters" prevails, the point is moot: Whether the U.S. intended to commit genocide or not, it succeeded in doing so. Moreover, this set of events left, in its wake, an array of deeply institutionalized cultural attitudes. For instance, the notion that "the only good Indian is a dead Indian" is as much a part of the early "Westerns" as the good girl/bad girl, good guy/bad guy plot lines. This view was nurtured in many of the contemporary "Indian fighter" stories published for the pulp magazines back East. Even the cavalry diaries are more ambiguous. Many of these works have now been reprinted. For more information, see Calhoun (1979), Carter (1989), Ewert (1976), Noland, (1990), Simpson (1979), Smith (1989). Alexander (1977) gave a glimpse into the lives of wives of cavalry soldiers. Brown (1972) placed these events in a modern context.

[31]There are, of course, towns where, through things like "restrictive covenants," blacks and Jews were not driven out, they simply were not "let in." Such covenants, which are usually part of land deeds and leases, are now generally rejected by American courts, but they continue to exist. During the confirmation hearings that led to the appointment of William Rehnquist to the U.S. Supreme Court, it was discovered that he owned a property whose deed included a restrictive covenant.

or another of these patterns on them have been met with *self-isolation* and *rebellion*, as well as acceptance or resignation. The Black Muslim movement, for instance, clearly provides an example of the former, and the riots (uprisings?) in Los Angeles following the acquittal of the Los Angeles police officers involved in the Rodney King beating of the latter. The United States has a well-established history of accommodation and peaceful coexistence among ethnic groups and, at the same time, it has a well-established pattern of intergroup violence, rebellion, repression, and intolerance.

CONCLUSION: STRUCTURED INEQUALITY
AND SOCIAL GROUP FORMATION

The term "race," we have noted, has been used in a variety of different ways. Among scientists, there is a clear split between those who have used the term in a biological sense and those who understand it socially or socioculturally. Biological notions of race originate, in Western culture, in the notion of *"limpieza de sangre"*—or purity of blood—devised by the Inquisition during the period of the transformation of Spain into a modern nation-state. There is some considerable evidence of an explicit link between biological notions of race and nationalism and nation-state formation. By 1930, biological notions of race were in retreat among scientists; both the fixed-type and breeding population theories of racial difference had been substantially discredited because they had failed the elementary tests of parsimony, consistency, and falsifiability.

The modern tendency is to understand a "race" as one example of the complex social formations we refer to as "ethnic groups." These are socially constructed and, as such, are difficult to assess, because the boundaries between them are subject to substantial changes over time due to shifts in the social forces that produce them. As a result, contemporary researchers in the area focus their efforts on understanding the sources and consequences of group difference.

The predominant pattern in the relations between specific U.S. ethnic groups at any given point in time seems to depend on a number of things. The history of all American minority groups includes at least some examples of accommodation, assimilation, and conflict/rejection. There are several reasons for this.

The American hemisphere was settled through immigration and cultural adaptation. Even the very first settlers—hunters and gatherers who, we believe, crossed the Bering Straits from Siberia some 40,000 to 50,000 years ago—faced the problem of maintaining their group identity in the face of environmental pressures. Note, for instance, the extraordinary variation in the cultural patterns of native Americans that Western Europeans found arrayed from Alaska to Tierra del Fuego. As each immigrant group came in contact with the others, it was immediately faced with the problem of formulating and then reformulating its relations to the others and, hence, its own identity.

This process has been continuous throughout American history. In each case, there has been at least some influence of immigrating groups on those that were already settled here, and vice versa. The extent to which a given immigrating group had an impact on its environment depended on the conditions under which that immigration took place; the size of the immigrating group; the technology, skills, and cultural artifacts it brought with it; its organization; and where in particular it settled. The saliency of each of these factors differed for different groups. Obviously, the "first Americans" who crossed the Bering Straits differed from the others in that they were not in competition with previous groups for resources. People taken out of various African cultures faced different problems of group identity than did, say, German farmers from the Rhineland. Basques—a tiny immigrant group from a small population—had much less of an impact than did the thousands of Eastern European Jews who arrived after 1880. Peasants who immigrated whole villages at a time—as was the case with some German and Hungarian immigrants—had a quite different impact than those from sophisticated urban centers. Immigrant groups that were culturally internally divided and that, as a consequence, had to go through a considerable period of "melding," had a different impact than did those that were relatively culturally homogeneous.

The reactions on the part of groups of earlier immigrants to each of the subsequent waves of immigration depended, in large measure, on their own social positions and where and how new groups attempted to fit into American society. Competition for resources played a large role in this. Anti-Catholic riots occurred in Boston, for instance, at the time when Irish immigrants became serious competitors for unskilled jobs. Anti-Chinese legislation was passed after, not before, the initial reasons for recruiting Chinese laborers, such as the construction of the transcontinental railroads, were no longer present. Responses on the part of minority groups depended, in part, on cultural factors and their own respective abilities to mobilize resources. Chinese Americans, for instance, formed tight enclaves and developed their own institutionally complete communities. Japanese Americans, by contrast, dispersed geographically after World War II and now show a much higher degree of integration into the general labor market than Chinese Americans.

The outcomes in terms of group relations resulting from these processes have depended, in large measure, on a series of contextual factors. Immigrants who were culturally similar to earlier waves of immigrants and who migrated at a time of high demand for labor obviously had a much easier time than did culturally variant immigrants who came during periods of economic restriction. Rural–rural migrants encountered much less opposition than did rural–urban and urban–urban migrants. In each case, the *trajectory* of a given group in American society has reflected the complex interaction of these factors.

The current state of relations among American ethnic groups is mixed. Non-Hispanic European immigrants seem to be undergoing considerable assimilation and show considerable evidence of continuing cultural accommodation. Hispanics, most African Americans, and Southeast Asians are not included in this process to any significant degree. Chinese Americans, after decades in their ghettos, are moving out into the mainstream society. Japanese Americans are assimilating at an accelerating rate. Newly arrived immigrants from Eastern Europe and the Balkans are beginning to form the same kind of ethnic enclaves as did earlier groups, but older immigrant groups have been following the general pattern of suburbanization with its consequent breaking down of immigrant neighborhoods. Significant economic and social inequality exists between various ethnic groups and, in the case of African Americans and Hispanics, shows every sign of continuing to grow.

Ethnicity and ethnic group identity, then, continue to play important roles in U S. society. Thirty-five years ago, most sociologists believed that ethnicity was becoming a less pervasive and important aspect of U.S. life. They contended that ethnic communities—such as the Italian neighborhood described by the sociologist Whyte (1943) in *Street Corner Society*—had largely disappeared and that those that remained were on their way to extinction (Stein, 1960). Ethnic identification, itself, was weakening as a result of suburbanization. In effect, they argued, the American melting pot had done its work and created a new American alloy out of the disparate immigrant groups that had arrived on these shores.

Beginning in the early 1960s, a large number of scholars began to find empirical evidence that this process of "Americanization" and "massification" was far from complete. Gans (1962), a sociologist, discovered that Italian ethnic enclaves—and, hence, Italian ethnicity—persisted in the central city. Liebow discovered an African American street corner society that had strong parallels to Whyte's (Liebow, 1967). Indeed, in the course of the following two decades, ethnicity and ethnic communities were rediscovered among Ukrainian (Kuropas, 1991), Irish (Clark, 1991), Japanese (Fujita, 1991), Hispanic (Weyr, 1988), and Basque (Etulain, 1991) Americans, among others. Polish, Hungarian, Armenian, Greek, and Asian Americans carried on extensive campaigns to revitalize their communal institutions. Indeed, as Alba (1990) noted, it is becoming almost impossible *not* to assume an ethnic identity. Novak (1971) contended that the American melting pot has failed to melt ethnic identity even among "white," Western European immigrants.

Steinberg (1981), another sociologist, referred to this sudden outbreak of interest in ethnicity as "ethnic fever," and he maintained that it has been greatly overstated. He contended, moreover, that many of those things we took to be cultural products of ethnicity are really properties of the ways in which various ethnic groups became *structurally* embedded in U.S. society. This suggests that, as the situation of these groups becomes more structurally similar over time, the social bases for ethnic identity will disappear—and, in fact, has been disappearing.

In fairness, whether one agrees with those sociologists who have rediscovered ethnicity or feel, like Steinberg, that this "new ethnicity" is not real depends, in some large measure, on how one views group identity. Clearly, third-generation Slovak Americans have absorbed a great many cultural attitudes and practices from other immigrant groups. In this sense, their ethnic identity is not the same as that of their grandparents. But has their *ethnicity* been lost or diminished—or has it, as Wellman (1979) suggested, merely been transformed as part of a general transformation in the structure of urban life?

REFERENCES AND BIBLIOGRAPHY

Alba, R. (1990). *Ethnic identity: The transformation of white America.* New Haven, CT: Yale University Press.

Alexander, E. (1977). *Cavalry wife: The diary of Eveline M. Alexander, 1866–1867.* College Station: Texas A&M University Press.

Bannister, R. C. (1979). *Social Darwinism: Science and myth in Anglo-American social thought.* Philadelphia: Temple University Press.

Barkan, E. (1992). *The retreat of scientific racism.* New York and Cambridge, England: Cambridge University Press.

Barron, M. (1957). *American minorities.* New York: Knopf.

Berkowitz, S. D. (1982). *An introduction to structural analysis.* Toronto: Butterworths.

Blumenbach, J. F. (1825). *A manual of the elements of natural history.* London: W. Simpkin & R. Marshall.

Boas, F. (1940). *Race, language, and culture.* New York: Free Press.

Bonacich, E. (1973). A theory of middleman minorities. *American Sociological Review, 38,* 583–594.

Brown, B. (1978). *Found: Long term gains from early intervention.* Boulder, CO: Westview.

Brown, D. A. (1972). *Bury my heart at Wounded Knee: An Indian history of the American West.* New York: Holt, Rinehart & Winston.

Buffon, G. L. L. (1780). *Natural history, general and particular.* Edinburgh: William Creech.

Cain, W. (Ed.). (1994). *Teaching the conflicts; Gerald Graff, curricular reform, and the culture wars.* New York: Garland.

Calhoun, J. (1979). *With Custer in '74: James Calhoun's diary of the Black Hills expedition.* Provo, UT: Brigham Young University Press.

Carter, W. H. (1989). *From Yorktown to Santiago with the Sixth U.S. Cavalry.* Austin, TX: State House Press.

Chalfant, W. (1991). *Without quarter: The Wichita expedition and the fight on Crooked Creek.* Norman: University of Oklahoma Press.

Chamberlain, H. S. (1907/1968). *Foundations of the nineteenth century.* New York: H. Fertig.

Chambers, J. (1979). *The devil's horsemen: The Mongol invasions of Europe.* London: Weidenfeld and Nicholson.

Churchill, W. (1993). *Struggle for the land: Indigenous resistance to genocide, ecocide, and expropriation in contemporary North America.* Monroe, ME: Common Courage Press.

Clark, D. (1991). *Erin's heirs: Irish bonds of community.* Lexington: University Press of Kentucky.

Clark, K. B. (1965). *Dark ghetto: Dilemmas of social power.* New York: Harper & Row.

Coon, C. (1982). *Racial adaptations.* Chicago: Nelson-Hall.

Coon, C., Garn, S. M., & Birdsell, J. B. (1950). *Races: A study of the problems of race formation in man.* Springfield, IL: C. C. Thomas.

Count, E. W. (Ed.). (1950). *This is race.* New York: Shuman.

Curiel, R. (1990). *The Venetian ghetto.* New York: Rizzoli.

Darwin, C. (1859/1896). *The origin of the species by means of natural selection.* New York: D. Appleton.

Darwin, C. (1871/1883). *The descent of man, and selection in relation to sex* (2nd ed.). London: John Murray.

de Gobineau, A. (1854/1967). *The inequality of human races* [Essai sur l'inégalité des races humaines]. New York: Fertig.

Dobzhansky, T. (1973). *Genetic diversity and human equality.* New York: Basic.

Etulain, R. W. (1991). *Basques of the Pacific Northwest.* Pocatello: Idaho State University Press.

Ewert, T. (1976). *Private Theodore Ewert's diary of the Black Hills expedition of 1874.* Piscataway, NJ: CRI.

Flynn, J. R. (1980). *Race, IQ, and Jensen.* London: Routledge and Kegan Paul.

Fujita, S. (1991). *Japanese American ethnicity: The persistence of community.* Seattle: University of Washington Press.

Gould, S. J. (1981). *The mismeasure of man.* New York: Norton.

Graetz, H. (1891/1967). *History of the Jews* (5 vols.). Philadelphia: Jewish Publication Society of America.

Gumplowicz, L. (1885/1963). *Outlines of sociology.* New York: Paine-Whitman.

Hallwas, J. E., & Launius, R. (1995). *Cultures in conflict: A documentary history of the Mormon War in Illinois.* Logan: Utah State University Press.

Harrell, A. (1983). *The effect of the Head Start program on children's cognitive development: Preliminary report.* Washington, DC: Superintendent of Documents.

Harris, M. (1968). Race. In D. L. Sills (Ed.), *International encyclopedia of the social sciences* (Vol. 13, pp. 263–269). New York: Macmillan.

Hearnshaw, L. S, (1979) *Cyril Dart, psychologist.* Ithaca, NY: Cornell University Press.

Henthorn, W. E. (1963). *Korea: The Mongol invasions.* Leiden: E. J. Brill.

Herrnstein, R., & Murray, C. (1994). *The bell curve: Intelligence and class structure in American life.* New York: Free Press.

Hilberg, R. (1961). *The destruction of the European Jews.* Chicago: Quadrangle.

Hill, M. S. (1989). *Quest for refuge.* Salt Lake City, UT: Signature Books.

Hubbell, R. (1983). *A review of Head Start research since 1970 and an annotated bibliography of the Head Start research since 1965: Head Start evaluation, synthesis and utilization project.* Washington, DC: U.S. Department of Health and Human Services, Office of Human Development Services, Administration for Children, Youth and Families, Head Start Bureau.

Irons, P. (1989). *Justice delayed: The record of the Japanese American internment cases.* Middletown, CT: Wesleyan University Press.

Jaimes, M. A. (1992). *The state of native America: Genocide, colonization, and resistance.* Boston: South End Press.

Jensen, A. (1969). How much can we boost IQ and scholastic achievement? *Harvard Educational Review, 39*;1–123.

Jensen, A. (1973). *Educability and group differences.* New York: Harper & Row.

Jensen, A. (1974). Kinship correlations reported by Sir Cyril Burt. *Behavior Genetics, 4,* 1–28.

Johnson, R. A. (1980). *Religious assortative marriage in the United States.* New York: Academic.

Joynson, R. B. (1989). *The Burt affair.* London: Routledge.

Kaganoff, N., & Urofsky, M. I. (1979). *Turn to the South: Essays on Southern Jewry.* Charlottesville: University Press of Virginia.

Kamen, H. A. F. (1965). *The Spanish Inquisition.* New York: New American Library.

Kamin, L. (1974). *The science and politics of IQ.* New York: Wiley.

Korn, B. W. (1969). *The early Jews of New Orleans.* Waltham, MA: The American Jewish Historical Society.

Kuropas, M. (1991). *The Ukrainian Americans: Roots and aspirations, 1884–1954.* Toronto: University of Toronto Press.

Laumann, E. O. (1973). *Bonds of pluralism: The form and substance of urban social networks.* New York: Wiley.

LeSueur, S. C. (1987). *The 1838 Mormon War in Missouri.* Columbia: University of Missouri Press.

Liebow, E. (1967). *Tally's corner: A study of Negro streetcorner men.* Boston: Little, Brown.

Maccoby, E., & Zellner, M. (1970). *Experiments in primary education: Aspects of Project Follow Through.* New York: Harcourt Brace Jovanovich.

Marcus, J. R. (1951–1953). *Early American Jewry.* Philadelphia: Jewish Publication Society of America.

Mayer, E. (1985). *Love and tradition: Marriage between Jews and Christians.* New York: Plenum.

McCormick, M. (1975). *Primary education for the disadvantaged.* La Jolla, CA: Western Behavioral Science Institute.

Mendelsohn, J. (1982). *The judicial system and the Jews in modern Germany.* New York: Garland.

Montagu, A. (1964). *The concept of race.* New York: Free Press.

Morris, H. S. (1968). Ethnic groups. In D. L. Sills (Ed.), *International encyclopedia of the social sciences* (Vol. 5, pp. 167–172). New York: Macmillan.

Mueller, S. (1973). *The new triple melting pot.* Ann Arbor, MI: University Microfilms.

Noland, C. F. M. (1990). *Noland's Cherokee diary.* Spartansburg, SC: Reprint Co.

Norton, J. (1979). *Genocide in Northwestern California.* San Francisco: Indian Historian Press.

Novack, G. (1970). *Genocide against the Indians: Its role in the rise of U.S. capitalism.* New York: Pathfinder.

Novak, M. (1971). *The rise of the unmeltable ethnics.* New York: Macmillan.

Nussbaum, A. (1954). *A concise history of the law of nations.* New York: Macmillan.

Osofsky, G. (1966). *Harlem: The making of a ghetto.* New York: Harper & Row.

Porterfield, E. (1978). *Black and white mixed marriages.* Chicago: Nelson-Hall.

Proctor, S., & Schmier, L. (1984). *Jews of the South: Selected essays from the Southern Jewish Historical Society.* Macon, GA: Mercer University Press.

Ramati, A. (1986). *And the violins stopped playing: A story of the Gypsy holocaust.* New York: F. Watts.

Reichlin, F. (1987). *Les Amerindians et Leur Extermination Déliberée* [The Amerindians and their deliberate extermination]. Lausanne, Switzerland: P.-M. Favre.

Rhine, R. (1981). *Making schools more effective: New directions from follow through.* New York: Academic.

Rivlin, A. M., & Timpane, P. M. (1975). *Planned variation in education: Should we give up or try harder?* Washington, DC: Brookings Institution.

Rossi, P., & Williams, W. (Eds.). (1972). *Evaluating social programs: Theory, practice, and politics.* New York: Seminar Press.

Roth, C. (1946). *History of the Jews of Italy.* Philadelphia: Jewish Publication Society of America.

Simpson, H. B. (1979). *Cry Comanche: The 2nd. U.S. Cavalry in Texas, 1855–1871.* Hillsboro, TX: Hill Junior College Press.

Smith, S. L. (1989). *Sagebrush soldier: Private William Earl Smith's view of the Sioux War of 1876.* Norman: The University of Oklahoma Press.

Spickard, P. R. (1989). *Mixed blood.* Madison: University of Wisconsin Press.

Stallings, J. (1975). *Implementation and child effects of teaching practices in follow through classrooms.* Chicago: Society for Research in Child Development.

Stein, M. (1960). *The eclipse of community.* Princeton, NJ: Princeton University Press.

Steinberg, S. (1981). *The ethnic myth: Race, ethnicity, and class in America.* Boston: Beacon.

Stuckert, R. S. (1958). The African ancestry of the White American population. *Ohio Journal of Science, 55,* 155–160.

Svaldi, D. (1989). *Sand Creek and the rhetoric of extermination.* Lanham, MD: University Press of America.

Vander Zanden, J. W. (1983). *American minority relations.* New York: Knopf.

Wecter, D. (1937). *The sage of American society: A record of social aspiration, 1607–1937.* New York: Scribner's.

Wellman, B. (1979). The community question: The intimate networks of East Yorkers. *American Journal of Sociology, 84,* 1201–1231.

Westinghouse Learning Corporation. (1969). *The impact of Head Start: An evaluation of the effects of Head Start on children's cognitive and affective development.* Springfield, VA: Customer Services Clearinghouse, U.S. Department of Commerce.

Weyr, T. (1988). *Hispanic U.S.A.: Breaking the melting pot.* New York: Harper & Row.

Whyte, W. F. (1943). *Street corner society.* Chicago: University of Chicago Press.

Wirth, L. (1929). *The ghetto.* Chicago: University of Chicago Press.

Wirth, L. (1964). *Louis Wirth on cities and social life: Selected papers.* Chicago: University of Chicago Press.

Zigler, E., & Valentine, J. (1979). *Project Head Start: A legacy of the war on poverty.* New York: Free Press.

2

The Difference Race Makes:
Outcomes and Causes

James W. Loewen
The Catholic University of America
University of Vermont

THE UNITED STATES IS A MULTIRACIAL NATION

About 250 million people lived in the United States in 1990. Of these, almost 30 million (12%) were African Americans. Another 20 million (8%) were Hispanics with ancestors in Latin America. Asian Americans have been growing rapidly in numbers and totaled about 7 million (3%). More than 1.5 million Native Americans (0.6%) lived in the United States. Figure 2.1 shows how immigration changed in the 1980s, compared to the 1950s. Two out of three immigrants in the 1950s came

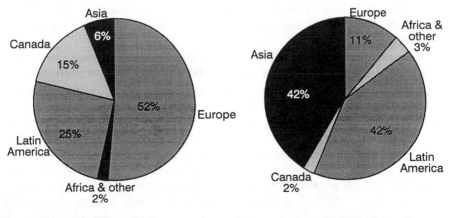

1951-1960   **1981-1989**

FIG. 2.1. Sources of U.S. immigrants, 1950s and 1980s. From O'Hare & Felt (1991).
Copyright 1991 by Population Reference Bureau. Reprinted with permission.

35

from Canada and Europe. In the 1980s, seven immigrants in eight came from Asia and Latin America. By the year 2000, Asian Americans will be at least 4% of the U.S. population, and Hispanics 10%. In some states, including California (the largest), whites will no longer be in the numerical majority. This has already happened in Hawaii. The United States is a multi-racial, multi-ethnic society, and it is becoming more diverse.

The previous paragraph relies on terms—*African Americans, Hispanics, Asian Americans, Native Americans*—that do not work very well. Classification is most difficult for Hispanics. Many Hispanics consider themselves—and are considered by others—to be people of color. But the term *Hispanic* does not refer to a racial category, and Hispanics can be of any "race." When asked, more than half classify themselves "white," about one tenth say "black," a few say "Asian," a few say "Native American" or "American Indian," and growing numbers say "other" or "Hispanic"—some because they do not agree with labeling people by race. Filipinos may end up being classified as Asian Americans or Hispanics. Hispanics vary from prosperous Cuban American business leaders in Florida and New Jersey, who usually vote Republican, to very poor Mexican and Mexican American migrant farm workers in California, who do not vote at all. Puerto Ricans, especially numerous in New York City and New Jersey, enter the United States without immigrating, because Puerto Rico is a commonwealth of the United States. Hispanics also include people from Spain who, like immigrants from Latin America, have Hispanic surnames and speak the Spanish language, but who resemble other European immigrants more closely than they do refugees from Central America. Some Hispanics use the term *Latino* to exclude Europeans.

Like Hispanics, Asian Americans come from many different countries. Large numbers originally came from Japan and China. Others are from the Philippines, Samoa, and other Pacific islands. Also, the Census Bureau now classes immigrants from India, Iran, Iraq, and nearby countries as "Asian Americans," although they are not "Orientals" according to the old "Negro–Oriental–Caucasian" racial classification.

Columbus named Native Americans "Indians" because he thought he had reached the East Indies, or at least wanted others to think so. In the last 20 years, some Indians in the United States have rejected the term and called themselves Native Americans. Others, including the American Indian Movement (AIM), stick with the term *Indians*. Because Native people use both, this chapter also uses both terms. As with other groups, Native Americans self-report their racial identity. Owing to intermarriage, increasing numbers of Indians also have European and African ancestors. During times in our history when to be Indian meant to face exceptional social pressure, the number of Americans who claimed to be Native declined. Since AIM, more Americans identify themselves as Native. Terms like *half-breed* are offensive, however, because they are typically applied to animals.[1]

---

[1] These terms also offend because they emphasize the biological component of "Indianness," whereas Native Americans stress that Indian identity is primarily social and cultural (Churchill, 1992a).

Majority and *minority* are other problematic words. Some people of color take offense when called "minority" Americans. They argue that people referred to in America as "minorities" are in the majority worldwide. They also note that conferring majority status on whites may imply that others are supposed to acculturate to white culture, whereas actually the majority culture has been influenced by all groups and is thus culturally plural.[2] At the same time, Caucasians assuredly are not translucent, and the term *people of color* is not an accurate synonym for *minority* either.

Thus, apparently simple matters like terms prove not to be simple at all. The census relies on self-identification, and people can misreport their race (and other facts) if they want to. Increasing numbers of people of mixed racial ancestry refuse to choose any one of their backgrounds listed on the census form, and instead select "other."

BUT WHAT IS "RACE"?

As the last few paragraphs imply, "race" is hard to define. Biologically, all humans are one species. In the 19th and first half of the 20th centuries, social scientists and biologists tried to define distinct races, by which they usually meant people who looked different and were presumed to behave differently, supposedly owing to different innate capabilities. Some proposed three races: "Mongoloid" or "Oriental," "Negroid," and "Caucasoid." Others pointed out that Australian Aborigines did not really fit into these three. The Khoisan people (Khoi and San, formerly called "Hottentots and Bushmen" by Europeans) in South Africa did not fit in either. Native Americans might be "Oriental," but the relationship is not very close, so some classifiers listed them as a distinct race. Some smaller groups, such as the Pygmies and Watutsi in Central Africa and Ainu in Northern Japan, also provided problems for the classifiers. Thus, depending on the scientist, there were three, four, five, or as many as three dozen distinct races.

What about ethnic groups? Were the Irish a race? In the 19th century some people called them one. Nazis claimed that the Jews were a race, as were the Rom (also called "Gypsies"). Finally, overt racists claimed that each group except their own had unfortunate characteristics, probably innate, and made racial and ethnic terms into slurs—for example, to "nigger-rig" (fix temporarily and poorly), "welsh" on a bet, to "jew" down a price, or to "gyp" someone.

Even before the horror of the Third Reich's "final solution" to its "Jewish" and "Gypsy problems" became clear, such racist thinking was losing prestige in the biological and social sciences. Anthropologists pointed out that, biologically, what we mean by a "race" merely indicates a period of relative isolation from the world's overall human genetic pool. Because this isolation has never been total, racial purity does not and cannot exist. Within the United States, at least 70% to 80% of "black"

---

[2]Following Nigerian American anthropologist John Ogbu and others, I still use the term *minority* but often substitute the term *people of color*.

people have some European ancestry, and at least 20% of "whites" have some recent African ancestry.[3]

Socially, the definition is clearer: A race is any group of people who share physical characteristics that are used to determine social status. Thus, the definition lies in the culture of the group doing the defining. In most countries that formerly practiced racial slavery, like Brazil and South Africa, persons of mixed African-European or African-European-Native American ancestry were assigned to positions between "black" and "white." The United States has been unusual in labeling people legally black if they had one eighth black ancestry—that is, if one of their eight great-grandparents were black. But because that great-grandparent may have been only one eighth black him- or herself, the definitions of black and white end up with inconsistent genealogical components. Some people thus designated black in the United States look entirely white.

The conclusion must be that the social meanings of race, not the biological, are the important ones (see Berkowitz & Barrington, chap. 1, this volume).

RACE IS MEANINGFUL IN THE UNITED STATES

Racial and ethnic group memberships, socially defined, assuredly influence basic life chances in the United States. For example, Anglos murdered Chinese Americans by the score in race riots in the West in the 19th century. The federal government interned California's Japanese Americans in what U.S. Supreme Court Justice Owen Roberts called "concentration camps" during World War II. White ethnic groups, such as Irish Americans in New England and Italian Americans in Louisiana, have sometimes faced severe discrimination in American society. Dwelling on victimization in the past is pointless, according to Huggins and Kilson (1971), black sociologists who liken it to "biting on an aching tooth, sucking pleasure from the pain" (p. 15). Thus, there is little point in playing the "who has been most victimized" game. Nonetheless, in his important book, *Minority Education and Caste* (1978), Ogbu observed that, historically, the United States (and its predecessor European colonies) systematically attacked Native Americans, Mexican Americans, and African Americans. Using force, European Americans took the land of the first two groups and the labor of the third. As part of the process of justifying American history, European Americans have therefore systematically stigmatized these groups as inferior. That is why Ogbu called Native Americans, Mexican Americans, and African Americans "caste minorities." *Caste* means a group locked in place in a hierarchy with almost no way for individuals to move up or down. This has accurately described these three groups for most of their history in the United States. Also, unlike Irish, Italian, Japanese, and Chinese Americans, until recently the caste minorities could not point to strong foreign

---

[3]Since humans probably originated in Africa, all of us have distant African ancestry.

nations as their point of origin.[4]

If, in the minds of whites, there is a stigma attached to being black, Indian, or Hispanic (particularly Mexican American), and if whites control most institutions in the society (most colleges, companies, religious organizations, governmental agencies, etc.), then to be defined as black, Indian, or Hispanic is a disadvantage. Race will then correlate with many other social variables.

Minorities have less than their fair share of power and receive less than their share of money, status, and other societal rewards. Median family income is even more important. Because money is the key to so many things in our society, median family income is probably the single most important statistic to examine. Figure 2.2 shows median family incomes for European Americans and for Ogbu's three caste minorities. These latter three groups—African Americans, Native Americans, and Hispanics—make far less money, on average, than do non-Hispanic whites. The median income of black families was only 57% of the income for white families. Indians and Hispanics averaged about 65% of white income per capita.[5]

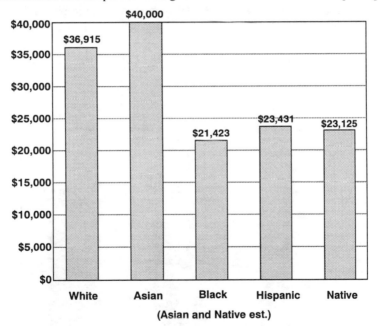

FIG. 2.2.   1990 median family income, by race. Data from Census Bureau.

---

[4]American Indian nations have not been independent since at least 1890 (Brown, 1971). Most African nations were under colonial rule until the 1960s and are still unequal partners in the global setting. Mexico has been independent but clearly under United States influence; the United States sent troops to Mexico 11 times during Woodrow Wilson's presidency alone. Of course, in the precolonial past all three groups can point to important accomplishments.

[5]Although some Hispanics do not fit Ogbu's definition of caste minority, sources usually describe Hispanics as a group. Mexican Americans comprise about 62% of all Hispanics, Puerto Ricans 13%, Cubans 5%, and those from other Latin American countries 12%.

Income buys access to everything from attorneys to the Boy Scouts to computer camps to dictionaries to x-rays to Yellowstone to zoos. African American, Hispanic, and Native American families lag in their use of all these things. Ultimately, money buys life itself, in the form of better nutrition and health care and freedom from danger and stress. Thus, it comes as no surprise that African and Native Americans have median life expectancies at birth that are several years less than that of whites (see Fig 2.3).[6]

Many of these differences in income and life expectancy come about because many people of color hold very low-paying jobs or no jobs at all. Figure 2.4 shows unemployment for African Americans and Native Americans, compared to European Americans. On some Indian reservations and in some urban ghettos, unemployment among young men reaches 75%.

In turn, young men without jobs are the group most likely to commit crimes. African Americans are arrested more, are convicted still more often, and serve longer jail terms than do European Americans. The statistics showing higher rates of incarceration among African Americans, summarized in Fig. 2.5, indicate different treatment by race within the criminal justice system but also reflect a

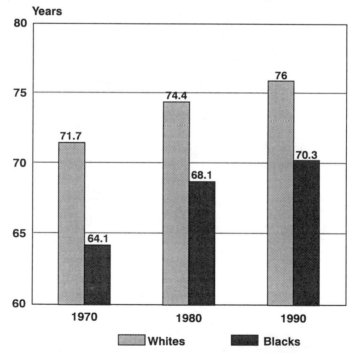

FIG. 2.3. Life expectancy at birth. Data from *Two Nations: Statistical Abstract.*

[6]European Americans' median life expectancy is 76, whereas African Americans (on average) die 6 years earlier, and Native Americans die younger still. Incidentally, these facts mean that Social Security is a massive transfer program, shifting retirement money away from African and Native Americans to white and Asian Americans.

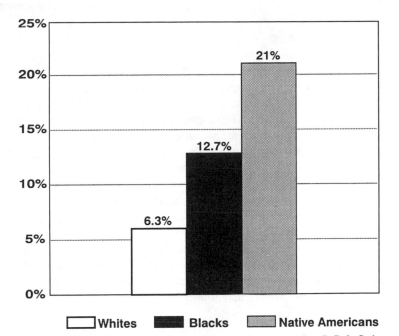

FIG. 2.4. Unemployment, by race (percentage of the labor force unemployed). B. L. S. data for December 1991 (projected for Natives).

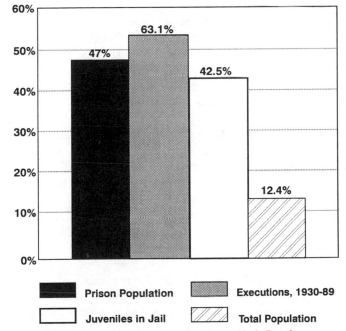

FIG. 2.5. Percentage of prison population categories who are black. Data from *Sourcebook of Criminal Justice Statistics.*

higher rate of criminal behavior.

In the short run, drug dealing and other criminal occupations can appear to be a rational response to the opportunity structure in ghetto neighborhoods. In the long run, however, criminal behavior rarely leads to satisfying lives, as the careers of the African American men described in the recent bestseller *Brothers* demonstrate (Monroe, Goldman, & Smith, 1988). Because most victims of African American criminals are themselves African Americans, criminal behavior cannot provide a route to upward mobility for the group as a whole.

The statistics in Fig. 2.5 are thus both a result and a cause of low family income. Elements of African American and Latino subculture also hold back African Americans and Latinos. An inner-city youth subculture has developed that denies the importance of white society and does not help individuals meet its standards. Many inner-city black and Hispanic adolescents do not work hard in high school and deride those who do so. This is understandable: Segregated housing projects like that depicted in *Brothers* offer few role models who might demonstrate that conventional routes to success work in the ghetto. Despite this, crime proves to be an inappropriate response even if the system is biased and one's prospects seem bleak (Monroe et al., 1988; Ogbu, 1990).

DO ALL THESE STATISTICS IMPLY
A RACIST SOCIETY?

Some observers place all the blame on the victim, believing that if African Americans, Native Americans, and Hispanics just "got their act together," they would face no more obstacles than anyone else in our society.[7] However, as we show in this chapter, various processes in our society still function to keep out African Americans, Hispanics, and Native Americans.

The word *racism* is a red flag to most white Americans, who apply it only to self- proclaimed white supremacists like David Duke (the former Ku Klux Klan leader who, in 1993, won 55% of the white vote for governor of Louisiana). Duke is a racist, to be sure, but the term has a broader meaning than merely a label for overt racial extremism. We must learn to use it not as a swearword but as an analytic term, and not as an explanation but as a description. Thus, the term should cause us to grow thoughtful rather than defensive.

The 1992 riots in Los Angeles and other cities, triggered by the verdict in the trial of police officers acquitted of police brutality toward Rodney King, point to the fact that the tragedies associated with intergroup hostility are too severe for some people to indulge in name calling or others in mindless defensiveness.

Sociologists Simpson and Yinger (1972) defined racism as "a complex of discriminations and prejudices directed against an allegedly inferior race" (p. 721). However, not all persons who discriminate against African Americans, for instance,

---

[7]Representatives of this point of view include Charles A. Murray, Thomas Sowell, and probably Supreme Court Justice Clarence Thomas.

do so because they believe them to be inferior. Lynch, a black Republican legislator from Mississippi during Reconstruction, summed up the argument of white supremacists as follows: "'We must proscribe the Negro because he is inferior and incapable,' but when he attempts to be successful, it says, 'We must proscribe the Negro, or he will equal us'"(Azug & Maizlish, 1986, p. 117). Thus, in 1911 the Kentucky Derby barred black jockeys, but not because anyone thought they were inferior—they had won 15 of the first 28 derbies!

Not everyone who discriminates realizes that he or she is doing so. Imagine that a personnel officer in charge of hiring census takers used a difficult aptitude test similar to the SAT, with complex math and verbal questions. Many white and Asian suburbanites would probably do well on it. Hiring applicants with the highest scores would virtually exclude inner-city African Americans, Native Americans, and Hispanics, even though the exam would have little directly to do with the skills required for successful census interviewing. Our census personnel officer who used the test to hire only whites and Asians shows that prejudice is not required for discrimination. Such an exam would be racist in effect, but probably not in intent. This example is not merely hypothetical: Educational Testing Service (ETS) and other test makers have prepared pencil-and-paper tests used for hiring for jobs ranging from welding to selling insurance to pumping gas. (A fairer welding test would be to ask the person to weld!)

A better operational definition of racism might be: treating people unfavorably because of their racial or cultural group membership, not because of any task-related qualifications. This definition says nothing about motivation; the unequal treatment can be on purpose or by accident. To the nonhired would-be census taker, after all, it makes no difference. Discrimination against racial or cultural groups who do not really vary physically from the majority (e.g., Jews) is included under this definition. Discrimination against people owing to other physically noticeable characteristics—gender, age, physical handicap—or owing to characteristics not so noticeable—sexual orientation or social class—shares many features of racism but should not be construed as racism itself. Becoming more aware of the processes linked to racism, however, usually helps one to become more aware of the very similar processes linked to discrimination along other lines. As with racism, discrimination owing to gender, sexual orientation, and so on may be inadvertent, cannot usually be defended as relevant to the task at hand, stunts careers, and amounts to a poor talent search for the society as a whole.

Many social scientists divide racism into three types: individual, institutional, and cultural. Acts of individual racism are committed by one or more persons to another person(s) and usually involve an element of intent. A landlord who refuses to rent an apartment to a couple because of their race would be an example.

Institutions and institutional policies can also be racist, however, without entailing individual racism. The hypothetical census personnel officer offers an example: Hiring on the basis of written aptitude test scores is not intentionally racist. It is racist in effect, however, because it makes hiring African Americans, Native

Americans, and Hispanics difficult. Thus, that census office would be institutionally racist, because it would treat people differently according to their color.

The third form, cultural racism, is built into our language, religion, etiquette,
law, and so on. It does not usually affect specific persons, such as job applicants,
but instead affects entire groups. For instance, all the images of powerful super-
natural figures in our culture are Caucasian, from angels to God to Santa Claus to
the tooth fairy. When pressed, to be sure, most Americans would probably claim
not to believe in a God or angels or a tooth fairy in human form, let alone in white
human form. Nonetheless, the images permeate our culture. To some degree, they
function to make people other than whites outsiders.

CAUSES OF RACIAL INEQUALITY
MUST BE STUDIED HISTORICALLY

At any given point in time, racial inequalities are evident even to casual observers
of our society. Their causes can be harder to understand, partly because inequalities
interconnect. For example, income buys education. Public high schools are far
better and classes far smaller in northern Long Island suburbs of New York City
than in the lower class parts of Brooklyn. Income buys suburban housing. After
graduation, affluent suburban high school children have a clear avenue to college,
paved by parental incomes, with green lights provided by high SAT scores. Poor
Brooklyn high school graduates have no clear path to any destination valued by the
larger society. This is one reason why many Brooklyn students do not choose to
work hard in high school. In turn, better education will help suburban Long
Islanders earn higher incomes, continuing the cycle.

A snapshot in time can make it look as if the downtrodden are oppressed owing
to their own fault. The visitor to Brooklyn may see children cutting school, dropping
out, even selling drugs or sex, and may conclude that more money spent on
education would only be wasted in the ghetto. In a now-famous book by the same
title, sociologist Ryan (1971) called this attitude "blaming the victim." Few social
scientists believe that genetic inferiority causes the lower incomes, shorter life
spans, lower IQ test scores, and poorer swimming ability that African Americans,
Native Americans, and Hispanics typically exhibit. Social scientists look for social
causes to explain these racial inequalities. The trouble with blaming the victim is
that it keeps us from perceiving the various processes in our society that work to
keep people underprivileged. To see race relations in our society from a better
perspective we need to take a longer view—a historical view.

Three groups in our history have been especially singled out for unfair treatment
by European Americans. First were the Native Americans, whose land was taken.
Several states continued to deny Native Americans basic civil rights, including the
rights to appear in court and to vote, until well into the 20th century. "The problem"
wasn't simply the Indians' "failure to acculturate" but continuing discrimination,
which still exists in many parts of the United States.

Second were Hispanics, particularly Mexicans and Mexican Americans who lived in and governed half of what we now call the United States—from Florida through Arkansas to San Francisco. After the Anglo settlers took the Southwest, they pushed most Mexican Americans off their land and denied them civil and legal rights.

Europeans brought African Americans here in chains. Throughout the United States, those who had become free were liable to re-enslavement until the Civil War. Slavery officially ended in 1863, but it left a legacy to the present: the ideology known as white supremacy. Immediately after the Civil War, there was a brief period (Reconstruction, 1863–1877) during which African Americans made significant gains in legal status. Soon, however, the federal government stopped enforcing the civil rights laws. African Americans then entered a period of regression called the "nadir of American race relations" by historian Rayford Logan. African Americans began to regain a measure of legal equality in the United States only after the 1954 school desegregation decision, *Brown v. Board of Education*, which helped trigger the civil rights movement. The three caste minorities are still far from achieving social or economic equality.

THE LEGACY OF PRIOR DISCRIMINATION LINGERS
TO AFFECT THE PRESENT

Faulkner once wrote that the past is never dead. It's not even past. About race relations, the most direct influence from the past is, literally, our inheritance. Whites inherit more when relatives die; before they die, whites get more assistance in buying a home, starting a business, or meeting family emergencies (Blau & Graham, 1990). Income is unequal by race in America, but wealth is far less equal, for the very good reason that people with low incomes cannot accumulate savings, and in order to transfer wealth across generations you must accumulate it. Thus, the median African American family has just one tenth of the total wealth amassed by the median white family. Similarly, Native Americans and Hispanics control very few assets. Figure 2.6 shows wealth by race.

Along with name, race, and religion, parents pass this financial inequality on to their children. Families translate their financial capital into human capital when they use their savings to send their children to camp, buy *Sesame Street Magazine*, or take their tyke to the symphony. Parents are supposed to do what they can for their children, and some parents can do vastly more than others. Children in families worth $3,397—the median African American family net worth—do not get the same childhood that affluent children receive. Moreover, 30% of black families and 24% of Hispanic families have a negative net worth (Blackwell, 1990).

Because money purchases opportunity, children raised with more money are likely to receive better training in skills ranging from swimming to computer awareness. Thus, even if all racial discrimination had miraculously ceased when students entering college in the year 2000 were born 18 years previously, caste

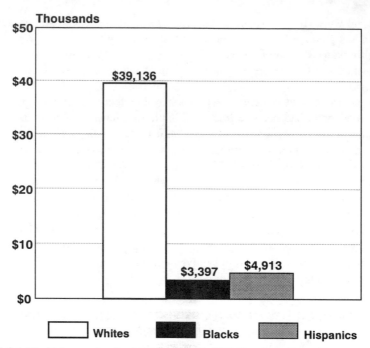

FIG. 2.6. Wealth by race (median family net worth), 1986. Data from Census Bureau.

minority children on average would still be way behind—particularly in academic vocabulary—owing to discrimination in their parents' generation. Partly as a result of their better skills training, whites' SAT scores in the late 1980s averaged 160 points higher than those of African American children, 125 more than Hispanics, and 100 more than Native Americans (Rosser, 1989). Affluent European American children are not inherently more able than their caste minority peers, but SAT scores reflect socioeconomic background as well as racial and cultural test bias. Wilson (1978) and others who emphasize social class pointed out that much of the gap is related to differences in family income. Wilson's critics, like Willie (1986), pointed out that much is also related to continuing racial discrimination.

Regardless of the origin of the gaps, when colleges use SAT scores to help select their student bodies without considering the social and economic milieux in which students achieved their scores, the colleges are using past discrimination to justify denial of admission or rejection for scholarship aid. In turn, adults who do not get into college are more likely to raise children with low SAT scores, and the vicious circle repeats itself.

RACIAL DISCRIMINATION STILL GOES ON TODAY

Unfortunately, racial discrimination continues. In the area of sports, for example, Braddock (1990) studied the selection of coaches (head, offensive, and defensive coaches) in the National Football League in the 1970s. He looked at the race, education, leadership, and accomplishments of players to see which factors predicted promotion to coaching. He found that if race were not a factor, African Americans would occupy 102 of the 329 coaching positions. Instead, they held just 20. Race was a factor "even after black and white players' differences in educational attainment, leadership ..., and professional accomplishments have been equated or controlled [for] statistically" (p. 116).[8]

Bank credit is often a key to success in U.S. society, whether in small business or home improvement. Many banks draw a "red line" around neighborhoods that are not predominantly white and refuse mortgages for homes in those areas, even when the property is sound and the family's income, credit history, and assets equal those of white families who do get mortgages in the area. A 1992 study by the Federal Reserve Bank found that minorities were 60% more likely to be denied mortgages than whites, even when they were equally credit worthy ("Blacks' woes," 1991; Loewen, 1982; Zuckoff, 1992).

A segment shown in 1991 on television's "60 Minutes" titled "All American" documented straightforward discrimination at a large employment firm in New York City. Producers sent two young women with secretarial training to interview for jobs. They were matched as to age, educational background, and even beauty, but the African American had slightly better secretarial skills. Nonetheless, the agency gave the European American woman several referrals, whereas it told the African American woman "We'll call you." The segment showed how the company coded applications "AA" for "All-American" if the applicant was attractive and European American, but used different codings and treated the applicant differently if he or she was not European American and not attractive.

Overt racial discrimination is no longer legal, to be sure, but it is not easy to prove. The employment agency, having been caught on videotape by "60 Minutes," settled the lawsuit that plaintiffs then brought. However, more often in such cases an individual has only the uneasy feeling that he or she has not been treated equally, but no proof of discrimination and no systematic knowledge of how other applicants fared.

OTHER SOCIETAL PROCESSES DISCRIMINATE INDIRECTLY

Probably the most severe hurdles faced by African, Native, and Hispanic Americans today are more subtle than plain discrimination. Various processes operate in our society that treat whites better than other people. Institutions in our society operate to discriminate, with or without conscious design. These processes affect every

---

[8]Colleges and universities are reluctant to hire African Americans as head coaches, according to Reed (1990). Braddock used multiple regression and path analysis to examine the effects of several factors at once. He defined leadership operationally as "centrality of position," with quarterback, center, and coordinating defensive linebacker considered central positions.

institution in America, such as traditionally white colleges and universities, that does not take specific steps to overcome them. They combine to mock the slogan almost every college and large corporation applies to itself: "An Equal Opportunity Institution."

In this section we consider seven racist processes: historical, economic, psychological, cultural, social structural, ecological, and political. Each of these processes is racist, in that each affects other people differently and more harshly than it does Euro-Americans. Yet each is institutionally racist, not individually racist. Together they contribute to an overall condition: unequal opportunity.

Historical: High School History Encourages Identification With White Supremacist Heroes

The year 1992 marked the quincentenary of Christopher Columbus' arrival on Haiti,[9] whom the United States honors with a holiday. Recently I studied how 15 history textbooks used in U.S. high schools portray Columbus. They present him as a hero and invite us to identify with him (Loewen, 1992a).

The crossing of the Atlantic by Columbus and his conquest of Haiti can be seen as amazing feats of courage and imagination. The latter can also be understood as a bloody atrocity. When Columbus arrived, Haiti had a population of about 3 million (Cook & Borah, 1971). Sixty years later, owing primarily to Spanish wars against the Arawaks—when the Spaniards enslaved the Arawaks, interfered with their food production, and disrupted their culture—full-blooded Indians had disappeared from Haiti. Haiti under the Spaniards was the site of one of the biggest genocides in all of human history.[10]

Both views of Columbus are legitimate. Indeed, his historic importance owes precisely to his being both a heroic navigator and a distinguished plunderer. If he were only the former, he would merely rival Leif Erikson. Columbus shows us both meanings of the word *exploit*—a remarkable deed and also to take advantage of. Textbooks should no more guarantee his "rightness" by what they include and exclude than his "wrongness"—they should present both sides. They do not.

---

[9]Again, there are questions of terminology. What was the original name of the island Columbus named *Hispaniola*, now Haiti and the Dominican Republic? Perhaps *Haiti*, an Arawak word probably meaning "highlands." Perhaps *Bohio*, an Arawak word probably meaning "home." For that matter, *Arawak* may not be the best word for the Indians Columbus met; some scholars use *Tainos*.

[10]Some writers argued that *genocide* is too harsh a term. They maintain that since the Spanish profited from Indian labor on Haiti they didn't want to wipe out the Arawaks, and that many Indians died from diseases like malaria, which the Spanish introduced unknowingly. However, smallpox—the big killer of Indians elsewhere in the Americas—did not appear on Haiti until after 1516, suggesting that war and slavery played a larger role than disease between 1492 and 1515. Moreover, disease and forced famine were factors in other genocides, according to Ward Churchill (1992b). Churchill argued that Europeans' treatment of Indians can be compared with the Nazi Holocaust against Jews and Gypsies. In *American Holocaust: Columbus and the Conquest of the New World* (Stannard, 1992), David E. Stannard argued that the "destruction of the native peoples of the Americas was the most massive act of genocide in the history of the world."

Following are two stories written about Columbus and his arrival in the Americas. The contrast between them shows how our histories are still colonialist. The first story encourages identification with Columbus. The second one presents an Arawak view. It is part of a longer account, written shortly after the event, of an Arawak *cacique* (leader) who had fled from Haiti to Cuba.

A man riding a mule moved slowly down a dusty road in Spain. He wore an old and shabby cloak over his shoulders. Though his face seemed young, his red hair was already turning white. It was early in the year 1492 and Christopher Columbus was leaving Spain.
Twice the Spanish king and queen had refused his request for ships. He had wasted five years of his life trying to get their approval. Now he was going to France. Perhaps the French king would give him the ships he needed.
Columbus heard a clattering sound. He turned and looked up the road. A horse and rider came racing toward him. The rider handed him a message, and Columbus turned his mule around. The message was from the Spanish king and queen, ordering him to return. Columbus would get his ships. (Peck, Jantzen, & Rosen, 1987, p. 16)

Learning that Spaniards were coming, one day [the *cacique*] gathered all his people together to remind them of the persecutions which the Spanish had inflicted on the people of Hispaniola:
    "Do you know why they persecute us?"
They replied: "They do it because they are cruel and bad."
    "I will tell you why they do it," the *cacique* stated, "and it is this—because they have a lord whom they love very much, and I will show him to you."
He held up a small basket made from palms full of gold, and he said, "Here is their lord, whom they serve and adore .... To have this lord, they make us suffer, for him they persecute us, for him they have killed our parents, brothers, all our people .... Let us not hide this lord from the Christians in any place, for even if we should hide it in our intestines, they would get it out of us; therefore let us throw it in this river, under the water, and they will not know where it is."
Whereupon they threw the gold into the river. (Williams, 1963, pp. 92–93)

The first fragment comes from an American history textbook, in this case *American Adventures*. Most of what it describes never really happened (Peck et al., 1987).[11] Why was it included in *American Adventures*? It creates a mild air of suspense, although we know everything will turn out all right in the end. Certainly it encourages identification, making Columbus the underdog, riding a mule and dressed in a shabby cloak. It puts us on his side.

As best we can tell, the incident described in the second story did happen. It was written down by Bartolomé de las Casas, whose summaries of Columbus' original

---

[11]The only accurate details would be that Spanish roads were sometimes dusty, Columbus' hair had turned white, and it did take 5 years to win the support of the monarchs. Columbus was not poor, he was not leaving Spain, and there was no last-minute message (de Madariaga, 1940/1967; Sale, 1990).

journals are the best record we have of these crucial undertakings. He apparently learned it orally from Arawaks in Cuba (Williams, 1963). Unlike the mule story, the *cacique*'s story teaches important historic facts—that the Spanish sought gold, that they killed Indians, and that Indians fled and resisted. (Indeed, after futile attempts at armed resistance in Cuba, this *cacique* then fled "into the brambles." Weeks later, when the Spanish finally caught up with him, they burned him alive.) No history textbook includes the *cacique*'s story.

These passages show how our textbooks omit any story that might undermine the moral or technical superiority of Europeans. Including the perspective of the colonized people, rather than just the conqueror's, might help students understand both sides of the story. Excluding the second passage and including the first amounts to colonialist history. Such writing invites European Americans to feel comfortable in "their" country. Leaving out other points of view implies that American history is European American history and invites other Americans to feel *un*comfortable. Presentations like these have prompted outcries from African Americans for history viewed from an Afrocentric point of view.

Economic: Unequal School Finance Hampers Inner-City Schools

Inner cities connect many school-age children with few tax dollars. Many families live in large apartment buildings. Some of these are publicly owned, whereas others are in such poor condition that they have low valuations for tax purposes. As transportation has shifted from rail to truck and air, industries have moved to the suburbs, so cities cannot tax them. Meanwhile, cities continue to house government agencies, hospitals, and universities, which either are not taxed at all or pay only nominal fees. As a result, cities have had to tax private property at high rates in order to afford even mediocre school systems (Kozol, 1991).[12] When they do this, they find themselves in a dilemma: High taxes induce more businesses to move to the suburbs, where taxes are lower, and the urban tax base erodes further. In *Savage Inequalities*, Kozol (1991) related how industries in the East St. Louis area even incorporated their own tiny towns, partly so that they would not have to pay to support East St. Louis schools, which are 98% African American (Kozol, 1991).[13]

In contrast, affluent suburbs boast single-family homes valued at between $150,000 and $750,000. When a new industry moves to a suburb, the school district can afford to lower its tax rate, while still taking in enough revenue for splendid teachers and equipment. Figure 2.7 compares the result for Manhasset, a suburb of New York City, and the city's school system.

Kozol (1991) showed similar disparities in the metropolitan areas of San Antonio, St. Louis, Chicago, Boston, and Camden, New Jersey. Figure 2.8 shows the resulting disparity nationally in just one variable: access to computers in school.

---

[12]A few large city school systems maintain excellent "flagship" high schools, like Bronx Science or Boston Latin. Nevertheless, these systems are known for overall mediocrity, partly caused, according to Jonathan Kozol (1991), by the extra attention and expenditures they lavish on the flagships.

[13]Kozol also showed how our tax system offers enormous subsidies to wealthy suburbanites.

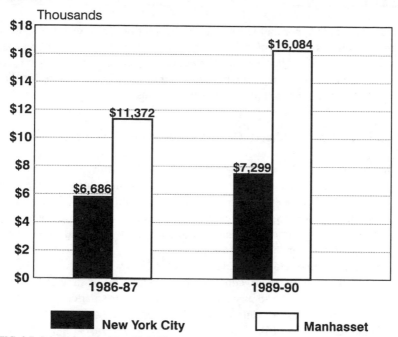

FIG. 2.7. School funding, New York City versus suburb, spending per pupil. Data from Kosol, *Savage Inequalities. (1991).*

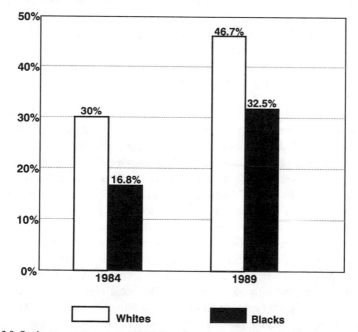

FIG. 2.8. Student computer use at school. Data from *Statistical Abstract: Digest of Educational Statistics.*

So much for equal opportunity in education. In addition, because houses cost so much and sometimes because of racial "steering" by realtors, people of color are often shut out of suburbs. Thus, because they cannot live in a suburb, they are shut out of its excellent school system, and because their urban schools are inferior, they are shut out of occupations that pay well. It is a vicious cycle.

Cultural: Stereotypes of "Place" Cause Whites to End Up on Top

According to Burns (1991), who made a public television series on the Civil War, the black–white rift "stands at the very center of American history. It is the great challenge to which all our deepest aspirations to freedom must rise." And he warned "If we forget that—if we forget the great stain of slavery that stands at the heart of our country, our history, our experiment—we forget who we are, and we make the great rift deeper and wider."

The key idea we inherited from slavery is that whites were meant to be on top and blacks on the bottom. In its core, our culture tells all of us that Europe's domination of the world came about because Europeans were smarter. Many whites and some non-whites who have internalized their oppression believe it. Martyred South African leader Steve Biko wrote of the colonialized black man who "has become a shell, a shadow of a man, completely defeated," blaming "himself for not having been educated enough" (Biko, 1979, pp. 28–29). African American writers like Ntozake Shange (*For Colored Girls Who Have Considered Suicide/When the Rainbow Is Enuf*) and Ralph Ellison (*Invisible Man*) described the wounds inflicted on the psyche when this low sense of self-esteem is absorbed from the surrounding culture (Ellison, 1952; Shange, 1977). More remains to be written about the damage to the *white* psyche from absorbing the racism that still permeates our slavery-influenced culture.

Thus, lawyers in a big city firm do not really notice that all the partners are European American, whereas half of the secretaries and all the people who clean up are African American or Hispanic. Whites do not notice because they do not really think about it. It seems natural because American culture has handed us a set of stereotypes about people of color that we have come to believe. Native Americans are often thought of as "drunken Indians." Mexican Americans may be pictured at siesta time—"Do it *mañana*." Announcers laud African American athletes for their "natural ability," but not for their brain power.

European Americans, on the other hand, so often head social institutions that we do not think this is unusual. Instead, we consider it unusual for a Hispanic, African American, or Native American to actually lead a university or company. The first two years of a recent advertising campaign, "The Most Beautiful Women of the World Wear Revlon," portrayed four different light-skinned white women in almost every panel, implying over the seasons that almost all of the most beautiful women are white and most of them are blonde. From Dr. Doolittle to Dr. Seuss, white male characters dominate the classics of children's literature.[14] Even the lowly Band-Aid plays a role in maintaining our "white is right" syndrome: We have no name for its color except "flesh color!"[15]

To some degree, these ways of thinking get internalized by minority and majority groups alike. Then they operate to make it harder for people of non-European descent to break out of the mold and challenge the stereotype. The same process also hinders disabled people, who report that they face *two* handicaps: their actual physical or mental impairment, and the stereotyped views of the rest of us as to their limitations.

Psychological: Differing Teacher Expectations Hurt Caste Minority Children

Within classrooms, from kindergarten on, teachers expect more from some students than from others. Unfortunately, like the rest of us, teachers are products of our culture. Therefore, like the rest of us, teachers are likely to think it is usual for whites to be on top. As a result, many teachers expect less from minority students, without even realizing it, unless the students are of Asian descent—in which case teachers often expect more. Over time, many students internalize these expectations. Similarly, from subtle ways in which teachers treat them, female students can infer that they are bad at math—so that they *become* bad at math. It is a self-fulfilling prophecy. The fact that most physical scientists, engineers, and architects are male does not help girls develop confidence that they are equal to boys in math. The fact that most highly educated and influential people in our society are white does not help caste minority youth develop confidence that they are as capable academically as are whites. Thus, "evidence" from society reinforces these lower expectations from teachers.

In May 1964, two social scientists, Rosenthal and Jacobson (1968a, 1968b), began an experiment to show the power of expectations. They gave an IQ test to classes of kindergarten through fifth-grade students at the Oak School in San Francisco. But they duped the teachers and students into believing that the exam identified students in each grade who were about to spurt. When school opened the next fall, Rosenthal and Jacobson casually mentioned to the teachers the names of four or five children in each classroom who were likely to show unusual intellectual

---

[14]Visiting an all-black kindergarten in Illinois, Kozol watched a teacher read from a "worn and old" Mother Goose book and noted, "Mary is white. Old Mother Hubbard is white. Jack is white. Jill is white. Little Jack Horner is white. Mother Goose is white. Only Mother Hubbard's dog is black" (Kozol, 1991; p. 45).

[15]Some corporations have broken out of this "appropriate place" corral. Benetton deliberately includes all groups in its "United Colors of Benetton" ads. Digital seeks women for traditionally male technical jobs, people of color for traditionally white management positions, and people with physical handicaps for jobs previously thought to require able-bodied workers. Revlon, too, finally desegregated its "Women of the World" campaign.

gains in the year ahead. Actually, the spurters had been chosen randomly.[16]

At the end of the school year, Rosenthal and Jacobson retested the students (see Fig. 2.9). In the first two grades, the experiment had clearly worked. Spurters in first grade gained an average of 27 IQ points. How had this happened? The researchers concluded that through "tone of voice, facial expression, touch," and other means, teachers communicated different expectations to different children. The Oak School findings have been called the *expectancy effect* and are considered a classic example of a self-fulfilling prophecy.

Other researchers have shown that when African American children excel they are *less* liked by their teachers, whereas when white children excel they are *more* liked (Brophy & Good, 1974). Even Hispanic and African American teachers sometimes participate in expecting more from European American children. Thus, individual racism may not be the culprit; rather, teachers have a sense for the "right order," "the way things should be." Students who are "not supposed to" know the right answer do not get rewarded the same way as students who are supposed to know. What is the "right order"? Harvey and Slatin (1975) showed photographs of children to teachers, and found the teachers all too willing to predict different levels of school performance based solely on snapshots. "White children were more often

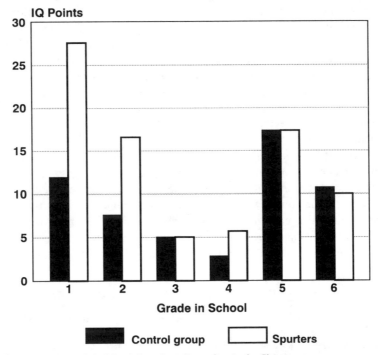

FIG. 2.9. IQ gains at Oak School. Data from *Pygmalion in the Classroom.*

---

[16]This research led to more than a thousand subsequent studies. Although some researchers questioned the findings, enough studies confirmed them to give reason to believe in their generality.

expected to succeed and black children more often expected to fail" (p. 141), Harvey and Slatin reported.

Special note must be taken of the expectations placed on Asian Americans. Many European Americans stereotype Asian Americans as a "model minority"—studious, docile, hardworking. Although this image is generally positive, it still constrains and limits Asian Americans. Some Asian American students report that their high school teachers always expected them to know the right answers, especially in math and science classes, so that they had to be extra prepared. At the same time, some whites point to Asian academic success as proof that "the system works," America is no longer racist, and the problem really resides within those *other* minorities. Research by Tang indicates that a "glass ceiling" keeps Asian American engineers from advancing to management, however. Thus, the stereotype that "Asians are good at math" cuts both ways, enhancing and limiting Asian American careers. In reality, Asian American success partly underscores the power of expectation. This point was brought home to me while I was researching in Mississippi, when I discovered that children of mixed African and Chinese ancestry excelled in then-segregated black schools, because their black teachers expected them to always know the right answer (Loewen, 1988).

When different expectations by race, class, or gender dominate a classroom, students do not have an equal chance to succeed. Such a classroom does not provide equal educational opportunities to all its students.

Social Structural: Segregated Networks Keep Opportunity Within the In Group

According to information circulated by American Express in 1985, 85% of all jobs are not advertised but instead are filled by word of mouth. This is the meaning behind the old cliché "It's not what you know but who you know that counts" (Baber & Waymon, 1992; Granovetter, 1973).

Many college students have used networking to land summer jobs. Their parents may have suggested that they contact a friend of the family, told them of a company that was hiring, or put in a good word for them so that they would be hired. Networking also helped many of them learn about specific college opportunities in the first place: A friend went there, or a counsellor knew the campus and passed on the word.[17]

Networking is also a way of life in the faculty. Professors in departments with entry-level openings contact friends in large graduate departments to learn of their recent Ph.D.s. Through countless informal connections like these, people learn about the vacancies, decide to apply, get recommended by people known to the senior faculty, and get hired. There is nothing intrinsically wrong with this informal process: Often professors learn more about a candidate from an informal phone call

---

[17]Compare this to Malcolm X's high school English teacher, who suggested that he become a carpenter although he excelled academically (Malcolm X, 1964).

than they ever could through a formal application. Because America is still racially segregated, however, networks are separated by race (Korte & Milgram, 1970). And because most professors are white, most of their informal connections are with white colleagues, so word of job opportunities often does not cross over effectively into the minority networks. Many departments make special efforts to get the word out to such groups, such as advertizing in *The Black Scholar* or sending notices to predominantly black colleges, but the informal networks still have a powerful impact on academia and corporate life.

Perhaps the gravest barrier people who are segregated face is their social isolation. Residential segregation locks African Americans into ghettos, Hispanics into barrios, and Native Americans onto reservations and into inner-city neighborhoods. Their parents and neighbors do not know employers with whom they could "put in a good word." Thus, in conjunction with racial segregation in residence and occupation, networking works to help whites get in and keep others out. This holds true whether we are talking about summer jobs, university professorships, or positions in corporate America.

Ecological: Minority Neighborhoods Are More Likely to Suffer From Industrial Pollution and Inferior City Services

In almost every major city, residential neighborhoods adjoin heavy industry. Kozol (1991) described one such scene in 1989: "On the southern edge of East St. Louis, tiny shack-like houses stand along a lightless street. Immediately behind these houses are the giant buildings of Monsanto, Big River Zinc, Cerro Copper, the American Bottoms Sewage Plant, and Trade Waste Incineration" (p. 15). According to an inspector, the entire city of 55,000 people is contaminated. The industries did not set out to make such people sick; they merely located where zoning allowed them to locate. Some companies now look to Indian reservations to dump their waste. White suburbs use their greater legal and political clout to exclude heavy industry or limit it to areas that are far from residential neighborhoods.

Sometimes government itself is the culprit. In 1992, New York City made headlines because crews sandblasting the Williamsburg Bridge sprayed lead-based paint chips over a wide residential area in Brooklyn. Testing revealed that even before the bridge work lead levels had already been far higher than allowable limits. Although this episode was new, the problem was old: 20 years earlier, William Ryan (1971) began his bestseller, *Blaming the Victim*, with a description of criminal levels of lead poisoning that caused hundreds of thousands of inner-city children to grow up mentally retarded and physically ill.

Dinuba, California, a town of about 12,000, lies in the fertile San Joaquin Valley, southeast of San Francisco. It has more Mexican Americans than Anglos in its population. Mexican American neighborhoods look very different from Anglo neighborhoods, however, because municipal services are so unequal. From streetlights to storm water drainage, the city does a better job in Anglo areas. Table

2.1 shows just one variable, the condition of sidewalks. The overall pattern forces the conclusion that municipal services are not provided equally, without regard to race, in Dinuba, California. Residents in Hispanic neighborhoods have the right to feel cheated by this obviously unequal expenditure of tax dollars. All across America, non-white neighborhoods face similar inequalities in city services ranging from zoning to hospital location to sewage water backup (Banfield, 1961; *Hawkins v. Shaw,* 1972; Kozol, 1991; Loewen, 1992b).

TABLE 2.1
Condition of Sidewalks In Dinuba, California,
by Residential Composition of Neighborhood

Condition	Anglo	Mixed	Hispanic	Total
Excellent	88.7%	59.6%	36.8%	60.1%
Good	11.3%	30.9%	38.5%	27.6%
Holes, etc.		3.2%	8.5%	4.2%
Poor		6.4%	16.2%	8.1%
	100%	100%	100%	100%
N	97	94	117	308

Political: White Bloc Voting Coupled With At-Large Elections Keeps City Councils Anglo

Why do people who are discriminated against not take advantage of the political process and elect officials who will give their neighborhoods a better break? Bloc voting by whites often makes this difficult. In some communities and for some offices, whites have proven willing to vote for candidates of another color. Andrew Young captured 51% of the white vote when he won the election for Congress in his Atlanta-based district (*Busbee v. U.S.*, 1982). Douglas Wilder captured about 40% of white votes when he won the governorship of Virginia in 1989. An African American is mayor of predominantly white Seattle. In most cities, towns, and counties, however, whites bloc vote for European American candidates, even when African American or Hispanic candidates have equal or better qualifications for office (Davidson & Grofman, 1995; Loewen, 1990a, 1991). Overall in 1993, African Americans controlled 2% of the governorships, 1% of the U.S. Senate, about 8% of the House, and perhaps 1.8% of state and local positions, even though they comprised 12% of the population. Hispanic representation lagged even further behind the 8% of the population that Hispanics now constitute. Figure 2.10 shows percentages of elected officials who were black, from 1964 to 1990.

Dinuba exemplifies this process. In 1990, the city was about 60% Mexican American. Voters, however, were only 35% Mexican American, because Anglos comprised a higher proportion of the adult population, had higher voter registration, and had higher turnout on election day. Anglos also voted overwhelmingly for Anglo candidates. Because Dinuba elected its city council at large rather than from districts, often all five members were Anglo. If Dinuba elected its city council by district, as many cities do, Hispanics would probably elect two of five councilors. These officials might then be able to bargain politically to improve their neighborhoods.[18]

In 1993, in response to a suit filed by Mexican American plaintiffs, Dinuba finally gave up its at-large voting system, and more Hispanic candidates began to win elections. Nationally, African Americans, Latinos, and Native Americans won lawsuits that led to winnable single member districts from Los Angeles to Boston, Florida to Illinois. As a result, the proportion of public officials elected from these groups rose. Minority candidates never won office in proportion to their share of the population, however, and in the mid-1990s a spate of lawsuits by European Americans challenged even these gains. These plaintiffs argued that districts constructed to put people of color in the majority disadvantaged the white minority. By this argument, most districts in the United States disadvantaged people of color, since they were in the minority. Nevertheless, the Supreme Court accepted the whites' argument, so many districts had to be redrawn to put whites in the majority again.

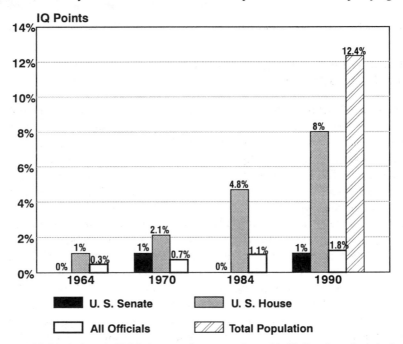

FIG. 2.10. Black elected officials (percent of category who are black). Data from *Statistical Abstract, Joint Center for Political Studies.*

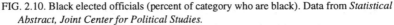

[18]Mexican Americans held 17.9% of city council positions before 1993. However, the occasional Mexican American candidates who won knew that they owed their success to Anglo voters as much as to Hispanic voters, so they could not do much to improve conditions in the barrios. In 1993, in response to a suit filed by Hispanic plaintiffs, Dinuba finally changed its at-large voting system, and more Hispanic candidates began to win elections.

THE OVERALL PROCESS: UNEQUAL OPPORTUNITY

These seven processes of institutional discrimination, other processes that could be described, the legacy of prior discrimination, and the direct individual racial discrimination that still goes on all combine to form what we can call "unequal opportunity." We can trace some of the interconnections if we follow two imaginary children, Dick and Jane, from birth to the age at which they might attend college. Jane lives in a mixed African American and Hispanic part of Brooklyn. Dick lives in suburban Darien, Connecticut.

Before they are even born, they are treated unequally. Dick's mother sees her obstetrician regularly and receives current medical advice ("Stop smoking, stay active, watch your weight gain …"). Her general health, fitness, and nutrition are good. Jane's mother has no health insurance and gets no medical care. Her diet is loaded with sugars and starches, cheaper than the produce that costs 20% more in cities than in the suburbs (Caplovits, 1967). She meets an intern at the hospital emergency room and gives birth under anesthesia; Jane has to be spanked into consciousness. Dick's mother follows the instructions of her Lamaze group and has "natural" childbirth; Dick arrives fully conscious.

The infants go home, but to very different homes. Jane's has lead in the atmosphere and the ground; her walls were painted long ago with lead-based paint. Dick enjoys his mother's company all day and his father's on weekends, although they soon place him in a nearby Waldorf school for a few hours of "enrichment play" each week. Jane's mother works 5 days a week, so she leaves Jane with a neighbor who watches children while also watching television. Jane's father is not a factor in her life, so she gets no verbal stimulation from him, and her mother is usually too tired for much verbal play when she comes home in the evening.

Dick and Jane enter first grade. Dick's school in Darien recently won a national award for excellence in math instruction. It has a computer for every child. Jane's school has just one computer, used for demonstrations in the library. Some of Jane's first-grade classmates need more attention than do Dick's. Nevertheless, Jane's first-grade class has almost twice as many students. Dick's school system enjoys a rich property tax base, owing to splendid residences and corporate headquarters. Jane's school is part of a city system that is still struggling out of a barely averted bankruptcy years ago.

As the children progress through school, Dick's teachers expect him to know the right answer. They perceive the upper middle-class signals he gives off by his dress, bearing, and "show-and-tell" stories (Todd, 1986). Jane's teachers praise her for being attentive, a "good student," but they do not really expect her to be excellent. She shows a real flair for English, always picking the longest book she can find to meet reading assignments, but her math teacher subtly expects her not to know the right answer. Each summer, Dick's parents enroll him in different activities, such as creative dramatics, computer camp, Outward Bound. Once Jane goes to Vermont for 2 weeks as a Fresh Air Child, but otherwise she plays with her friends on the block.

In his junior year of high school, Dick takes the PSAT and the SAT for the first time. His SAT scores are below average for Darien, totaling just under 1,000, so his father enrolls him in the Princeton Review coaching course, which costs about $500 and promises average score gains of more than 100 points. "Of course" Dick is going to college, hopefully to his father's Ivy League alma mater, "if he can get his scores up."

In the fall of their senior years, Dick and Jane take the SAT "for real," Jane for the first time. Her main reason for taking it is that it is required of all students in certain high schools that have been placed on academic probation by the district board. Dick's scores total 1,120, about average for Darien, and his father suggests he apply to the University of Vermont in case he does not make it into the Ivy League. Jane scores 600 in English, the highest score from her high school in 2 years, but only 430 in math. Nonetheless, her English teacher suggests she apply to the University of Vermont, which recently sent a recruiter to a metropolitan college fair he attended.

Which student has more "aptitude?" If the university were to base its admission primarily on SAT scores, can we say that Dick and Jane have enjoyed equal opportunity? We know that poor prenatal nutrition inhibits intellectual performance (Loehlin, Lindzey, & Spuhler, 1975).[19] We know that the absence of fathers hurts SAT scores (Deutsch & Brown, 1967). We know that enriched preschooling causes some of the difference in scores between whites and people from deprived racial groups (Deutsch & Brown, 1967). We know that absence of summer programs helps explain why test scores of African American, Hispanic, and Native American children drop back in the summer (Hayes & Grether, 1975). We know that many math teachers subtly challenge boys to work on their own more than they do girls (Sadker & Sadker, 1986). We know that coaching, especially Princeton Review coaching, increases SAT scores and is less available to children from disadvantaged backgrounds (Hammer, 1989). In addition, Dick is familiar with the test, is better motivated to take it, is more aware of the test makers' vocabulary and subculture, and enjoys dozens of other advantages compared to Jane.

Thus, even though universities and the U.S. government officially treat people equally, opportunity remains decidedly unequal, particularly for caste minorities. Thus, "equal opportunity"—the elimination of all *formal* barriers based on race or sex—masks and maintains unequal opportunity.

HOW CAN THE VICIOUS CYCLE OF UNEQUAL OPPORTUNITY BE BROKEN?

Many institutional processes combine to make equal opportunity a myth, so that even if we stopped discrimination against others, everyone would not become equal automatically. We have not *been* discriminating, at least not intentionally. Institu-

---

[19]Let me hasten to add that the process is reversible: Good nutrition leads to >10 point increases in IQ.

tional processes have kept our universities, some suburbs, and corporate board-rooms white. To diversify we must change our institutional processes. It is as simple as that.

Where might these cycles of inequality be broken? In theory, we might begin at any point. For example, we might seriously try residential desegregation, so that minority children did not have to grow up in ghetto housing projects. In 1977, the Chicago Housing Authority was found guilty of deliberately segregating African Americans by locating public housing in areas already overwhelmingly black. As a remedy, the court required the authority to locate families in white neighborhoods in Chicago and its suburbs. Rosenbaum studied the outcomes for families placed in white neighborhoods. He found that being exposed to new surroundings had transforming effects on these families: 95% of their children graduated from high school and 54% went on to college. (Both of these rates were higher than those for European Americans nationally.) He concluded that residential segregation was itself the problem, promoting hopelessness and keeping poor black families from connecting with the larger society in ways that might help them obtain jobs or see the point of schooling. Unfortunately, only about 4,000 families have been thus desegregated in Chicago. Other cities and suburbs—absent a court order—have not been willing to accept such levels of class and racial desegregation.[20]

In theory, we might organize our public schools so that, from kindergarten on, they compensated for the inferior childhoods that ghettos supply. We could put some of our best teachers in interracial primary schools and make sure they had libraries and learning labs at least as good as those in white neighborhoods. As we have seen, however, ghetto schools not only do not make up for bad earlier conditions, they perpetuate the inequality. Parents of African American and Latino students have sued, claiming that the inequalities their children faced, as a result of unequal school financing, constituted a fundamental denial of equal opportunity. In 1973 in *San Antonio Independent School District v. Rodriguez* (1973), however, the Supreme Court denied their claim, holding that education "is not among the rights afforded explicit protection under our Federal Constitution, [n]or do we find any basis for saying it is implicitly so protected." In a few jurisdictions, state law provides a possible remedy. In 1981, parents in the New Jersey municipalities of East Orange, Camden, Irvington, and Jersey City filed a *Rodriguez*-type suit under the New Jersey state constitution. In 1990, they finally won. However, Justice Thurgood Marshall, dissenting in *Rodriguez*, pointed out that several white subur-ban school districts filed *amicus* briefs justifying the inequalities that the plaintiffs were attacking, which implies that districts like these will not give up their unequal finance privileges without a struggle (*Abbott v. Burke*, 1990; Kozol, 1991).

In theory, we might change our admissions policies in colleges and universities to extend more opportunity to caste minority students when they graduate from high school. Admissions policies could take into account the unequal conditions that have affected many caste minority children in their first 18 years of life. This

---

[20]See "A House Divided," which appeared on CNN's "The Nation's Agenda," September, 1992.

alternative is often called *affirmative action*. Affirmative action goes beyond treating all races "alike," which on the surface might seem fairer, but which results, as we have seen, in using inequalities in the first 18 years of life as the reason to extend less opportunity to racially disadvantaged people when they graduate from high school. Affirmative action compensates for the fact that society is patterned by race and gender in order to make opportunity within it more equal. Thus, affirmative action works as an antidote to institutional discrimination in our society.

Affirmative action is not new. Most institutions of higher learning already practice it in some form. State schools act affirmatively on behalf of their residents, admitting in-state students with lower grades and test scores. Many colleges act affirmatively on behalf of donors' families, children of alumni, and other special constituencies. Still others do so for students with special skills—athletes or musicians. Universities do all this because they believe that they have a duty to define themselves by defining their student bodies.

Such affirmative action is rarely controversial—until it concerns race. Nonetheless, many universities have passed resolutions calling for affirmative action to bring more minority students and faculty onto campus. Often, however, they have not made the institutional changes necessary to make these resolutions reality. The result of 20 years (1970–1990) of "equal opportunity/affirmative action" at the University of Vermont has been that an overwhelmingly white campus stayed overwhelmingly white. To be sure, almost half of its students come from the state of Vermont, where in 1990 among 562,758 residents, African Americans numbered only 1,951; Hispanics 3,661; and Native Americans (mostly Abenakis) 1,609. But the other half come mostly from the metropolitan areas of the east—Washington, Philadelphia, New York/New Jersey, and Boston. Almost one of every three high school graduates in these metropolitan areas is a caste minority.

Affirmative action began at the University of Vermont in 1970. In the 1969–1970 school year, the university had endured a year of controversy centered on "Kakewalk," a ritual deriving from blackface minstrel shows in the 19th century. The turmoil culminated in students abolishing Kakewalk. In the aftermath, considerable antiracist idealism remained, especially in the student body, admissions office, and school of education, prompting the university to increase the number of black professors from 2 to 10 and the number of black students from 6 to 75. After 1975, however, the university gradually stopped acting affirmatively. Admissions recruiters stopped seeking Hispanics or African Americans, visiting high schools in the suburban fringes instead. Thus, the numbers dwindled: By 1988, the student body included only 28 African Americans. Nationally, commitment to affirmative action dwindled during the Reagan–Bush years, and so did the number of African American undergraduate and graduate students (Gates, 1988).[21]

In the late 1990s, the Supreme Court seemed to be moving toward a ruling that to act affirmatively on behalf of racial minorities is illegal. Since the United States

---

[21] A diminishing pool of high school graduates was not the problem, for the proportion of African Americans graduating from high school rose from 79% in 1972 to 86% in 1991.

has not remedied the seven processes of institutional discrimination described earlier in this chapter, such a termination of affirmative action would exclude the three caste minorities—African Americans, Mexican Americans, and Native Americans—from many colleges and graduate programs almost completely. The effect of this exclusion on American society would be to move the United States backward, toward the days of segregation, as if integration had never really happened.

INTEGRATION REQUIRES INSTITUTIONAL CHANGES

Indeed, at many institutions, integration never really got off the ground. One of the problems at the University of Vermont and at many other schools across the nation has been the retention of minority students. At overwhelmingly white universities, students from other racial groups may feel uncomfortable because they have so few students of their group with whom to socialize. If some drop out, that only makes the problem worse for those who stay. Conversely, white parents often feel quite comfortable with the schools their children attend. Many colleges and universities in America are located in relatively small towns, such as Eugene, Oregon; Storrs, Connecticut; Chapel Hill, North Carolina; and Burlington, Vermont. Their children will be safe at college, these parents reason, because they are isolated from big-city problems. Thus, the "safe" image of these institutions draws more white applicants. And exactly that same image deters caste minorities, because a homogeneous environment that is safe and comfortable for a European American may be uncomfortable, even dangerous, for them. This is a vicious cycle operating within institutions of higher education—in addition to the societal processes that adversely affect children discriminated against by the time they are 18—to keep white colleges white.

Beyond this, because many predominantly European-American universities have so few students of non-European descent, some faculty members feel that they need not make any special effort to incorporate perspectives other than that of the dominant culture into their courses. (Those who make this argument fail to understand that diverse perspectives are important for *white* students.) Then the converse argument is also made: Why bring more "minority" students here, when we have so little to offer them? Again, a vicious cycle, this time of rhetoric.

Courses on Milton or periods of European history have proven popular with white students. But courses on Native American writers or periods of African history might also draw white enrollment. A course treating the particular health problems faced by Americans other than those of European descent might attract premedical students who foresee locating in multiracial metropolitan areas. Overwhelmingly white faculties have often not developed such courses. When universities hire new professors, they usually take the curriculum as "given" and hire people who can teach it. Professors whose background and interests are not Eurocentric may appear less qualified. Thus, a Eurocentric curriculum inadvertently helps maintain a Eurocentric faculty, which helps maintain a Eurocentric curriculum—another vicious cycle.

For a school to move beyond token desegregation to real integration requires institutional changes—developments that will benefit all students and our nation as a whole. It is difficult for education to be truly effective when it occurs in a segregated setting. Education does not just take place from faculty to students, but among students as well. If all students in a given place are alike—in age, race, and social class—their ideas and experiences tend toward homogeneity as well, thus impoverishing their dialogues with one another. Students at more diverse institutions get broader views of the world and can see issues from new perspectives. Therefore, as we achieve more diversity in our student bodies, in some respects teaching will become easier. At least in literature and the social sciences, the presence of students from a variety of backgrounds can help make us better understand how society works. Students in all disciplines will graduate into a multicultural world in which Wyoming ranchers hire cowhands from Latin America, and computer manufacturers in Vermont consult via modem with programmers in India. As our country grows increasingly diverse, educational policies that encourage us to be more accepting of others are surely in our national interest.

This chapter began with statistics showing how diverse our nation is and how diverse it is becoming. Most other nations are more uniform in their racial and ethnic makeup. Transportation and communication link us ever more tightly, however. From the Netherlands to Australia, nations that were once overwhelmingly white now have increasing numbers of immigrants who are racially and ethnically distinctive. The United States is merely the portent of things to come. Early in this century, DuBois said, "The problem of the twentieth century will be the problem of the color line" (p. 209), and he has been proven correct. Unless we change our institutions to counteract the patterns of institutional discrimination that still pervade our society, the color line will surely continue to generate riots, wars, and quiet desperation in the next century as well. If the United States can develop a multicultural society that works, however, other nations might copy our race relations policies as they now imitate our music and blue jeans. That would be a legacy to the world of which we could be justly proud.

REFERENCES

Abbott v. Burke, 119 N.J. 287 (1990).

"All American" (1991). "60 Minutes." Chris Whipple (Producer). New York: CBS.

Azug, R., & Maizlish, S. (Eds.). (1986). *New perspectives on race and slavery in America*. Lexington: University Press of Kentucky.

Baber, A., & Waymon, L. (1992, October). Making the connection. *Sky*, p. 16.

Banfield, E. (1961). *Political influence*. New York: Free Press.

Biko, S. (Ed. by A. Stubbs). (1979). *I write what I like*. London: Heinemann.

Blacks' woes in borrowing. (1991, May 8). *New York Times*, p. D13.

Blackwell, J. E. (1990). Current issues affecting Blacks and Hispanics in the educational pipeline. In G. E. Thomas (Ed.), *U.S. Race Relations in the 1980s and 1990s* (pp. 35–52). New York: Hemisphere.

Blau, F. & Graham, J. (1990). Black–White differences in wealth and asset composition. *Quarterly Journal of Economics, 105*: 325, 334.

Braddock, J. H. II. (1990). Sports and race relations in American society. In G. E. Thomas (Ed.), *U.S. race relations in the 1980s and 1990s* (pp. 105–120). New York: Hemisphere.

Brophy, J., & Good, T. (1974). *Teacher–student relationships.* New York: Holt.

Brown, D. (1971). *Bury my heart at Wounded Knee.* New York: Holt, Rinehart & Winston.

Burns, K. (1991, Sept. 12). Speech presented at the University of Vermont, Burlington.

Caplovits, D. (1967). *The poor pay more.* New York: Free Press.

Churchill, W. (1992a). Nobody's pet poodle. *Z., 5,* 68–72.

Churchill, W. (1992b). Deconstructing the Columbus myth. In J. Yewell, C. Dodge, & J. DeSirey (Eds.), *Confronting Columbus.* Jefferson, NC: McFarland.

Cook, S., & Borah, W. (1971). *Essays in population history: Mexico and the Caribbean.* Berkeley: University of California Press.

Davidson, C., & Grofman, B. (Eds.). (1995). *Quiet revolution.* Princeton, NJ: Princeton University Press.

de Madariaga, S. (1940/1967). *Christopher Columbus.* New York: Ungar.

Deutsch, M., & Brown, B., (1967). Social influences in Negro–White intelligence differences. In M. Deutsch (Ed), *The disadvantaged child* (pp. 295–307). New York: Basic Books.

DuBois, W. E. B. (1965). "Forethought" to The souls of black folk. In *Three negro classics.* New York: Avon. (Original work published 1903)

Ellison, R. (1952). *Invisible man.* New York: Random House.

Gates, H. L., Jr. (1988). On the rhetoric of racism in the profession. In B. J. Craige (Ed.), *Literature, language, and politics* (pp. 20–26). Athens: University of Georgia Press.

Granovetter, M. (1973). The strength of weak ties. *American Journal of Sociology, 78* 1360–1380.

Hammer, J. (1989, April 24). Cram scam. *New Republic,* pp. 15–18.

Harvey, D., & Slatin, G. (1975). The relationship between child's SES and teacher expectations. *Social Forces, 54,* 141.

Hawkins v. Shaw, MS [437 F.2d 1268 (5th Cir. 1972)].

Hayes, D., & Grether, L. (1975). The school year and vacation: When do students learn? In A. Montagu (Ed.), *Race and IQ.* New York: Oxford University Press.

Huggins, N., & Kilson, M. (1971). *Key issues in Afro-American experience.* New York: Harcourt, Brace.

Korte, C., & Milgram, S. (1970). Acquaintanceship networks between racial groups. *Journal of Personality and Social Psychology, 15,* 101–108.

Kozol, J. (1991). *Savage inequalities.* New York: Crown.

Loehlin, J., Lindzey, G., Spuhler, J. N. (1975). *Race differences in intelligence.* San Francisco: Freeman.

Loewen, J. (1982). *Social science in the courtroom.* Lexington, MA: Heath.

Loewen, J. (1988). *The Mississippi Chinese: Between black and white.* Prospect Heights, IL: Waveland.

Loewen, J. (1990). Racial bloc voting and political mobilization in South Carolina. *The Review of Black Political Economy, 19,* 23–37.

Loewen, J. (1991). Preliminary report on racial bloc voting and political mobilization in Virginia. (Filed with the United States Department of Justice, July, 1991). Burlington, VT: MSS.

Loewen, J. (1992a). *The truth about Columbus.* New York: New Press.

Loewen, J. (1992b). Preliminary report on Dinuba municipal services. MSS, Burlington, VT.

Malcolm X. (1964). *The autobiography of Malcolm X.* New York: Grove.

Monroe, S., Goldman, P., & Smith, V. E., et. al. (1988). *Brothers, black and poor.* New York: Morrow.

Ogbu, J. (1978). *Minority education and caste.* New York: Academic.

Ogbu, J. (1990). Racial stratification and education. In G. E. Thomas (Ed.), *U.S. race relations in the 1980s and 1990s* (pp. 24–25). New York: Hemisphere.

O'Hare, W., & Felt, J. (1991). *Asian Americans: America's fastest growing minority group* (Population Trends and Public Policy Series). Washington, DC: Population Reference Bureau.

Peck, I., Jantzen, S., & Rosen, D. (1987). *American adventures.* Austin, TX: Steck-Vaughn.

Reed, W. (1990). Equality begins at home. *Sports Illustrated, 73,* 138.

Rosenbaum, J. (1995). Changing the geography of opportunity by expanding residential choice: Lessons from the Gautreaux Program. *Housing Policy Debate, 6* (1), 231–269.

Rosenthal, R., & Jacobson, L. (1968a). *Pygmalion in the classroom.* New York: Holt.

Rosenthal, R., & Jacobson, L. (1968b). Teacher expectations for disadvantaged students. *Scientific American, 248,* 21–25.

Rosser, P. (1989). *The SAT gender gap.* Washington, DC: Center for Women Policy Studies.

Ryan, W. (1971). Blaming the victim. New York: Pantheon.

Sadker, M., & Sadker, D. (1986). Sexism in the classroom: From grade school to graduate school. *Phi Delta Kappan, 67,* 512–515.

Sale, K. (1990). *The conquest of paradise.* New York: Knopf.

San Antonio Independent School District v. Rodriguez [411 U. S. 1–137]

Shange, N. (1977). *For colored girls who have considered suicide when the rainbow is enuf: A choreopoem.* New York: Macmillan.

Simpson, G., & Yinger, M. (1972). *Racial and cultural minorities.* New York: Harper & Row.

Stannard, D. E. (1992). *American holocaust: Columbus and the conquest of the New World.* New York: Oxford University Press.

Todd, R. (1986, March). Darien, Connecticut. *New England Monthly,* pp. 37–43, 86–87.

Williams, E. (1963). *Documents of West Indian history.* Port-of-Spain, Trinidad: PNM.

Willie, C. (1986). The inclining significance of race. In K. Finsterbusch & G. McKenna (Eds.), *Taking sides: Clashing views on controversial social issues* (pp. 180–185). Guilford, CT: Dushkin.

Wilson, W. J. (1978). *The declining significance of race.* Chicago: University of Chicago Press.

Zuckoff, M. (1992, October 9). Study shows racial bias in lending. *Boston Globe,* pp. 1, 5.

3

Teaching the Conflicts: Race and Ethnic Relations

Moustapha Diouf
University of Vermont

THE BROWNING OF AMERICA

Race and ethnicity are at the center of a polarizing issue in the United States. This issue is likely to become even more central to conflicts in U.S. society in the near future, given a rapidly changing demographic environment marked by trends toward what can be called the "browning of America." According to the most recent U.S. population projections, by the year 2020 white Americans will become a statistical minority in the United States. In fact, current trends in both immigration and birth rate show that, by the end of the 20th century, Asian Americans will increase by an estimated 22%, Hispanics by 21%, blacks by almost 12%, and whites by only a little more than 2% (Loewen, chap. 2, this volume).

This browning of America raises some critical questions that affect the current state of race relations in the United States. It induces a climate of fear and suspicion within the dominant group—a fear of losing traditional "white skin privileges" and a suspicion that minority groups will come to form a counterhegemonic block to the traditional white power base. Indeed, this browning of America raises the issue, in a very direct way, of a sharing of this country's wealth and resources by its diverse sociocultural groups. Such a sharing runs counter to the perceived interests of dominant group members who are ill prepared to deal with it because they have been subject to secular socialization by a white-only power structure within a unicultural milieu.

In such a context, a class on race and ethnicity in America is increasingly likely to become politicized to the point where instructors are drawn into confrontations with students pursuing one particular agenda or another.[1] Because knowledge is a

---

[1]Being a black professor teaching race and ethnicity in an overwhelmingly white environment becomes a very delicate task, given the emotionally charged state of race and ethnic relations in this

social product developed in the interaction between students and an instructor, the knowledge base for a course of the kind described here is subject to a continuous challenge in terms of "how do we know we know" those facts and theoretical constructs through which we engage students in the classroom.

A REFLECTIVE PEDAGOGY

In order to convey an intellectual message that enables students to critically reflect on deeply structured racial, class, and gender inequality, we must identify a key set of pedagogical issues. In pursuit of this, it is pedagogically important to bear in mind that, as Habermas (1971) contended, we cannot separate our intellectual and cognitive structure from the prevailing social arrangements: We cannot escape the fact that, as scholars, we are embedded in a political, social, cultural, and economic context that shapes and influences our ontological assumptions. Moreover, we ought to use our dialectical imagination to challenge the assumed neutrality of knowledge to show that, by adopting this view, we are assuming a specific intellectual position, whether or not we recognize it as such.

An instructor in this type of course should engage students in a reflective thought process that challenges underlying assumptions such as, for example, the relative openness or closedness of the opportunity structure in U.S. society and whether or not it is based on meritocratic criteria. Within such a framework, the next step is to delineate the ground rules for the class by emphasizing the need for inclusion and openness and to set the intellectual parameters for a *negotiated order* based on respect for one another's opinions. We may know the historical genesis of a given racial configuration, but we should consider the ultimate implications of a particular set of socially constructed racial identities to be questions open to further investigation.

I believe it is important, from the very beginning, to make it clear to students that although it is problematic that we can teach racial sensitivity, the intellectual processes through which we engage students are not simply theoretical and abstract. The critical dialogue initiated during such a course is based on a fusion of social

---

country. In fact, as a faculty member of color, I experience a role conflict, ultimately illustrated by the fact that being black raises expectations of "loyalty" to one's "people"—in the way one presents the facts, and the advocacy role one is supposed to take in the classroom. By contrast, as instructors we are supposed to promote objectivity, reliable data, and academic rigor in the discussion of the theoretical and methodological issues involved in race and ethnicity. In many respects, this very "objectivity" can be seen as a way of avoiding the real issues by some minority students who have already made up their minds about what racism is all about and, therefore, adopt a defensive posture *vis-à-vis* any form of intellectual discussion of it. This refusal to engage in "abstract theorizing" about racism—on the grounds, for instance, that being black gives one moral authority in relation to issues because one experiences racism—rests on an essentialist argument that is a major challenge instructors must face in the classroom. Indeed, those students who adopt this militant posture often try to ideologize the discussion. And, as a black faculty member, not taking a favorable stand on an Afrocentric agenda is often interpreted as a "sell out." Moreover, as a black educator teaching race and ethnicity, in some cases one is perceived as a "white basher" by some white students who feel uncomfortable addressing the issue. They tend to see any attempt to discuss this issue as anti-white.

theory and praxis that must be translated into concrete, accessible activities in the classroom. It is equally important to stress the fact that no individual or group can claim a monopoly over knowledge. The primary reason for teaching race and ethnic relations is to raise awareness about racism as a dehumanizing ideological construct—an ideology grounded in perceptions of one particular group's racial superiority that has been used to rationalize the deprivation of minority groups and to legitimize the foundations of a given social order. Because knowledge itself represents a powerful tool for social change, it tends to become the center of ideological contradictions and political struggles.

DEMYSTIFYING THE RECEIVED VIEW
OF THE DOMINANT GROUP

A discussion of the U.S. ideology of "equal opportunity" can help us to clarify some of the misleading assumptions underlying the received views of many, if not most, students who take a race and ethnicity course. Many students—particularly those who are part of the dominant group—believe that America is an open society that provides a great deal of evidence of equality and social mobility. They assume an individualistic framework in which individual effort, hard work, ambition, and the acceptance of personal responsibility will lead to success in various aspects of American life. They believe, moreover, that there is relatively easy access to education in the United States for those individuals who have the ability. Within this context, most students assume that the state plays a neutral, impartial role in defending and promoting the interests of the collectivity as a whole.

This received view of the United States as a meritocracy is a critical building block in a larger ideological structure that validates and supports the position of the dominant racial group in American society. By confronting students with concrete data on social stratification in the United States—such as statistics on employment and income, education, rejection rates in home mortgage applications, residential segregation, or the criminal justice system—it becomes possible for them to cut through this distorted image of the United States as an equal opportunity/open society, and to juxtapose their received views with evidence suggesting that racism, class oppression, and sexism are central features of American society.

THE SOCIAL CONSTRUCTION OF RACISM

The *raison d'être* of racism is to provide an ideological justification for domination and oppression by using prejudiced and stereotypical constructs to rationalize the unequal treatment of supposedly inferior races. A racist ideology usually begins with labeling that, according to Becker (1963), is based on the power of the dominant group to define the realities of subordinate groups and, through these mechanisms, to shape the mainstream values of a society.

The use of stereotypes or negative labels by the dominant group has serious consequences for the groups so defined and labeled. For instance, in the United

States, traditional white Anglo-saxon Protestant norms still influence the structure of race relations and shape the social definitions of racial categories. Blacks, Native Americans, Asians, and Latinos have begun to resist such falsely defined realities and to recapture or recreate their own. However, a racist ideology can be so pervasive that some members of subordinate groups will internalize their own "inferiority" as defined by the dominant group. This creates false consciousness within subordinate groups that does not allow them to deal effectively with the objective reality of their own deprivation and oppression.

It is important in a course on race and ethnicity to engage students in an analysis of the sociological meaning of this minority/majority group distinction. As sociologists use the terms, *majority* and *minority* are defined in terms of the control exercised by various groups over institutional power and resources—not the relative size of these groups within a given population. This is why sociologists increasingly tend to use the term *dominant* rather than *majority* when referring to groups exercising differential power within a society (Vander Zanden, 1996).

This differential power allows dominant groups to adopt and implement decisions that affect the life chances of other racial and ethnic groups who are relatively less able to control institutional resources. A good way of demonstrating this is to lead students to explore the relationship between race and the state of the economy, particularly in periods of heightened fiscal crisis, economic depression, and/or high unemployment, which intensify intergroup competition for jobs. Comparative studies indicate that, under these circumstances, there is a direct association between difficulties within a given economy and increasing hostility directed against minorities or other subordinate groups (De Rudder, 1991; Schaefer, 1997). In France, African immigrants have been made the scapegoats for the economic crisis and the shortage of jobs for "real French" people. In England, such scapegoating is commonly known as "Paki-bashing." Recent racist attacks against immigrant workers in both Germany (Turkish) and Italy (African) are symptoms of a socially sanctioned institutional policy that is reminiscent of the exclusion and genocide practiced under fascism in the 1930s and 1940s.

In general, as the economic pie shrinks and competition for jobs becomes fiercer, corporations initiate a policy of divide and rule that fractionalizes the labor movement along racial lines and pits each group against the others in order to secure a more favorable operating environment. As Bonacich (1972) argued, under conditions of fierce economic competition, a split labor market generates antagonistic relations among members of different racial and ethnic groups.

It is important to recognize that race only becomes an important factor within a society because of its social definition and the meanings people attach to it (Berkowitz & Barrington, chap. 1, this volume). "Race" is not a phenomenon *sui generis*, but becomes meaningful only when it is ingrained within the fabric of a society. If we examine the different stages in the history of the evolution of race relations in the United States, we can see that, from the early days of slavery to the postbellum period, to the Supreme Court's separate but equal ruling in *Plessy v.*

Ferguson (1896, cited in Rothenberg, 1992) to the entrenched segregation policy of the 1950s, to the comprehensive civil rights bill of 1964 and, more recently, to the Rodney King tragedy, U.S. society is characterized by structured inequalities in power focused along racial and ethnic lines.

THE DECLINING/INCREASING SIGNIFICANCE OF RACE DEBATE

Given this context, the debate between Wilson and Willie about the declining/increasing significance of race is a valuable entry point for engaging students in a range of issues. I have found that it sheds light on the interconnection between race and class, and allows students to examine the contending assumptions, as well as the sociopolitical forces, that shape the current black experience. The principal pedagogical value of this debate is that it provides students with an opportunity to reflect on questions such as what the overall impact of affirmative action has been on the structural location of blacks in the labor force.

Both sides of the issue are well argued. Wilson's approach goes beyond the narrowness of a simple Afrocentric perspective in that it provides an in-depth structural analysis of social stratification along class lines and a look, for instance, at the internal differentiation that results from the expansion of an economy and the consequences for the black community of state intervention—via its affirmative action policies—within it. Thus, for Wilson, contemporary patterns of black occupational mobility lend credence to the contention that class location in the economy has become more important than race in determining job placement: "In the economic realm, then, the black experience has moved historically from economic racial oppression experienced by virtually all blacks to economic subordination for the black underclass" (Wilson, 1992, p. 139).

Wilson further contended that this decline in the economic significance of race opens up the opportunity for a more differentiated black class structure, with black life chances becoming more a consequence of class position than race.

Willie's theoretical posture is grounded in the assumption that, regardless of their social class, blacks are still exposed to increasing discrimination and racism. Willie supported his argument—that blacks and whites with similar credentials fare differently—with a careful examination of data on income, education, and housing. He suggested that there is evidence for, in effect, a "racial tax" levied on blacks for not being white. For Willie, by exclusively focusing on individual mobility, Wilson tended to ignore the existence of institutionally based opportunities such as being of the "right race," attending the "right school," seeking employment with the "right company," and so on (Willie, 1992).

Through a critical comparison of the opposing views presented by Wilson and Willie, students can discover for themselves that race interacts with class in shaping the current black experience. Once these epistemological constructs of race and class are clearly identified and understood, one can begin to address other important theoretical dimensions in the study of race and ethnicity, such as gender stratification and its impact on life chances. It is not analytically defensible to teach race and ethnic relations from a purely essentialist perspective by ignoring the intricate interconnection among race or ethnicity and class and gender. Indeed, racism shares an ideological foundation with both class oppression and sexism and, for this reason, we need to develop an integrative theoretical framework capable of addressing these issues, simultaneously, as part of our teaching praxis.

RACE, CLASS, AND GENDER STRATIFICATION

There is a debate within the black movement over whether it should expend its energy attempting to establish equality of the genders as well as trying to eliminate racial and ethnic inequities. For Ladner (1986), black women face a double disadvantage in that they experience differential treatment on the basis of both race and gender. But, from her point of view, issues of sexual equality are minor by comparison to the oppressive forces faced by black men, women, and children together in all the various facets of their lives. For advocates of Afrocentrism, feminism deflects women's attention away from the primary struggle for the survival of the race and represents a divide-and-conquer strategy serving the interests of the dominant group. Thus, such advocates argue, all the forces and energies of both males and females should be joined to eradicate institutional racism. Other minority women, such as Vasquez (1970), focus on gender role stratification and advocate a struggle for sexual equality. But as hooks (1992) contended, "A focus on patriarchal domination alone masks the reality of racial and class oppression; thus feminism, as a liberation struggle, must exist apart from and as part of the larger struggle to eradicate domination in all its forms" (pp. 442–443).

In presenting a discussion of race, ethnicity, class, and gender, we should avoid economic determinism and a class reductionist approach such as Wilson's. Despite his thoroughly structural account of inter- and intragroup socioeconomic inequality, Wilson tended to ignore the extent to which racial affiliation molds people's life chances. Similarly, one should avoid a one-dimensional approach à la Hacker, which basically simplifies the issue of race and ethnicity into one major racial cleavage between blacks and whites (Hacker, 1992). Such oversimplifications of the issue negate the relevance of other minorities (Native Americans, Latino Americans, and Asian Americans) that constitute integral parts of the cultural mix in U.S. Society. It also alienates members of these groups who feel that too much emphasis has been put on the black–white dichotomy while the browning of America indicates the need to be even more inclusive than in the past. In other words, in presenting the facts, we should avoid cultural reductionism, which sees race and ethnicity as purely essentialist and self-evident constructs.

My argument here is that racial categories should not be seen as simply more powerful analytic tools for understanding the black experience than are class and gender. It is extremely important in a course on race and ethnicity to examine clearly the ways in which other structural factors—such as class location and gender—affect the definition and use of the notion of race. Racism, class oppression, and gender inequality constitute an interlocking system of domination and, for this reason, race alone (or any of the other variables alone) cannot provide a comprehensive view of the ideology of racism and the function it plays in the reproduction of the social order.

MULTICULTURAL VERSUS UNICULTURAL EDUCATION

One pertinent question regarding multicultural education that can be discussed in the class is whether or not a curriculum dominated by "the canon" (i.e., the study of core texts written by dead white European males) can accurately represent the life experiences of members of non-white social categories. Because the traditional canon is based on a received Eurocentric ideology, it is necessary to enlarge the set of appropriate texts to include contribution by scholars and by other voices from different cultural milieux (e.g., Africa, Asia, and Latin America).

In addressing issues of this type, I maintain that one should not take a purely Afrocentric approach. In the words of Asante (1993), such an approach focuses on the concept of "centeredness." For this reason, it may be seen as a form of cultural separatism and racial chauvinism despite the fact that it is a legitimate attempt to free African American scholarship from the intellectual bonds of traditional white academia, and provide African Americans with the analytical tools necessary to study their own historical social, cultural, and political life. The intricate, increasingly alienated and hostile relations between racial and ethnic groups in the United States creates a "confrontational" environment in the classroom. The basis for such an environment in this type of course is, as Cose indicated, a difference in the vision and understanding of the nature of America's social reality and the place different racial groups occupy within it (Cose, 1993).

The Rodney King incident illustrates these differences. Both blacks and whites saw a group of white police officers continuously strike Rodney King. But, as Cose observed, most whites saw the beating as a "shocking but isolated incident." By contrast, for most blacks, the brutality they saw poignantly reflected the broader issue of race-based inequity within the criminal justice system. After the nonguilty verdict for the four white L.A. police officers involved in the beating, blacks and whites surveyed about their opinions regarding this verdict had different reactions. To the question as to whether or not the verdict showed that blacks cannot get justice in this country, 78% of black respondents agreed with the statement, whereas only 25% of whites did (Cose, 1993). This difference in vision and understanding of American social reality between blacks and whites clearly demonstrates that race and ethnic relations can no longer be taught in a purely "objective" and "neutral" fashion. As West (1992) contended following the Rodney King tragedy:

> To engage in a serious discussion of race in America, we must begin not with the problem of black people but with the flaws of American society—flaws rooted in historic inequalities and longstanding cultural stereotypes. How we set up the terms for discussing racial issues shapes our perception and responses to these issues. As long as black people are viewed as a "them", the burden falls on blacks to do all the "cultural" and "moral" work necessary for healthy race relations. (p. 22)

Problems, such as family breakdown, urban decay and violence, teenage pregnancy, and other socioeconomic ills that affect most minorities in this country should not be seen as peculiar symptoms of the pathologies of some "underclass," but as inherent structural dysfunctionalities of late capitalism and its secular policies of racial exclusion and class oppression. Teaching the conflicts involves teaching these facts.[2]

As we move toward the 21st century, the issue of racial and ethnic tensions is likely to gain more attention. The implications of the browning of America in terms of a reallocation of power are likely to generate further tensions, if not conflict. The major questions—such as how to build a multiracially integrated society and how to effectively combat racism—will be likely to recur. Exposing students to these issues and creating an intellectually engaging environment conducive to critical examination of these social problems will become crucial. This kind of theoretical praxis, as advocated by Althusser (1969), is part of an "emancipatory project" that has as its goal the elimination of racism in all of its forms and the creation of new structures based on principles of equality, respect, and solidarity.

REFERENCES

Althusser, L. (1969). *For Marx*. London: Allen Lane, Penguin.

Asante, M. K. (1993). *Malcolm X as cultural hero, and other Afrocentric essays*. Trenton, NJ: Africa World Press.

Becker, H. (1963). *Outsiders: Studies in the sociology of deviance*. New York: Free Press.

Bonacich, E. (1972). A theory of ethnic antagonism: A split-labor market. *American Sociological Review. 37*, 547–559.

Cain, W. (Ed.). (1994). *Teaching the conflicts; Gerald Graff, curricular reform, and the culture wars*. New York: Garland.

Cose, E. (1993). *The rage of a privileged class*. New York: HarperCollins.

De Rudder, V. (1991). Le racisme dans les relations interethniques. [Racism in interethnic relations]. *Annales: Économies, Sociétés, Civilisations, 4* (46), 855–857.

Habermas, J. (1971). *Knowledge and human interests*. Boston: Beacon.

Hacker, A. (1992). *Two nations: Black and white, separate, hostile, unequal*. New York: Scribner's.

hooks, b. (1992). Feminism: A transformational politic. In P. Rothenberg (Ed.), *Race, class and gender in the United States: An integrated study* (pp. 441–448). New York: St. Martin's Press.

Ladner, J. (1986, September–October). Black women face the 21st century: Major issues and problems. *Black Scholar,* pp. 12–19.

---

[2]The notion of "teaching the conflicts" derives from the work of Gerald Graff (see Cain, 1994).

Rothenberg, P. S. (1992). *Race, class, and gender.* New York: St. Martin's Press.

Schaefer, R. (1997). *Racial and ethnic groups.* New York: HarperCollins.

Vander Zanden, J. (1996). *Sociology: The core.* New York: McGraw-Hill.

Vasquez, E. (1970). The Mexican-American women. In R. Morgan (Ed.), *Sisterhood is powerful* (pp. 379–384). New York: Random House.

West, C. (1992, August 2). "Learning to talk of race." *New York Times,* pp. 24–25.

West, C. (1993). *Race matters.* Boston: Beacon Press.

Willie, C. (1992). The inclining significance of race. In K. Finsterbusch & G. McKenna (Eds.), *Taking sides: Clashing views on controversial social issues* (pp. 141–145). Guilford, CT: Dushkin.

Wilson, W. J. (1992). The declining significance of race. In K. Finsterbusch & G. McKenna (Eds.), *Taking sides: Clashing views on controversial social issues* (pp. 132–140). Guilford, CT: Dushkin.

II

Approaches

4

Comparative Literature and Politics: A Transdisciplinary Approach

Mbulelo Mzamane
University of Fort Hare
University of Vermont

> *I am paid by Her Majesty's government. I couldn't possibly teach any of this anti-British propaganda.*
>
> *Who doesn't know that African oral literature is nothing more than the noise monkeys make?*

The first statement was uttered by my English professor in the 1960s, the decade of Africa's independence. His outburst was occasioned by the meeting of the department at the University of Botswana, Lesotho and Swaziland to consider revisions to the curriculum. The proposal involved the inclusion of literature from the LACAAP countries—Latin America, the Caribbean, Africa, Asia, and the Pacific—to balance our overwhelmingly Anglocentric and Eurocentric course offerings. The second statement, which echoes the anti-African sentiments of Trevor Roper of Oxford and, before him, the German philosopher Hegel (Ngugi, 1983), was made in the 1980s by one of my British colleagues at Ahmadu Bello University, Nigeria, when a course on orality and popular consciousness was proposed to balance our emphasis on elitist or high culture.

Such bigotry can be replicated in many places around the world, particularly among people of Anglocultural persuasion in their relationship to people who belong to other cultures. Such attitudes fly in the face of all common sense, however, especially in a country such as the United States, whose greatest asset is its cultural diversity from which it has profited more than any other nation on earth.

My teaching in more than two decades—in Africa, Europe, and North America—has often pitted me against such jaundiced and jingoistic views, which it is the function of education to cure. In addition, my teaching has ranged over fields as diverse as international studies, PanAfricanism, and comparative literature. Each one of my courses in these areas sheds some light on race and ethnicity, so that even before there was a requirement for such a course at the University of Vermont (UVM), I was already fully operational in the field. I had been appointed, originally, as a visiting professor in the fall of 1988 and, subsequently, on a permanent footing in the 1990–1991 school year to develop and teach such courses in the Department of English and in the International Studies Program.

Beside race and ethnicity, my courses also deal with the intersection of other variables such as gender, class, and caste—all of them factors in oppression universally. When UVM began its race and ethnicity requirement, however, there was a debate about the advisability of restricting our new requirement to race and ethnicity or not. The argument that prevailed was that race and ethnicity needed to be confronted headlong, without the kind of dilution that would result from including everything. Some of us remain convinced, however, that oppression is indivisible and that the courses should focus on the construction of, and the interplay between, "self" and "otherness" in U.S. society. Many of my students, black and white, from impoverished and from working-class families (mainly in Vermont) feel left out of a discourse that privileges some forms of deprivation, as if their particular predicament does not count for much. From such a feeling of exclusion, they become resentful and thus less receptive to attempts to sensitize them to ways in which marginalization works in society. In other words, their experiences are rejected as legitimate sounding boards for an investigation of oppressive forces in society. We may thus be failing to connect with many of them by such an exclusive emphasis on race and ethnicity.

There are other missing dimensions from our required courses, but many of us try to plug these gaps as creatively as we can. One of these is the failure to require that we all foreground our discussions in some concrete understanding of the dynamics of race and ethnicity worldwide. We can probably do better still by situating our arguments within a global rather than a strictly U.S. frame. Whatever the course, I always try to set an international context, against which my students can examine local or national issues.

This was another area regarding which faculty could not reach agreement. The side that prevailed insisted that to dwell on the international scene would detract from the specific manifestations, in the United States, of the problems being examined. The opposite seems true: To ignore international events creates the impression that such problems as exist elsewhere do not quite manifest themselves in the same way here. We must, therefore, be thankful that we are Americans, without the problems that afflict lesser nations.

There are other limitations to our understanding that we impose on ourselves by ignoring comparable phenomena elsewhere. By being inattentive to international events, most people miss out on significant changes in ruling class attitudes that may be anticipated in even the slightest shifts in the official lexicon. For example, we are hearing less these days about how the various African peoples should not have been trusted to govern themselves because they are driven by abiding tribal hatreds to kill and murder each other from one end of the continent to the other. One supposes that we are hearing less of this because various "tribes" of Caucasians have also taken to killing and murdering each other from the Danube to the Caucasus. As we all know, these various groups of Caucasians are not "tribes."—they are "ethnic groups." As nearly as can be judged, given their comparable savagery, the difference between a tribe and an ethnic group is that an ethnic group has both tanks and spokespeople who appear on "Nightline."

When the events in Yugoslavia first broke out, by bringing them to my students' attention I was able to make them better understand a concept developed in Berkowitz and Barrington (chap. 1, this volume): that race and ethnicity everywhere are social constructs, often manipulated by ruling classes for their own ends.

In my own courses, therefore, I always insist on including the international dimension and expanding my students' intellectual horizons. Their comprehension, not only of how race and ethnicity manifest themselves in American society, but of oppressive forces everywhere, is greatly enhanced by such exposure. They also come to understand that people have triumphed over their oppression because they have been creative fighters—a point that is exemplified by 20th-century struggles for emancipation.

THE 20TH CENTURY AND THE UNFOLDING OF EMANCIPATIONIST IDEALS

I begin most of my courses by arguing that every epoch has its characteristic preoccupations. In Western society, for example, the 18th century, which gave us Hegel, was the Age of Enlightenment, of *idealization*; whereas the 19th century can be characterized as the era of *reconceptualization*—that is, in the 19th century Marx and Engels translated Hegel's dialectics and idealism into dialectical materialism. Other materialist views of history were articulated by such thinkers as Darwin. All this set the stage for the 20th century era of *emancipation*—soon to give way to the age of *consolidation* in the 21st century.

A lively debate in my class usually follows in which we might modify my categories somewhat, but we usually agree that every age seems to produce its own dynamics that, if we understood better, would help explain the characteristic movement of that epoch.

We then focus on the 20th century—as the race and ethnicity course requirement stipulates—for an elaboration on the thesis that our century has been characterized by the unfolding of liberation struggles everywhere. Despite the tendency in Western society to underplay its importance, the Bolshevik revolution marked a break with Russia's czarist past, a significant step on the road to emancipation. The Chinese revolution was another leap forward for the Chinese people, whatever else it might appear to be today. The two Great European wars were fought to roll back the gains of Fascism and Nazism. The second of these wars unleashed other struggles for freedom—by the colonial victims of the very powers that had united most of the world in the fight against totalitarianism and expansionism. We further deal with women's struggles against patriarchy and how, in the 1920s and 1930s, U.S. workers in such industries as car manufacturing and shipbuilding had to fight exploitation by both the establishment and organized crime. From such a perspective, we interpret the fall of the Berlin Wall as yet another manifestation of unfolding emancipationist ideals and the completion of an agenda, begun during the Bolshevik revolution, but later hijacked by self-serving party bureaucrats and elites.

Such an approach usually challenges students to question many of the assumptions by which we live, including traditional views about the nature of the Cold War. We also reexamine claims made by some leaders, such as President Clinton's statement at his first inauguration that the United States was the oldest democracy in the world—despite the fact that women in New Zealand first voted in 1914, 6 years before women could vote in the United States, and despite evidence that blacks in such places as the South did not vote until the 1960s. Most of this leads us to better understand our own efforts as regards the United States and its real successes and failures in creating a just social order.

By thus developing students' capacities to challenge utterances that purport to be authoritative, we develop their own critical faculties. Their contribution to society may, as a result, become more significant in future because of their understanding that democracy is not a finished product—that in its formulation and application it may be more developed in some places than in others because it has had a head start, but nonetheless, like socialism, it is a process, always evolving perhaps but still in a formative stage.

PANAFRICANISM AND CULTURAL AFFIRMATION

My other courses on African American, African Caribbean, and African Studies usually revolve around PanAfricanism and cultural affirmation, as a case study of the unfolding of emancipationist ideals in the 20th century. We begin our discussions with the formation of the PanAfrican Congress in 1900, under the leadership of people such as W. E. B. DuBois, Booker T. Washington, and the Trinidadian lawyer H. Sylvester Williams. The formation of the National Association for the Advancement of Colored People (NAACP) in 1908 is shown as an outcome of the Congress. We study the Harlem Renaissance in the 1920s as a cultural expression of the same emancipationist impulse among African Americans. This takes us all the way to the civil rights and black power era of the 1950s and 1960s—whose significance, beyond the African American community, was in bringing together other freedom struggles such as feminism and gay rights.

Our understanding of these struggles in the United States, however, is incomplete without our appreciation of the interplay of various struggles by people of African descent internationally. Although students may be familiar with the legacy of Martin Luther King, Jr., they often have little knowledge of his indebtedness to the African experience. The civil rights era in the United States got underway 5 years after the Defiance Campaign in South Africa, which introduced the tactics that King was to adopt and which were derived, in turn, from the *satyagraha* (passive resistance) philosophy of Mahatma Gandhi, which first emerged in South Africa in the early 1900s. In addition, the inspiration for the civil rights struggle was the process of decolonization then underway worldwide, especially in Africa. These struggles fed off one another and explain the affinity that African Americans have, and the empathy other freedom-loving people in the United States feel, for the liberation struggle in South Africa.

Students are then challenged to explain the Rodney King phenomenon that rocked the United States, despite the passage of successive civil rights laws. Facts at our command begin to contradict generally accepted views on the subject: How could a "riot" in which 50% of the participants were Hispanic, 40% black, and 10% white have been described as "black"? How does one explain the fact that there are more blacks in America's prisons than there are in the nation's colleges and universities? If the passage of successive civil rights laws is everything that it was made out to be, what then do we make of the increase in poverty among African Americans in areas such as Atlanta since the 1960s? What truth is there to allegations that the civil rights struggles, along with affirmative action policies, have benefited white women more than black people?

At this point, we usually turn to a comparison between North and South, because students brought up in the North generally have little understanding of the South. My UVM students are often startled by the revelation that today the South generally has the more politically progressive environment. Mississippi—the scene, on June 21, 1964, of the civil rights murders of Mickey Schwerner, James Cheney, and Andrew Goodman (the subject of the movie *Mississippi Burning*) and, until recently, the state that prided itself on being the most unreconstructed in the nation—had, by 1989, 600 elected black officials, more than any other state. In 1964, 5,000 blacks could vote in the state. By 1989, 600,000 were registered and they used their ballot. When Ray Mabus ran for governor in 1987 on a platform of "basic, drastic change," whites were 2 to 1 against him; he won the state by carrying the black vote 9 to 1. In 1980, Mississippi still had no public kindergarten and no compulsory schooling—6,500 children each year did not go to first grade. All that was altered by the Education Reform Act, which was the first such state act in the United States (Kornbluth, 1989).

These are the type of issues I usually assign my students to research further. In some instances, when a student's interest and competence in the subject are amply demonstrated, I encourage him or her to pursue the subject as an independent study, whereby the student may then register the following semester for an independent study course designed to encourage just such innovative work. A student may take away more on race and ethnicity from such a class than from one that is more formally structured, even though such courses are not yet recognized as meeting the race and ethnicity requirement.

The understanding that emerges from our reading of world events is that phenomena such as the South Central Los Angeles "riots" represent the unfinished agenda of the 20th century in the sense that the United States has yet to resolve its own problems of discrimination based on race and ethnicity. Such a reading of contemporary events in the United States also enables students to feel less smug and complacent about their society. They then begin to see the study of other societies and diverse American subcultures as providing a window into their own souls.

Cultivating such an introspective perspective might then lead to a discussion of what the greatest challenge facing these students might be, as a group destined to be the first adult generation of the 21st century. Perhaps, it could be suggested, this new century will focus on *consolidating* all the imperfect but significant gains made in the previous one. This gives students a handle on life at the same time as it leads me to increasingly ask myself what my function as an educator is and whether there is much usefulness in simply imparting to my students what I have learned. This may have served me well in my time, but may be of limited value to them. I thus encourage my students to see me as a peer enquirer—rather than as a guru with all the answers—engaged in seeking meaningful ways to translate rhetoric on cultural diversity into the very substance and defining feature of U.S. nationhood and global citizenship.

COMPARATIVE CULTURAL STUDIES

A standing joke in my department—not particularly amusing to many, I am sure—is that everybody teaches British and American literature and I teach the rest of the world. The question that is often asked is how I do it. The unspoken assumption among many in academic circles is that one needs to receive formal training in a given area before one can teach it with reasonable competence. My own training in Southern Africa and England was, in many respects, more traditional than that received by my American colleagues. In addition, I had to contend with colonial education. I came into African and comparative literature, and then into international studies, through my own efforts. Its liberating impulse has been most profound for me. I thus cherish such perspectives as I have developed as a comparativist, not so much for the answers supplied as for the questions raised.

Several things are possible when a comparative approach to cultural studies is adopted. One is able, for instance, to identify progressive and regressive strains among the cultural practices of the privileged and underprivileged alike. One is also able to reaffirm the dignity and humanity of oppressed and marginalized people, for one then deals not so much with the deficit model of the problems they create, but instead with their contributions and creativity. One is thus able to assert, along with President Clinton, that "Surely the lasting legacy of such traumatic events as the Rodney King trial ought to be a determination to reaffirm our common humanity and to make a strength of our diversity. And if we can do that, then we can get on about the business of this great land" (Gerth, 1993).

Understanding the context within which each cultural group operates becomes necessary in defining new paradigms of nationhood. In defining such new paradigms, students come to realize that no single group's culture is complete in itself. A national culture is like a jigsaw puzzle: It is only through the interplay of disparate subcultures that a wholeness can be achieved. National culture becomes a composite process and an amalgam of various cultural configurations.

My teaching in comparative cultural studies is also designed to get students to appreciate the fact that, at any given moment, our collective identity is a combination of both fragments of tradition and the changes we are experiencing. The dividing line between tradition and change, however, is not always clear. But if we can be selective in the values that we adopt and if we can preserve the best of our heritage, then we need have no worry or guilt about appropriating everything our country has to offer. Once students grasp this central precept of culture as a dynamic and not a static phenomenon, their apprehensions about their threatened cultural identity and heritage are soon dispelled and a new sense of Americanness takes root.

The major thrust of cultural studies and policies—and of studies and policies in the area of race and ethnicity—should be the eradication of ethnocentrism. As we rid ourselves of cultural imperialism (the insistence by members of a culturally dominant group that their ways of doing things are superior), we should not be enticed into substituting cultural domination by one group with some other form of cultural hegemony. "No one has a monopoly on truth and beauty; and there is room for us all at the rendezvous of victory" (Cesaire, 1971, p. 34).

REFERENCES

Cesaire, A. (1971). *Cahier d'un Retour au pays Natal*. [Notebook of a return to my native land]. Paris: Presence Africaine.

Gerth, J. (1993, April 18). Verdict in Los Angeles: Clinton satisfied by jury's decision. *The New York Times* (late edition), Sect. 1, p. 34.

Kornbluth, J. (1989, July 23). The '64 civil rights murders: The struggle continues. *The New York Times* (late edition), Sect. 6, p. 16.

Ngugi wa Thong'o. (1983). *From the barrel of a pen: Resistance to repression in neo-colonial Kenya*. London: New Beacon Press.

5

Why, What, and How I Teach African American Literature

Mary Jane Dickerson
University of Vermont

WHY

Cudjoe (1980) opened his essay "What I Teach and Why" with these words: "I teach Afro-American literature because I am trained in the area of literature and because it is the literature of my people" (p. 362). Whatever authority I have as a white teacher with traces of a North Carolina drawl comes, of course, from a different context. I teach African American literature because I am trained in literature and because it is the literature *about* my people. Toni Morrison (1990) said it best: "Africanism is inextricable from the definition of Americanness—from its origins on through its integrated or disintegrating twentieth-century self" (p. 65).

Like many in my generation of American literature teachers, I recognized early the serious disadvantages of never having studied African American writers. Morrison and I both wrote master's theses on William Faulkner in the 1950s—she at Cornell, I at the University of North Carolina. This was about as close as the academy then allowed either of us to come to the study of the African presence in American literature. In the years since, Morrison has written herself into a major place in African American and world literature and was the recipient of the 1993 Nobel Prize for literature. Since the publication of *The Bluest Eye* (Morrison, 1970), she has enjoyed an incredibly wide audience. In those same years, I spent much of my time studying and teaching the many stories Faulkner could not write, always filling serious gaps in my own education because I have not wanted my predominantly white students to graduate from the state university in the whitest state in the United States as ignorant as I was at their age; educated, as I was, during the death throes of segregation. Also, it is the most demanding, the most exhilarating, and the most painful work I have done since 1970—and the most important.

WHAT

African American literature at the University of Vermont is a two semester survey course open to juniors and seniors. The first semester covers writers from Phyllis Wheatley and Olaudah Equiano in the 18th century, 19th-century writers such as Frances E. W. Harper and Charles W. Chesnutt, and such 20th-century writers as Jean Toomer, Nella Larsen, Langston Hughes, and others who shaped the Harlem Renaissance. The second semester includes writers such as Claude McKay, Richard Wright, Ann Petry, and Ralph Ellison, all of whom anticipated the decades of civil rights and black power; James Baldwin's essays; Audre Lorde's poetry; Toni Morrison and Alice Walker's fiction; Julie Dash's film; and bell hooks' cultural work. In recent years, groundwork laid by Mary Helen Washington, Hortense Spillers, and Henry Louis Gates, Jr., has expanded the available selections of African American writers from the 18th and 19th centuries. The 20th century has witnessed an outpouring of African American literature, so that selecting texts allows teachers to be truly creative, freely varying topics and approaches from year to year. I frame the reading and day-to-day lecture/discussion sessions so as to emphasize the culture that both shapes the literature and is shaped by it.

Whatever the choices of texts, course chronologies reflect a historical bias. This is especially significant for my approaches, because the historical bias embeds itself into the literature with both form and content marked, from its beginnings, by a history my students seldom know anything about beyond the word *slavery*. They know little about the complex relationships between enslaved people and their enslavers. In each semester's text selections, I try to offer students ways to understand how literary traditions develop and how recursive and complicated major themes such as freedom, orality and literacy, individual autonomy, and communal consciousness become focused as they emerge through the lens of the literary imagination. Cultural study always relies heavily on understanding the effects of history.

During both semesters, I make extensive use of video and audio materials to contextualize the written works: Paul Robeson's recordings of spirituals; Alan Lomax's landmark Jelly Roll Morton recordings; Public Television's production on the Underground Railroad; the two Civil Rights Movement series; the recent Malcolm X documentary titled "Malcolm X: Make It Plain"; the contemporary writers interview series; and the 18th-century engravings of male and female figures in shackles, on their knees before their master and mistress, with the words underneath reading "AM I NOT A MAN (WOMAN) AND A BROTHER (SIS-TER)?" (Andrews, 1988; Yellin, 1989). Students reflect on these materials in journal writing, and integrate discussion of their responses in class. They are also encouraged to attend campus events (e.g., the Negro Ensemble Theater, a Cornel West lecture, a Gwendolyn Brooks reading, or Mbulelo Mzamane speaking on the South African elections) to enrich their reading and discussion.

Both courses contain much that emphasizes the uses of history and the intersections of the historical with the personal in constructing identities. Students study how the autobiographical, closely tied to the historical, dominates literary production from the narratives of former slaves through many late 20th-century texts such as Charles Johnson's novel *Middle Passage*: The personal is the historical, and the historical assumes the personal (Johnson, 1990). Students need to develop an awareness of how African American writers mine the past to draw on a rich oral tradition and history that illuminate the present.

To accomplish these goals, I rely on a variety of tools and techniques to historicize the literature in both courses, titled "African American Literature Through the Harlem Renaissance" and "African American Literature Since the Harlem Renaissance," respectively. The following discussion necessarily focuses on sample moments in each course.

HOW

Besides organizing material to develop historical consciousness, I assign students work that causes them to interact constantly with course materials, with each other, and with the "other" they gradually locate within themselves. As one student observed recently in his journal: "Ellison is going to open my mind to the experiences of many types of humans including myself." Students learn through group oral and written work, in assignments that range from informal writing in the course journal to formal extended essays, and from group informal discussion to formal oral presentations.

Divided into small groups of four to six, (depending on class size), students regularly receive assignments that require them to investigate, for example, the relationships between white and black women in *Incidents in the Life of a Slave Girl* (Jacobs, 1861) or representations of Africa in the poems of Countee Cullen and Langston Hughes—with each group briefly contributing the results of its findings to the whole class. Each group also makes a class-period-long presentation on a topic related to the work of one of the writers we are studying, such as the Civil Rights Movement in the work of James Baldwin or oral traditions in Ellison's *Invisible Man*.

Students write two essays from six to eight pages in length, sharing ideas and drafts in progress within their small groups. The first piece is a standard critical essay, focusing on a central idea that offers a critical reading of one or more of the texts (e.g., "White References in Douglass, Brown, and DuBois"). The second is a personal response that asks students to construct something from their own experiences that connects with one or more of the texts (e.g., "Spirit Murder: An Evening in Penn Station With Patricia Williams"), as described in my critical essay (Dickerson, 1989). Because their course journal encourages them to record personal as well as interpretive responses, many students have kernels of material to shape into richly textured and critically informed essays. The personal response essay always causes important shifts of location for many students, enabling them to see themselves in the world differently. Writing autobiographically *about* African American literature underscores the significance of autobiography as a major genre from early scenes of writing to the present.

From the initial class meeting on, students begin such shifts in location as they enter into the process of becoming racialized selves. In the first semester, they encounter a terrorizing new world after being forcibly torn from the familiar; in the second semester, they confront racial and cultural differences through others' eyes. To initiate the process, in the first semester we might begin with a collective reading of Phyllis Wheatley's "On Being Brought From Africa To America" (1773; see Shields, 1988)—a poem with much to discuss because Wheatley herself was brought to America when she was only about 7 years old, torn from her family and thrust into another language and onto a New England landscape. In her brief lyric, Wheatley pulls the reader into the immensity of these vast physical, psychological, and cultural distances. In the lyric's closing lines, Wheatley called into question Christian practices of "other" African peoples: "Remember, *Christians, Negroes* black as Cain/May be refined and join the angelic strain" (see Shields, 1988, p. 18).

We might, as an alternative, begin with Robert Hayden's 20th-century narrative poem "Middle Passage," in which he explored the triangular slave trade from many perspectives—the American, the Portuguese, the ship's captain, the slave trader, and the sailor—to suggest the human complexity within the historical details. Through a group reading, students begin to understand something of the Middle Passage as a "Voyage through death/ to life upon these shores" (Hayden, 1966, p. 70). Students thus approach North America from these directions and from these varied locations.

In the first semester, students immerse themselves in the study of the most distinct literary genre produced in the history of human rights' struggles: the narrative written by the former slave, or "the slave narrative" as it is popularly called. Before students begin reading from texts such as Frederick Douglass' *Narrative of The Life of Frederick Douglass* (1845) or Harriet Jacobs' *Incidents in the Life of a Slave Girl* (1861), they spend time in the library reading accounts of former slaves' lives collected by the Federal Writers' Project of the Works Progress Administration (Douglass, 1845; Jacobs, 1861). These accounts alert readers to the subtle but telling ways in which these elderly African Americans responded to overwhelmingly white interviewers, and former slaves' varied attitudes toward their memories of childhood enslavement, enclosed as they were within the harsh realities of continued economic and social enslavement worsened by the Great Depression. Some accounts represent dialect in respectful ways; other accounts translate such traces of orality into a standard written English that distances the reader from the teller of the tale. Students observe how such conditions mediate and influence what they read, and prepare them for the many instances when African American texts of all kinds are marked by the dominant culture, from abolitionist editors to the generic conventions of the sentimental novel. Students readily perceive how these former slaves cling to and project their humanity despite great odds: Each one emerges from the account speaking in a distinctly human and original voice.

Moving from these oral accounts transcribed largely by others into the "authenticating" letters that introduce readers to Douglass' and Jacobs' narratives plunges readers into the significance of the intersections of freedom, literacy, and individual autonomy. Historical documentation—such as the South Carolina slave codes that addressed restrictions of movement and disallowed legal marriage, especially the anti-literacy law of 1740 that severely punished anyone who fostered reading and writing among slaves—provides students with disturbing historical contexts. Reading autobiographical narratives and fiction that emerge from slavery amply defies slave owners' insistence of their slaves' lack of intelligence and demonstrates the subversive power of the pen in the service of freedom.

Other useful texts studied in the first semester are William Wells Brown's *Clotel* (1853/1990), Frances E. W. Harper's *Iola Leroy* (1892/1990), Charles Chesnutt's *Marrow of Tradition* (1901/1990), and W. E. B. DuBois' *Souls of Black Folk* (1903/1969). DuBois' words, in particular, resonate into the closing years of the 20th century: "The problem of the Twentieth Century is the problem of the color line" (1903, p. xi). Holloway (1993) urged that we not "mask the color line" because to do so is to put our cultural literacy at risk: "The challenge of the twenty-first century is to claim its potential as the potential of the colors of our cultures" (p. 617).

Students respond in powerful ways to DuBois' *Souls of Black Folk* with its interesting collage of the polemical, the historical, and the personal. They especially get the point of DuBois' central question: "Why did God make me an outcast and a stranger in mine own house?" (1903, p. 45). As well, students readily understand the subtleties of DuBois' exploration of what he called "this double-consciousness, this sense of always looking at one's self through the eyes of others" (1903, p. 45), seeing it at work in a range of texts from James Weldon Johnson's *Autobiography of an Ex-Colored Man* (1912; see Johnson, 1965) to Langston Hughes' "Cross" (1959) and Ellison's *Invisible Man* (1952). The harsh realities of the Jim Crow laws enacted after Reconstruction and the *Plessy v. Ferguson* ("separate but equal") Supreme Court decision of 1896 hovered over the texts from the late 19th century through the early decades of the 20th century.

Concluding the first course with the Harlem Renaissance heralds a developing cultural literacy coupled with a consciousness of community. Alain Locke's "The New Negro" (1976; originally written in 1925) and Langston Hughes' "The Negro Artist and the Racial Mountain" (1976; originally written in 1926) contributed to the ongoing identity formation of both communities and their artists with the shifting African American populations from the agrarian South toward the industrialized urban centers. Alongside this demographic shift was another expansion of consciousness toward what Locke (1976) described in this way: "In terms of the race question as a world problem, the Negro mind has leapt, so to speak, ... and extended its cramped horizons. In so doing, it has linked up with the growing group consciousness of the dark-peoples" (p. 55). In contrast to the political identities with which Locke's essay concerns itself, Hughes' words sounded as a clarion call to the work of the artist to forge an identity: "We younger Negro artists who create now intend to express our individual dark-skinned selves without fear or shame. ... and we stand on top of the mountain, free within ourselves" (1976, p. 309) Langston Hughes' poetry and Jean Toomer's *Cane* accompanied by William Greaves' documentary "From These Roots" suggest the scope of the Harlem Renaissance and its enduring effects on later 20th-century African American writers—a good way to end the course "African American Literature Through the Harlem Renaissance."

To introduce "African American Literature Since the Harlem Renaissance," Zora Neale Hurston's short essay "How It Feels to Be Colored Me" draws readers into the dynamics of constructing racial difference and introduces an important writer whose work breaks many silences of race and gender: "I remember the very day that I became colored. ... I was not Zora of Orange County any more, I was now a little colored girl. I found it out in certain ways. In my heart as well as in the mirror, I became a fast brown—warranted not to rub nor run" (1985, pp. 1649–1650). In this brief essay, Hurston herself wrote from dual perspectives—that of the anthropologist and that of the woman of color—illustrating how the multicultural may voice itself in American texts.

In addition to the historical and its effects on questions of identity (both male and female), the literary period from the 1930s to the present has encouraged grouping texts to gain understandings from perspectives of how gender and genre interact; how matters of race, gender, and class interact; and how the problems of the color line permeate all facets of American consciousness. The course also examines what all these issues mean with regard to power, who wields it, and how. For example, studying James Baldwin's *The Fire Next Time* (1962), Alice Walker's *Meridian* (1976), and John Edgar Wideman's *Brothers and Keepers* (1984) in juxtaposition encourages students to see the civil rights period from the 1960s into the 1970s as a complex time in which issues of identity, autonomy, freedom, racism, classism, and sexism (heterosexism as well) intersected to complicate American society and to interrogate democracy itself. Studying Claude McKay's *Banana Bottom* (1933/1970), June Jordan's "Report From the Bahamas" (1985), and Jamaica Kincaid's *Lucy* (1990) further complicate student awareness of the Africanist presence in African American literature.

An excerpt from a student's journal entry on *Meridian* illustrates what can happen when reading takes place within such contexts:

> In the beginning of Meridian I was interested in one passage [that] seemed to capture a feeling in Meridian which I feel may have been shared by others during the Civil Rights Movement: "But what none of them seemed to understand was that she felt herself to be, not holding on to something from the past, but held by something in the past: by the memory of old black men in the South who, caught by surprise in the eye of a camera, never shifted their position but looked

directly back." I think that many Civil Rights volunteers took on their responsibilities out of sympathy for disenfranchised blacks or out of anger at the atrocities inflicted upon blacks. They, those volunteers, were holding onto ideas and memories, which gave them their drive. Meridian, on the other hand, was held by those people, not by memories and anger. It was the bond between Meridian and those who were oppressed which was the force behind her actions. It is almost as if she did not volunteer for her part in the movement, but, rather, was bound to the movement and had to play a role whether she felt like it or not. Therefore I must ask the question: Did volunteers hold to the past, or were they held by the past? I think many, themselves, held onto the past and an elite few were held. I thought this passage told a lot about Meridian and also tapped into a question concerning the Civil Rights Movement as a whole. (March 4, 1994)

This student's words about Alice Walker's fictional character Meridian express more than anything I might add about the ways in which students shift their own locations for understanding literature and its shaping contexts. She learned something of what it means for African Americans to look into the lens of white eyes while gaining a deeper understanding of DuBois' perceptive "double consciousness."

What do I *most* want students to take away from these courses in African American literature? First, I want them to realize that although the Middle Passage, the lynching of Emmett Till, or the Civil Rights Movement happened in the past, their implications for the present eliminate an "us" and "them" perspective, because we live each day drenched in history with our individual identities always connecting us to a shared past and thrusting us into a future all of us will shape. Those in my classes who are white, always the majority, must move beyond only viewing racial selves located in others and learn to examine constructions of whiteness within themselves and what it means. Students and teachers in predominantly white universities must also consider the implications of the question that ended Hazel V. Carby's essay "The Multicultural Wars": "Have we, as a society, successfully eliminated the desire for achieving integration through political agitation for civil rights and opted instead for knowing each other through cultural texts?" (1992, p. 17). I believe cultural literacy should manifest itself in thoughtful material acts for social change and in thoughtful consideration of what artificially constructed differences such as "race" mean in our personal, national, and global locations. Most of all, I wish students a lifetime of reading African American writers, because these writers never let us forget who and what we ought to be—and their words give us ways to greet the 21st century.

REFERENCES

Andrews, W. L. (1988). *To tell a free story: The first century of Afro-American autobiography, 1760–1865.* Urbana: University of Illinois Press.
Baldwin, J. (1962). *The fire next time.* New York: Laurel.

Brown, W. W. (1990). *Clotel; or, the president's daughter.* In H. L. Gates, Jr. (Ed.), *Three classic African-American novels* (pp. 3–223). New York: Random House. (Original work published 1853)

Carby, H. V. (1992). The multicultural wars. *Radical History Review, 54,* 7–18.

Chesnutt, C. W. (1990). *The marrow of tradition.* In H. L. Gates, Jr. (Ed.), *Three classic African-American novels* (pp. 465–747). New York: Random House. (Original work published 1901)

Cudjoe, S. R. (1980). What I teach and why. *Harvard Educational Review, 50,* 362–381.

Dickerson, M. J. (1989). Writing the personal essay. In A. Biddle & T. Fulwiler (Eds.), *Reading, writing, and the study of literature* (pp. 1729–1737). New York: Random House.

Douglas, F. (1997). Narrative of the life of Frederick Douglas, an American slave, written by himself. In W. L. Andrews & W. S. McFeely (Eds.), *A Norton critical edition* (pp. 302–369). New York: Norton. (Original work published 1845)

DuBois, W. E. B. (1903/1969). *The souls of black folk.* New York: New American Library.

Ellison, R. (1952). *Invisible man.* New York: Random House.

Harper, F. E. W. (1990). *Iola Leroy, or shadows uplifted.* In H. L. Gates, Jr. (Ed.), *Three classic African-American novels* (pp. 225–463). New York: Random House. (Original work published 1892)

Hayden, R. (1966). *Selected poems.* New York: October House.

Holloway, K. F. C. (1993). Cultural politics in the academic community: Masking the color line. *College English, 55,* 610–617.

Hughes, L. (1959). *Selected poems.* New York: Knopf.

Hughes, L. (1976). The Negro artist and the racial mountain. In N. I. Huggins (Ed.), *Voices from the Harlem Renaissance* (pp. 305–309). New York: Oxford University Press. (Original work published 1926)

Hurston, Z. N. (1985). How it feels to be colored me. In S. M. Gilbert & S. Gubar (Eds.), *The Norton anthology of literature by women: The tradition in English* (pp. 1649–1653). New York: Norton. (Original work published 1928)

Jacobs, H. A. (1987). *Incidents in the life of a slave girl.* (J. F. Yellin, Ed.). Boston: Harvard University Press. (Original work published 1861)

Johnson, C. R. (1990). *Middle passage.* New York: Atheneum.

Johnson, J. W. (1997). The autobiography of an ex-colored man. In H. L. Gates, Jr. & N. Y. McKay (Eds.), *The Norton anthology: African American literature* (pp. 777–861). New York: Norton. (Original work published 1912)

Jordan, J. (1985). *On call: Political essays.* Boston: South End Press.

Kincaid, J. (1990). *Lucy.* New York: Farrar Straus Giroux.

Locke, A. (1976). The new Negro. In N. I. Huggins (Ed.), *Voices from the Harlem Renaissance* (pp. 47–56). New York: Oxford University Press.

McKay, C. (1970). *Banana bottom.* New York: Harcourt Brace. (Original work published 1933)

Morrison, T. (1970). *The bluest eye.* New York: Holt, Rinehart & Winston.

Morrison, T. (1990). *Playing in the dark: Whiteness and the literary imagination.* New York: Random House.

Shields, J. C. (Ed.). (1988). *The collected works of Phyllis Wheatley.* New York: Oxford University Press.

Walker, A. (1976). *Meridian.* New York: Harcourt Brace Jovanovich.

Wideman, J. E. (1984). *Brothers and keepers.* New York: Holt, Rinehart & Winston.

Yellin, J. F. (1989). *Women & sisters: The antislavery feminists in American culture.* New Haven, CT: Yale University Press.

6

Law, History, and Political Science: Attacking the Architecture of Race in America—and More

Howard Ball
University of Vermont

Racism is still very much a defining aspect of life in the United States. This is true because although some progress has been made in diminishing some of the most blatant effects of racism in the last 40 years, what Toni Morrison called the "architecture of race in America" remains substantially unchanged. As the *Washington Post* noted in a 1992 editorial: "More than 125 years after the Emancipation Proclamation, race still matters greatly in this country" (p. 28).

It is important to focus on this "architecture of race" when teaching about the law and politics of racism in the United States. In 1998—over *40 years* after the U.S. Supreme Court overturned *Plessy v. Ferguson's* (1896) "separate but equal" racist precedent in its historic *Brown v. Board of Education* (1954) ruling—an aggressive, virulent racism still pervades our society. Henry Louis Gates, Jr., a respected scholar of African American studies, echoed these sentiments when he recently observed that "[he had not] ... felt this depressed about race relations in the United States since the assassination of Martin Luther King" (Gates, 1992, p. 48).

It is this racism—and its structural supports—that *must* be attacked in our classrooms if change is to occur. Some educators are profoundly skeptical about whether this can be done. They feel that, after almost half a century of trying, little has been accomplished. They observe, as Orfield (1993) did, that "The country and its schools are going through vast changes without any strategy. The civil rights impulse from the 1960s is dead in the water and the ship is floating backward toward the shoals of racial segregation."

Racial injustice is, clearly, America's heaviest burden. Public leaders—and such leaders must include faculty—bear the responsibility for devising ways to overcome the reality of the great racial divide in America and responding to the sometimes fashionable, bitter rhetoric of racism, as exemplified by demagogues such as Khalid Abdul Muhammad.

Toni Morrison's metaphor is, thus, quite appropriate. She urged us "to rethink the architecture of race" and to "convert a racist house into a race-specific, non-racist home" (Winkler, 1994, p. 11). At this time in American history, educators have a responsibility to respond to her. The main purpose of institutions of higher education has always been—and must continue to be—to stimulate the analytical and the creative powers of students. For educators, the clear challenge is to teach students about racism and then provide these same students with tasks that enable them to go beyond the simple analysis of American racism to a deeper and more complete understanding of it.

Initially, students must thoroughly understand, in an analytical fashion, the role played by racism in American history. Deconstructing the architecture of race means, at bottom, examining the historic role of law in our society and how law, morality, and politics interact to form the essential basis on which society rests. Only through a historical analysis of the architecture of racism of this kind can we, through our students—the future architects of their societal home—reconstruct it as a nonracist one. But in order for students to come to *want* to do this, they must come to understand the ravages of racism in a more direct and intuitive fashion.

THE TWIN CHALLENGES FACING THE INSTRUCTOR AND THE STUDENT IN UNDERSTANDING THE ARCHITECTURE OF RACISM

Anyone teaching an undergraduate course on civil rights in America must draw on, and then combine, knowledge about race and racism generated by scholars in a range of the humanities and social sciences. Most of these scholars have a great deal to learn from one another about how racism is developed and maintained. Ideally, a course on civil rights should be team taught with at least two faculty—one from political science and the other from history—working in tandem to provide students with inclusive knowledge about racism drawn from a number of disciplines. This means that, in addition to these core faculty, it is necessary to bring into the classroom persons such as sociologists, lawyers, psychologists, policy analysts, ethicists, artists, poets, littérateurs, and people representing other disciplines cross-cutting the humanities and social sciences. To fully understand the traumatic impact of race in American history, instructors must make a concerted effort to move away from the traditional vertical, or "silo," educational model and toward a horizontal pedagogy that brings students into contact with a broad range of knowledge.

After analyzing the interactions between law and politics over time, our second task in a course on civil rights is to try to get students to empathize with the innocent people who, as victims, have been caught up in the powerful vortex of law, politics, and race. The first challenge, when overcome, provides students with an analytic understanding of the role played by racism in American law and politics. But analytic understanding alone is not enough to generate a new culture of tolerance and nonracism in our society. American education must go beyond analytic observation of the issue of racism: There must be an active intermingling of academic analysis with social responsibility. This second challenge, then, gives rise to a second task: We must develop a sense of social responsibility in students that they must exhibit if liberty is to continue to flourish in our society. If this second task is successfully addressed, then instructors will have moved students to the point where they can actively participate in creating an America where men and women are judged on the quality of their intellect and their character rather than the color of their skin.

If educators, in the final analysis, cannot take students beyond the analytical and into a normative, ethical, or socially responsible understanding of the architecture of racism, then students cannot become partners in the reconstruction of the society and, in some sense, we will not have succeeded in leading them to understand the impact that law and politics have had on the development and maintenance of racism in America.

Clearly, as scholars such as Hacker (1992) have noted, racism is alive and well in contemporary America, and the task of providing students with the analytic tools needed to address racism, in itself, is by no means an easy one. Teaching about civil rights—and civil wrongs—in America does not make one sanguine about the problems faced by minorities. Instructors walk into an undergraduate classroom, whether in political science or history, and are immediately greeted by students who are bright, somewhat literate, but, for the most part, profoundly ahistorical and anti-intellectual. Undergraduates in the 1990s were born after the societal traumas of Vietnam and Watergate. They, for the most part, have absolutely no sense of what went on during the Civil Rights Movement of the 1950s and 1960s except as depicted in Hollywood films such as *Mississippi Burning* or *In the Heat of the Night*. These same undergraduates—including many minority students—have little or no sense of the rhetoric and the strategies of the various Black Nationalist Movements in the 1960s and 1970s, except for what they can appreciate through Spike Lee films such as *Do The Right Thing* and *Malcolm X*. Most do not have any sense of the rhetoric and ideology of the leaders and the movements in the period from the 1980s to the present.

Given this, one can imagine how little knowledge these same undergraduates have about large-scale historical changes of the kind initiated by *Plessy v. Ferguson* (the 1896 case in which the Supreme Court placed its imprimatur on the rhetoric and reality of "separate but equal" facilities) or how *Plessy* led to Jim Crowism and to, de facto, totally segregated environments in some parts of the United States.

Despite this lack of background (or, perhaps, because of it) educators must find ways not only to fill in the gaps in students' knowledge, but also to help them to come to understand something of the context of the events and times that led to the various developments in civil rights law that they are discussing.

THE ANALYSIS OF RACISM IN LAW AND POLITICS
ACROSS AMERICAN HISTORY

The description of the course I teach recognizes that racism has been an ugly part of the American legal, political, and economic landscape for hundreds of years. This recognition underscores the fact that the centerpieces of the analytic component of a course on civil rights are law, history, and public policymaking. Although there is a critical need to go beyond this core and bring in complementary knowledge about racism, it is also clear that students must really come to grips with the impact of law on politics and on history.

I find it desirable, if possible, to have a legal scholar—a philosophy professor whose area is jurisprudence, a law professor, or a legal practitioner, preferably a civil rights attorney—participate in my course at the very beginning, if only as a lecturer for the first or, better yet, the second week. It is very important that students analyzing racism come to understand the critical roles played by legal precedent and federal judges (especially the formidable role of the U. S. Supreme Court) in the entire process. Given the essential and inescapable connection between racism and gender stereotyping, such a course must contain information about the psychology and sociology of racism. This, ideally, should be brought into the class via guest lecturers from these departments.

The central task of the instructor or instructors in a civil rights course, however, is to get the students focused on the law, politics, and history of racism. The center of this segment of the course—an understanding of the history of racism in America—should be a tripartite one.

As I teach it, the first segment of the course, which deals with the pre-Civil Rights Movement era, examines slavery and its manifestation in the concept of race that emerged in 17th- and 18th-century colonial America. It highlights the leadership role that black ministers played in their communities, and gets students to understand the reasons for the creation of the National Association for the Advancement of Colored People (NAACP) by whites concerned about the cruel treatment of blacks across the nation, in 1909.

The second segment focuses on the growth of the Civil Rights Movement embodied in such organizations as the Southern Christian Leadership Conference (SCLC), the NAACP, the Student Nonviolent Coordinating Committee (SNCC), and other groups that emerged to try to give direction to black efforts to overcome segregation, including black militant movements in the mid-1960s.

The final segment in this analytical/historical portion of the course focuses on the state of civil rights in America, beginning with the Reagan and Bush administrations. It follows legal, political, and economic events and issues since then, including controversial issues such as affirmative action and voting rights.

I have very explicit historical material that I cover in each of these segments. In dealing with the pre-Civil Rights Movement era, I attempt to provide students with a succinct analysis of the development of the concept of racism, through the institution of slavery and as incorporated into the Constitution; congressional efforts to limit its expansion into a growing, expanding nation in the period prior to the Civil War; the Civil War, the amending of the Constitution with the addition of the Civil War Amendments, followed by passage of civil rights statutes that attempted to implement these amendments, and the negative impact of the Supreme Court when adjudicating the constitutionality of these civil rights acts, as seen in the 1883 Civil Rights Act cases; the watershed 1896 *Plessy v. Ferguson* litigation and the ensuing rapid development of a profound pattern of *de jure* segregation and Jim Crow statutes based on the *Plessy* concept of "separate but equal" facilities for blacks and whites; and the leadership role played by black ministers, the creation of the NAACP in 1909, and the Back to Africa Movement of Marcus Garvey in the 1930s.

As I teach it, the second segment of the analytic/historical component of the course deals with the Civil Rights Movement that emerged, fully, in the 1950s and 1960s, including the Emmett Till Murder and the Birmingham Bus Boycott, the twin events that led to the growth of the modern movement for civil rights in America; the growth of the civil rights protest "Movement" and civil disobedience, including freedom rides, freedom summers, teach-ins, pray-ins, and sit-downs—especially in relation to the emergence of the NAACP, SNCC, SCLC, the Urban League, Congress of Racial Equality (CORE), and other civil rights groups; the U.S. Supreme Court responses to litigation, especially after Earl Warren became Chief Justice in 1953—including the higher education cases in 1950, followed by the 1954 and 1955 *Brown* decisions of a unanimous Court; National legislative and executive efforts to address de jure racism, including civil rights and voting rights legislation, the creation of the Civil Rights Commission, the Equal Employment Opportunity Commission (EEOC), and the Federal Office of Federal Contract Compliance Programs, (OFCCP); evasion, avoidance, and delay by affected local communities, actions that blunted legal efforts to end segregation and the badges of slavery that had continued to exist long after the Civil War ended; and the growth of Black Nationalist Movements—in particular the Nation of Islam and the Black Panthers—in response to the evasion, avoidance, and delay exhibited by whites.

The third segment of this portion of the course deals with the post-Civil Rights Movement, from 1981 into the early 1990s, focusing on race, law, and the politics of race as practiced by the Reagan and Bush administrations between 1981 and 1992 and the politics of race engineered by Democratic President Bill Clinton (1992–). A great deal of what I do here points out why it was that civil rights activity reached a low ebb during this period.

Instructors will find that readings, films, music, and documents—especially those internal files of the justices of the U.S. Supreme Court available from the

Library of Congress—are all useful in fleshing out students' understanding of the context within which these events took place.

There are a number of different kinds of books that can be used in this way. Anthologies, such as Weisbrot's *Freedom Bound* or Carson et al.'s *Eyes on the Prize: Civil Rights Reader*, are good books for undergraduates, especially first-year students (Carson, Garrow, Gill, Harding, & Hine, 1991; Weisbrot, 1990). Instructors should also examine some of the many case books on civil rights law or, alternatively, using a reproduction service, put together a book of relevant civil rights cases that fully covers the three analytic segments of the course.

There are a number of biographies that can have a major impact on students who take the time to read them. Moody's (1968) searing and poignant memoir, *Coming of Age In Mississippi*, grabs the students from the very first page to the last. It is an absolutely first-rate book, written by a young black woman who wrote about the dilemmas she encountered when she was growing to womanhood in rural, segregationist, pre-Movement Mississippi.

Malcolm X's autobiography is another book students find engrossing. Martin Luther King's autobiography, *Stride Toward Freedom*, is equally moving and informative (King, 1958). David Hilliard's book about his time in the Black Panthers, entitled *This Side of Glory*, provides students with a no-holds-barred view of that radical black militant movement during the late 1960s and early 1970s (Hilliard & Cole, 1993).

Duberman's (1988) biography, *Paul Robeson*, offers students a view of racism in the period prior to the development of the Movement in the 1950s. Civil rights leaders, including Ralph Abernathy of SCLC (*And the Walls Came Tumbling Down*, 1989), and Mary King of SNCC (*Freedom Song*, 1987), have provided us with well-written autobiographies based on their lives in the Movement at that time.

There are many, many excellent histories of civil rights in America. One or two of these should, I believe, become required reading for students in a course of the kind we have been discussing. For the pre-Civil Rights Movement segment, there is Joel Williamson's (1984) *The Crucible of Race: Black–White Relations in the American South Since Emancipation*. Stephen Whitfield's (1988) excellent book, *A Death in the Delta: The Story of Emmett Till*, instantly impels students into a dynamic discussion of racism, racial violence, and the impact of racial-sexual stereotypes on the problem of racism. This is an important issue that needs to be discussed when addressing the growth of white fears of blacks.

Taylor Branch's (1988) award-winning book on the growth of the Civil Rights Movement, *Parting the Waters: America in the King Years, 1954–1963* is an excellent historical resource for students in the course. David Garrow's (1986) Pulitzer Prize-winning book, *Bearing the Cross: Martin Luther King and the Southern Christian Leadership Conference* is another outstanding secondary source for students. Fred Powledge (1991), a reporter for the *New York Times* during the Movement era, wrote an excellent book, *Free At Last? The Civil Rights Movement and the People Who Made It*. Richard Kluger's (1976) book, *Simple*

Justice, tells about how the Supreme Court dealt with the school segregation cases that led to the Court's watershed decision in the *Brown v. Board of Education* case, and gives students a very clear account of the interaction of pressure groups using litigation as a form of lobbying, the Solicitor General's Office, and the Supreme Court justices and their law clerks.

At a minimum, a course of the kind we are discussing should include a civil rights law casebook, either a published one or one created by the instructor. The advantage in using a compiled reader is that the instructor can add an introduction that focuses on the nature of constitutional interpretation and on how the justices of the Supreme Court decide cases brought before them. For most students in the course, this information will be invaluable.

It is extremely useful in a course of this kind to also include a "civil rights" reader that provides students with primary sources drawn from history, politics, literature, poetry, sociology, and other disciplines, including excerpts from Movement literature and the speeches and writings of civil rights leaders.

In addition, it is useful in a course on civil rights to assign at least one biography—Moody's, for example—with others placed on reserve. I have found that a first-person perspective dramatically assists students to transcend a purely analytic stance and move toward otherness and empathy. Finally, a secondary source, such as Whitfield's account of the Emmett Till murder, should be required for the course because of its interpretative power.

In addition to books, instructors should review the great variety of video- and audiotapes, films, CDs, and CD-roms that complement these readings. PBS television series, such as "Eyes on the Prize, I and II," are excellent supplementary materials (WGBH Boston, 1986–1987).

FROM ANALYSIS TO SYNTHESIS:
THE "EMPATHY PAPER" REQUIREMENT

The most important of the papers I assign in the course is what I call the "empathy" paper. *Empathy* is defined as the quality or process of entering fully, through imagination, into another person's feelings or motives or pains. For a student to empathize is to have that student project into or identify with a person—to leap beyond the analytical into intimate, subjective "otherness" in order to become one with another. Students can display empathy by discussing their feelings about an actual action or a historical event. In doing this, they are encouraged to creatively identify with others through "diary" entries, letters, short stories, art, music, essays, and other means by which students can put themselves into the shoes of minority group members.

A natural way for students to engage the empathy assignment is to take incidents they have encountered in the analytical/historical segments of the course—from the readings, films, lectures, discussions, or whatever—that have had some impact on them and then to have them enter the event through the assignment. Students, for example, will have seen a film in class about the Movement's use of the media to arouse the national community against segregation in Birmingham, Alabama. In the film there is a scene showing a vicious, violent white mob harassing and then attacking a well-dressed black man who, in the film, seemed to be trying to mind his own business and get out of the area as quickly as possible. He, however, had no options once the mob descended on him. He could only take their abusive language and hope to get away without a beating or worse. If he had in any way actively defended himself, the mob would have seriously injured him—or worse. In this case, students could imagine themselves to be that black man. Would these events have humiliated him? Would he be angry at his inability to defend himself from that horde of white racists bent on hurting blacks who were trying to desegregate a local lunch counter? Would he have understood that the white mob wanted to make him appear ineffectual, impotent, and subservient to them?

Students viewing this film could seize on that one brief incident and put themselves in the place of that middle-class black person caught up in the anger of the moment. After putting themselves in the place of that person— or, for instance, in the place of Emmitt Till's mother after her dead son's body was recovered from the Tallahatchie River—students can then take on the task of expressing themselves as the "other" through a variety of methods.

By completing the empathy assignment—and, ideally, there should be assignments of this kind at the end of each of the three analytical segments of the course—students are forced to confront their feelings concerning the incidents about which they write and what they say about racism in America. For example, by focusing on the event in which the mob attacked the middle-class black man and then describing it from his perspective, students have to confront and then analyze not only facts but also personal thoughts and feelings about it.

CONCLUSION: BEYOND DECONSTRUCTION TO THE TASK OF REBUILDING A NONRACIST AMERICAN HOME

The chief aim of a course on civil rights is to analyze the history of race in America. This can be done, principally, by examining the interplay between law and politics throughout our history. Students should be able to hone and then use their critical faculties through such an analysis. This should cause barriers to begin to come down. To use Morrison's metaphor, the old, racist walls of the building *have* to come down.

The second task of the course, the one addressed by the empathy exercises, is to have students overcome stereotypes by creating an intimate and personal "otherness" experience. With empathy, students can say: "This is not the way the world is supposed to be. Let's work to fix it." With that task accomplished, one can, with the students, begin the task of building a nonracist home.

REFERENCES

Abernathy, R. (1989). *And the walls came tumbling down: An autobiography.* New York: Harper & Row.

Branch, T. (1988). *Parting the waters: America in the King years, 1954–63.* New York: Simon & Schuster.

Brown v. Board of Education, 347 *US* 483 (1954).

Carson, C., Garrow, D. J., Gill, G., Harding, V., & Hine, D. C. (Eds.). (1991). *The eyes on the prize: Civil rights reader.* New York: Penguin.

Duberman, M. B. (1988). *Paul Robeson.* New York: Knopf.

Garrow, D. J. (1986). *Bearing the cross: Martin Luther King, Jr. and the Southern Christian Leadership Conference.* New York: Morrow.

Gates, H. L., Jr. (1992, May 11). [Quoted in] The King Verdict. *Newsweek*, 48.

Hacker, A. (1992). *Two societies: Black and white, separate, hostile, unequal.* New York: Scribner's.

Hilliard, D., & Cole, L. (1993). *This side of glory: The autobiography of David Hilliard and the story of the Black Panther party.* Boston: Little, Brown.

King, M. L., Jr. (1958). *Stride toward freedom.* New York: Harper.

King, M. (1987). *Freedom song: A personal story of the 1960s Civil Rights Movement.* New York: Morrow.

Kluger, R. (1976). *Simple justice: The history of Brown v. Board of Education and Black America's struggle for equality.* New York: Knopf.

Moody, A. (1968). *Coming of age in Mississippi.* New York: Dial.

Plessy v. Ferguson, 163 *US* 537 (1896).

Powledge, F. (1991). *Free at last?: The Civil Rights Movement and the people who made it.* Boston: Little, Brown.

Weisbrot, R. (1990). *Freedom bound: A history of America's Civil Rights Movement.* New York: Norton.

WGBH Boston. (1986–1987). *Eyes on the prize: America's civil rights years, 1954–1965* (Videorecording). Alexandria, VA: PBS Video.

Whitfield, S. J. (1988). *A death in the Delta: The story of Emmett Till.* New York: Free Press.

Williamson, J. (1984). *The crucible of race: Black/white relations in the American South since Emancipation.* New York: Oxford University Press.

Winkler, K. (1994, Mary 11). The significance of race. *The Chronicle of Higher Education*, A10.

7

Race Relations: Theory and Classroom Applications

Nicholas L. Danigelis
University of Vermont

Since the early 1970s, I have taught introductory, intermediate, and advanced undergraduate courses as well as a graduate-level seminar in race relations. The political, cultural, and social climates have changed during this period, so that one teaches race relations somewhat differently today than during the 1970s. Nevertheless, the core concepts and paradigms that any sociological treatment of race relations must address have remained relatively constant during this period. Furthermore, certain principles of classroom dynamics that worked in the 1970s are still quite relevant in the 1990s.

My experiences in teaching race relations are best understood in terms of two conceptual objectives I bring to each of my race relations courses, regardless of level, and the strategies I use to transmit these objectives to my students. The first conceptual objective is *distinguishing theory from ideology*, a necessary precursor to developing a sociological handle on intergroup relations. The second conceptual objective is *framing the key concepts* that form the basis of any sociological study of intergroup relations. Strategies focus on *applying ideas about race in the classroom*, with special emphasis on colleagues, local history, and structured conflict.

DISTINGUISHING THEORY FROM IDEOLOGY

For most undergraduate students in the 1990s, nothing appears to be quite as boring as theory. At their most naive, students want quick visuals and sound bites describing "race relations: the abridged version." A small number of students will tolerate a bit of theory if it does not interfere with talking about problems of intergroup relations. Nevertheless, both groups need to understand the difference between theory and ideology before they can understand anything about race relations. Therefore, I make a deal with my students: In exchange for my leading discussions early and often about contemporary intergroup issues of concern, I extract their agreement to pay attention to a brief introductory discussion of theory and ideology.

At this point, I define a theory as a set of logically related hypotheses that represents a description of some part of social reality based on the past or portending the future. It purports to tell us the way thing are and therefore is amenable to scientific testing. Ideology, too, represents a view of social reality, but it prescribes rather than describes, telling us what ought to be, rather than what is (Newman, 1973). A major case in point concerns the nature of contact between different racial or ethnic groups (excellent summaries are in Feagin & Feagin, 1996; Marger, 1997). As Gordon (1961, 1964) explained, the theories of assimilation, the "melting pot," and pluralism developed out of the ideologies prevalent at various times in U.S. history. For example, at the turn of the century, while Madison Grant was decrying the "passing of a great race," European immigrants to the United States were expected to shed the ways of the old world and conform as quickly as possible to American cultural values and norms.

In contrast to this confining view from the host culture were voices from the 19th-century American frontier and early 20th-century presidential propaganda, promoting a vision of U.S. society as a "melting pot" that argued all immigrant peoples gave as well as received culture to produce a new complex of ideas and behaviors that were wholly American. As dissenting voices on behalf of the immigrants themselves came arguments promoting cultural pluralism from early 20th-century Jewish intellectuals who asserted the importance of immigrant culture and the benefits of retaining much of it in the new world.

Despite their ideological flavor, the assimilation, melting pot, and cultural pluralism arguments also came to dominate sociological thinking about the facts concerning intergroup relations until the late 1960s. Since then, conflict models of intergroup relations have been offered as counterpoint to these basically function-alist perspectives (see, e.g., Blalock, 1967; Doob, 1993; Geschwender, 1978; Newman, 1973). Today, thankfully, sociologists are examining intergroup relations through a broad range of theories.

Nevertheless, assimilationist ideology and, to a lesser degree, melting pot and pluralist ideologies tend to have a restricting effect on what the average student will see as the nature of intergroup contact. In order to attack the constraining influences of these ideologies, I try to have my students separately address the questions of what they want to see regarding intergroup relations and what they are seeing, especially as we contrast the experiences of Euro-Americans with those of African, Latino, and Asian Americans.

FRAMING THE KEY CONCEPTS

I discuss three sets of concepts with my students early in my courses. The first speaks to the meaning and measurement of the defining characteristics that produce intergroup relations: *race*, *ethnicity*, and *minority*. The second represents the key terms that produce the negative relations among groups: *racism*, *prejudice*, and *discrimination*. The third reflects a confusion in intergroup contact outcomes that students of intergroup relations must clear up in order to promote positive social change: *pluralism* and *segregation*.

Race, Ethnicity, and Minority

Because race and ethnicity are discussed in enough detail in Berkowitz and Barrington (chap. 1, this volume), not much needs to be added, except to say that using the term *ethnicity* exclusively makes a great deal of sense to me in the abstract. Nevertheless, practically speaking, both terms are in the public domain and distinguished in people's minds, so I use them both.

Before moving on to *minority*, a note about *race*: Geneticists have been telling us for quite a while that it is impossible to consistently distinguish among races in terms of any sort of differences among isolated gene pools, because isolation is impossible. The history of white–black relations from slavery onward in this country is testimony to the lack of genetic isolation in this country. Therefore, I use the term *race* to refer to social categories and emphasize the ways in which it varies from any biologically based notion of race.

The social definition, of course, is basically what societal values and norms at the moment support and, at the individual level, what each person presents to be true and has accepted as true. In the case of individuals whose skin color and general features approximate a race that they are trying to adopt, they are members of that race if others believe them to be. Even though it is an unreliable scientific yardstick, the social definition of race is the basis on which people and their societal representatives judge and act toward one another.

Minority is a term that has come under a great deal of fire in recent years. Our intermediate course offering in intergroup relations had had the name "Minority Groups" since before I arrived on campus. Moreover, there are excellent contemporary texts on the subject of intergroup relations that use the term *minority*. Nevertheless, in today's politically charged climate on campuses, many students of color believe the term to be denigrating in the extreme and reject its use.

I found this out firsthand a couple of years ago in my course on "Minority Groups." The main text was called *Minorities in American Society* (Marden, Meyer, & Engel, 1992). One of my students of color objected to the term in the course title, the title of the text, and my description of those ethnic and racial groups whose economic, social, and political positions in society were being contrasted to that of the "majority" group. In her eyes, the term *minority* was a slap at people of color and further proof that White America was continuing to persecute them. After all, people of color make up the majority of the world's population, not a minority.

My response and the subsequent arguments within the class actually produced some of the best discussions of the semester. The term has an important sociological use in distinguishing among the relative power positions of racial and ethnic groups that are objects of prejudice and discrimination ("minorities") and the group that benefits from the invidious distinctions ("majority") *in a particular social, economic, and political context*. I still think the term *minority* is a legitimate sociological concept, but I have become sensitized to an alternate interpretation that sees much more in it than was originally intended or than sociologists mean when employing it today.

Racism, Prejudice, and Discrimination

Most volatile among the commonly used terms in courses on race relations is the concept of *racism*. I strongly agree with Simpson and Yinger's (1985) argument that racism is a problematic concept for two reasons: First, it tends to be a swear word more than an analytical term, immobilizing races whom it sets into opposition with one another. Second, racism tends to prevent us from looking for solutions to the problems it highlights by being a kind of explanation in itself, without really taking us very far in that explanation.

This is not to deny the important distinctions that observers of intergroup relations have made about the historical basis of the term and its use to describe ideologies among competing racial groups (Doob, 1993) or the distinction between individual and institutional racism (Carmichael & Hamilton, 1967). Nevertheless, I ask my students to wait on definitions of racism until they understand two concepts that affect it so critically: prejudice and discrimination. Just as sexism and ageism tend to have both attitudinal and behavioral components, so too does racism. The attitude—prejudice—may sound a bit outdated to some, but I use it because students are able to relate to it without the kind of anger or defensiveness that the concept of racism provokes. In addition, prejudice has been studied objectively in such detail that we know a lot about its origins and maintenance. My main objective in discussing prejudice is to get my students to think how the concept applies to themselves as well as to other people they know.

Central to this goal is Allport's (1958) argument that prejudice is easily acquired because its essential elements, "erroneous generalization" and "hostility," are such clear human tendencies. Also, his notion of "re-fencing," a device by which any contrary evidence to our prejudices are listed as exceptions to the rule explains the durability of prejudices. In class, we work through examples from our own experiences. At this point, I share evidence from a social distance study of college students that showed how prejudices against known groups (e.g., blacks, Poles, Turks) extended to fictitious and therefore unknown groups as well (e.g., Daniereans, Wallonians; Hartley, 1946).

Over the years I have found little variability in the proportion of my students who believe themselves to be relatively free of prejudices (the range is between none and only a handful each semester). My goal is not to belabor the obvious fact that we all tend to have prejudices, but rather to explain the processes by which these prejudices come about and to raise questions in my students' minds about the validity of those prejudices.

Discrimination, as the behavioral component of racism, tends to be a different matter to students. Although there is a kind of comfortable feeling in believing that almost everyone is prejudiced, folks are reluctant to admit that they discriminate, a behavior that has legal as well as moral implications. In this context, Merton's (1949) classic typology integrating prejudice and discrimination is useful. The "active bigot" who is prejudiced and discriminates and the perhaps nonexistent "all-weather liberal" who is tolerant of all and treats everyone equally are easy to understand because both are consistent in attitude and behavior.

Nevertheless, argued Merton (1949), one may also be relatively unprejudiced yet discriminate ("fair-weather liberal") or be prejudiced but not discriminate ("timid bigot"). I believe that most of us, at one time or another, have lived the lives of the fair-weather liberal and timid bigot, so I discuss them in some detail with my students. Furthermore, I have found the fact that prejudice and discrimination may not work together consistently is a useful opening to a reasoned discussion of the meaning of racism. Once the students understand Merton's typology, it then becomes easier to discuss the contemporary distinctions between individual and institutional racism and the arguments about whether racism by racial minorities is possible.

Pluralism and Segregation

The ideology of pluralism has been popular among the many students who have passed through my race relations courses. As a humane and progressive view of intergroup relations, it has much to commend it; and as a hyphenated American, I find its promise of "live and let live" to be consistent with the values I was taught by my parents.

At the same time, many students, both black and white, interpret the desire of people of color to develop African American student groups on college campuses and to demand neighborhood control of their school systems, for example, as aggressive manifestation of the kind of segregation that blacks in this country have fought so hard to eliminate. Even Gary Trudeau, the cartoonist/satirist, has joined the debate with his running series on African American student demands for their own facilities, including segregated drinking fountains. Is the demand for race-homogeneous groups, neighborhoods, and institutions manifest segregation or is it pluralism?

As a partial answer, I introduce Schermerhorn's (1970) typology on majority and minority aims, which simultaneously considers the objectives of both the majority and the minority. If both desire the minority to assimilate, then what Schermerhorn called integration, or the absence of conflict, will result. If both groups desire that the minority retain its (cultural) identity, integration also results. On the other hand, situations in which the majority wants assimilation and the minority wants pluralism, and in which the majority wants the minority to retain its identity but the latter desires assimilation both lead to conflict.

How does the case of African American presumed self-segregation on campuses fit into the typology? Clearly, the minority wants pluralism. What does the majority want? I believe there is no simple answer, because elements of the majority want different things. On the one hand, some want black students to become an integral part of the student body through assimilation. On the other hand, those who would just as soon not have blacks on campus are not nearly so upset about black pluralism unless it highlights black presence on campus and poses a threat to whites. A few may genuinely understand the need for black students to maintain black groups on campus and not feel threatened.

The problem is that the pluralism of African American students means something quite different from segregation of black students by white students. Similar parallels can be made regarding community control arguments. In each case, the superficial layers surrounding a particular set of behaviors (e.g., a black student union) must be peeled away to find the fundamental goals that are represented by the behavior.

APPLYING IDEAS ABOUT RACE IN THE CLASSROOM

Over the years I have discovered the importance of three ways to maximize the likelihood that I will get my conceptual ideas about intergroup relations across to my students. The first is *being collegial*, by making and keeping in contact with colleagues who teach in the area of race relations, especially those folks from outside the discipline of sociology. Second, *using local history* makes national and global issues more meaningful to students. Finally, *structuring conflict* in the classroom around contemporary and historical issues that are problematic focuses attention on not just the obvious issues, but also the ones that are hidden.

Being Collegial

A recent insight for which I am thankful to our college's dean, the associate dean, and the college's race and ethnicity cohort colleagues from departments outside sociology is the critical role that other faculty play in the teaching of race relations. I am thinking of contexts other than the very useful traditional guest lecture. Let me describe one to illustrate what I mean.

The situation involves a couple of colleagues from sociology and another from anthropology, who are part of the cohort. During the spring semester a couple of years ago, the anthropologist invited the rest of us to share our early semester experiences over lunch, because she was having problems dealing with apparent political agendas that some of her students were attempting to follow. Her concern was that the class atmosphere was becoming so adversarial that all of her students would soon be alienated. The rest of us were experiencing similar problems and enthusiastically shared our own pains and sorrows.

In my own case, I was facing the polarization of my class into two very antagonistic groups. The first contained most of the students, almost all of whom were white and Anglo, whereas the second contained fewer than a half dozen, most of whom were students of color. The first group, despite my first day's talk on the need to confront issues and express opinions honestly, were reluctant to say almost anything for fear of being politically incorrect. The second group, which talked much more, felt alienated from the lack of response by students in the first group as well as from my sociological perspective. Despite my speaking individually outside of class with students from each group, class discussions became more and more one-sided.

Our lunch group continued to meet throughout the semester, benefiting us in two ways. First, of course, was the fact that misery loves company. We were relieved to find that all of us were sharing similar problems and could commiserate with each other over them. More important, however, by sharing our experiences we were able to brainstorm possible solutions. In my own case, it involved confronting my entire class for a whole 75-minute period about what I perceived to be happening in class. I wish I had done it earlier. From that moment on, the course began to come together, because students from both groups started communicating with one another. A great deal of the reason for the change in the course's direction is due to the lunchtime meetings.

Using Local History

A rather different device for applying concepts is sharing local history with students. In the case of Burlington, Vermont, and the University of Vermont, there are two ways to integrate local history into a course on intergroup relations. The first stems from a fairly decent community study done by Anderson (1937) on ethnic and religious cleavages in Burlington during the 1930s. I have my students read selected chapters in the book and compare what used to be with what Burlington is now like. Given the minuscule number of blacks in 1930s Burlington and the only slightly larger numbers today, the issues discussed tend to focus on the reasons for the paucity of African Americans in Burlington and the meaning of ethnic and religious cleavages 60 years ago and how they have played out in recent years.

The second example I use is Kakewalk, a winter festival and competition by the same name that characterized winter in Burlington, Vermont, from the turn of the century through the 1960s (an excellent description is in Loewen, 1991). The key element in Kakewalk was "Walkin' fo' de Kake," a competition of structured (and athletically demanding) dancing performed by two male partners dressed in brightly lavish tie and tales and wearing burnt cork "black face." The winners, judged by a blue-ribbon panel of local dignitaries, received a cake and trophy, along with the enduring gratitude of their sponsoring fraternity. Along with the walking were skits put on by the fraternities and snow sculptures erected by fraternities and sororities. In its heyday, Kakewalk probably was the premier university social event in the northeastern United States.

Despite its clearly negative stereotyping of African Americans, Kakewalk continued through much of the Civil Rights Movement into the early 1960s. Eventually, in response to strong pressures from within and without, Kakewalk came to an end, leaving a significant number of students and even more significant number of alumni frustrated and angry at this "innocent" carnival that had been taken away. Interestingly, the initial response by the university administration had not been to halt the "walkin'" but to put the walkers in "green face." Response from the campus community was almost uniformly negative, from those who thought dancing green men was absurd to others who, looking at the walkers from a distance, thought they were still seeing "black face." Officials then tried the dance competition without makeup, but that didn't seem right either, so, finally, Kakewalk was stopped.

There is a film from a local television station documenting the waning years of Kakewalk that I show to my classes. Afterward, we discuss the meaning of Kakewalk, both the good and the bad, trying to place it in the context of the conceptual issues we have been discussing in class.

The obvious advantage of using local material is that it easily engages the students' attention because, in one way or another, the history of the area and, in the case of Kakewalk, of the university, is familiar territory. A second advantage is that local history can throw a clearer light on the larger society (e.g., the community study of Burlington's focus on cross-cutting ethnic and class cleavages) or on a set of abstract issues (e.g., Kakewalk highlighting the distinction between manifest and latent functions).

Structuring Conflict

Every time I teach race relations, I structure conflict into it. For example, I ask essay questions on exams and organize oral reports that require students to consider both sides of an issue. I try to structure it also with guest speakers, especially colleagues of color, and media presentations. My favorite method, however, is to set up formal debates on a regular basis (i.e., every 2 or so weeks).

The debate requirements are fairly straightforward: There are two to four students per side, each side has a constructive presentation in which major arguments and evidence for the affirmative and negative are given, there is a brief break to prepare responses to the other team's constructive speech, and then each side presents its rebuttals and summaries. It is useful to augment the debates with a discussion afterward of which observing students' minds were changed by the debate, and why. I also ask my debaters to hand in a written summary of the debate along with source citations a few days after the debate, so that they can consider both sides of the issue in question.

Initially, I give students as much freedom as possible in choosing which topic to debate, and most get their first or second choice; but once assignments have been made to topics, I arbitrarily choose who debates which side. If I could guarantee it,

I would force everyone to take a side with which they disagree, because being forced to find arguments and evidence for a position with which one is not too familiar facilitates the learning process more than does the comfort of arguing a position that one believes from the outset.

Choice of topics can be left up to the students if topics are solicited early enough and students have enough knowledge about current issues. I prefer to give my students on the first day of class a questionnaire that contains a list of topics. For one thing, it allows me to direct the topic choices from the beginning, so that I can be sure key areas in the course are covered. In addition, student feedback to the questionnaire tells me whether the topic is likely to foster much disagreement. If a topic does not foster disagreement among the students, then I either abandon it as a debate topic but still discuss it where appropriate, or rephrase it to generate more disagreement.

My most recent race relations offering produced an example of the latter. I originally asked, "Should bilingualism be encouraged in our public schools?" My intention was to raise the question as to whether bilingualism was helping or hurting Latino students whose first language was Spanish. Instead, almost everyone in class interpreted the question to mean whether having two languages was a good thing, and responded "yes." When the class explained the almost uniform response, I raised the question that I should have asked in the first place: "Does bilingual education hinder children whose first language is other than English?" With this topic there was disagreement, so I included this second question as an issue to be debated during the semester.

Another topic produced a different kind of problem in the same class. The question was, "Are African Americans better off today than they were at the time of the Reverend Martin Luther King, Jr.'s assassination?" The student response was fairly evenly split. One can look at different kinds of evidence, indeed even the same evidence, and argue over what really has been proven.

Unfortunately, this was my polarized class and it was early in the semester. The two students I assigned to the affirmative (both white) argued the affirmative side tongue-in-cheek, because they honestly did not feel the evidence warranted the conclusion that black Americans had made significant gains during the past 25 years. I was rather dumbfounded by this tactic but, in a class that followed the debate, raised the issue with my students. In retrospect, I should have raised the issue at the time the students began their nonarguments, but I assumed, mistakenly, that the class would get around to raising affirmative evidence and arguments in the ensuing discussion.

The debates that followed later in the semester were significantly improved because of the public controversy generated by the second "nondebate." Students from both my quiet and vociferous groups contributed in significant ways during these subsequent debates. Overall, student evaluations over the years have consistently supported my feelings about structured debates. The insights learned from considering both sides of contemporary controversies usually outweigh the discomfort of performing before one's peers.

In summary, among all the topics addressed in university classrooms today, there is none that has the same potential as race relations for failed communication if the participants are inflexible and unwilling to deal with one another honestly. At the same time, there is no topic that possesses quite the potential of race relations to engage the minds and hearts of students and professors alike. Hopefully the conceptual objectives and suggestions for applying them in the classroom discussed in this chapter will help professors and students engage each other in intellectual good faith.

REFERENCES

Allport, G. W. (1958). *The nature of prejudice*. Garden City, NY: Doubleday.

Anderson, E. (1937). *We Americans: A study of cleavage in an American city*. Cambridge, MA: Harvard University Press.

Blalock, M. M., Jr. (1967). *Toward a theory of minority group relations*. New York: Wiley.

Carmichael, S., & Hamilton, C. V. (1967). *Black power: The politics of liberation in America*. New York: Random House Vintage Books.

Doob, C. B. (1993). *Racism: An American cauldron*. New York: HarperCollins.

Feagin, J. R., & Feagin, C. B. (1996). *Racial and ethnic relations* (5th ed.), Englewood Cliffs, NJ: Prentice-Hall.

Geschwender, J. A. (1978). *Racial stratification in America*. Dubuque, IA: William C. Brown.

Gordon, M. M. (1961). Assimilation in American life: Theory and reality. *Daedalus, 90*, 247–285.

Gordon, M. M. (1964). *Assimilation in American life: The role of race, religion, and national origins*. New York: Oxford University Press.

Hartley, E. L. (1946). *Problems in prejudice*. New York: Kings Crown.

Loewen, J. W. (1991). Black image in white Vermont: The origin, meaning, and abolition of Kake Walk. In R. V. Daniels (Ed.), *Bicentennial history of the University of Vermont* (pp. 349–369). Boston: University Press of New England.

Marden, C. F., Meyer, G., & Engel, M. (1992). *Minorities in American society* (6th ed). New York: HarperCollins.

Marger, M. N. (1997). *Race and ethnic relations: American and global perspectives* (4th ed.). Belmont, CA: Wadsworth.

Merton, R. K. (1949). Discrimination and the American creed. In R. H. MacIver (Ed.), *Discrimination and national welfare* (pp. 99–126). New York: Harper & Row.

Newman, W. M. (1973). *American pluralism: A study of minority groups and social theory*. New York: Harper & Row.

Schermerhorn, R. A. (1970). *Comparative ethnic relations: A framework for theory and research*. New York: Random House.

Simpson, G. E., & Yinger, J. M. (1985). *Racial and cultural minorities: An analysis of prejudice and discrimination* (5th ed.). New York: Plenum.

8

We Shan't Overcome This Way: Questions of Recontextualizing the Study of Liberal and Religious Reform Action

Robert Gussner
University of Vermont

The agendum for this chapter is to share my experience, and that of my students, in a course on race and religion in America that is one of several recently instituted to allow students to fulfill a new undergraduate degree requirement in multicultural education. The course has been offered twice: once in a seminar format (with 26 students) and once in a lecture/discussion-section format (with 42 students). In both instances, first-year students comprised about half the class.

My recent teaching has centered on three problems—*war*, with its corollaries of nuclear proliferation and life-draining expenditures; *overpopulation* and its associated hunger, infrastructure collapse, and dieback; and *environmental degradation* leading to fundamental shifts in planetary conditions—all as viewed by conservative, liberal, and mystical religious perspectives, together with their proposed solutions and the real-world obstacles to implementing those solutions.

For years I had approached religion and social issues from the standpoint of the prophetic social gospel of Christian liberalism. But I have come to realize that the idealistic liberal vision, which has so long served as inspiration and rationale for liberal education, social action, and the crusade for black rights (and now is supposed to shoulder the weight for a whole "new world order" of democracy and free enterprise) is actually ill-adapted in crucial ways to present realities, and even less to future ones. I have concluded that a new foundation must be put under the long effort—from the *Magna Charta* to *Roe v. Wade* and beyond—to extend more rights to more groups in more areas of life in order to empower them to pursue the liberal version of the good life. This thesis underlies the ways in which I teach my course "Race and Religion in America." Thus, I conclude this chapter with a discussion of liberal models of multiethnic education and why they are inadequate to the task. I then propose an alternative.

ORGANIZING THE COURSE

I opted from the outset against attempting to arouse student interest by assigning biographies of great figures in black history, such as Richard Allen, Frederick Douglass, Booker T. Washington, W. E. B. DuBois, James Weldon Johnson, Martin Luther King, Jr., Malcolm X, and Ralph Ellison. To me, this smacked of the outdated "great hero" approach to ethnic studies with its insidious implication that "These people in general may not have amounted to an awful lot, but even they have had outstanding leaders and it is nice to be a little familiar with their food and holidays." To me, this approach smacks of tokenism. That approach would also deflect attention away from the structural, collective nature of white oppression and black suffering and, moreover, make it difficult to deal with the full range of religious data and the several types of black religious life I wished to cover.

I also discarded a topical or thematic approach to the course, as well as a course centered on some controversial thesis like Wood's (1990) in *The Arrogance of Faith*: the thesis that Christianity is inherently and peculiarly racist in the curse of Ham, and, indeed, generally oppressive in both its way of life and scriptural word. This book fairly crackles with passion and is useful for term papers on Puritan and evangelical religious life. It is also good for an initial understanding of what it means to "be white," an important subject that surfaced during the course. But it seriously underplays the crucial role of the social Gospel, on which the leading edge of black leadership has so effectively drawn.

For a time the topical approach appealed to me, because C. Eric Lincoln's (1974) *The Black Experience in Religion* offered a hard-hitting, religiously comprehensive text. However, its strengths were also its weakness. Topics like the agenda for the black church, future church styles, the black sermon, and what African American music means, important as they are for understanding the experiences of black people in America, might not be as compelling for students unacquainted with traditional African American church services.

I finally settled for a standard chronological design—and about 65% black history, and 35% black religion—on the grounds that students, by custom and training, quite naturally attempt to understand anything really unfamiliar by starting with its historical origins and working from there. If the data were to be largely new, it seemed best to have a familiar framework in which to put them.

But a single good text for a chronologically organized course dealing with both race and black religion is hard to find. The first syllabus was a patchwork of chapters stitched together. Two textbooks, however, have remained serviceable: Sernett's

(1985) *Afro-American Religious History: A Documentary Approach* and Donald Niemen's (1991) *Promises to Keep*. Sernett's book lacks proper introductions to its "selections," and fails to typologize the numerous forms of religious life that it presents, but its selection of firsthand sources is superb and its short introductions adequate. Nieman's *Promises to Keep* deals with the Constitution and the Supreme Court in a manner that highlights black oppression and how resistance to this oppression came to be based in natural rights theory, prophetic liberation theology, and "Jesus as friend of the oppressed." It also shows how long and exhausting the road to equal treatment has been, and how central sheer terror has been in American life. It documents, moreover, how devious institutional resistance has been to letting blacks become part of American life.[1]

PERIODS OF BLACK HISTORY

Standard periods in American history serve fairly well for black studies, too. I initially divided the syllabus into six: the Colonial period (1619–1775); the period from the Revolutionary War to the end of the Civil War (1776–1864); the Reconstruction period (1865–1876); "Redemption" and the Jim Crow segregation period (1877–1954); the Civil Rights years (1954–1968); and, finally, the period of benign neglect and Southern electoral strategies (1969–). I have subsequently collapsed the last four periods into two: Reconstruction and the Jim Crow segregation period (1865–1954), and the Civil Rights struggle (1954–). Of my present four periods, the first takes 2 weeks to cover, the next two take 3 weeks each, and the last takes 4 weeks. The class meets 3 times a week, and there is generally a reading for each class. I prepare study outlines from the readings highlighting the major events, dates, persons, and trends.

In the second offering of the class I resorted to the flashback format by beginning with American racial realities in 1992: We undertook an historical survey only after weighing contemporary problems and options. We kicked off with "Eye of the Storm," a video about third graders in Iowa divided into good brown-eyed people and bad blue-eyed people, and with the 2-hour Phil Donahue video "The Issue Is Race," in which a panel of nine leaders reacted to three video "essays" setting forth differing strategies for progress: government spending (Sylvester Monroe of *Time* magazine), "buying black" (businessman Tony Brown), and forming alliances with other ethnic groups on the moral "high ground" of Christian love (Cornel West).

As we went through each of these periods of black history there were leading questions: How prevalent was brutality and sadism in the antebellum South? If you were living in the 1830s, which kind of abolitionism would you have advocated? Was Booker T. Washington wise to propose a "deal" with white America in which

---

[1]In addition to these texts, we have used chapters from Paul Escott's *Slavery Remembered* (1979), John Blassingame's *The Slave Community* (1972), Albert Raboteau's *Slave Religion* (1978), Andrew Hacker's *Two Nations* (1992), and James Loewen's "The Difference Race Makes in the United States: An Introduction to Outcomes and Causes" (chap. 2, this volume).

blacks would forgo seeking the vote and social integration in exchange for economic opportunity for educated blacks and fairness in the courts?

Another issue that arose might be framed this way: In the civil rights period, which was really most effective in bringing constructive change: black adherence to nonviolence, the threat of black violence waiting in the wings, public backlash against white violence, or actual black violence showing itself willing to tear a city apart? For example, would the Voting Rights Act of 1965 have been passed if the nation were not in mourning for James Reeb, a white Unitarian minister clubbed down by whites in Selma?

Also of interest were questions of the extent of prejudice in students' own families and home communities. Most placed the percentage of bigots in the population well above the core 10% found in studies from 1945 to 1985. Many reacted to Sister Soulja's remark that blacks could not be racist. Most felt that there could be individual black racism, defined in James Loewen's paper as "unfavorable treatment by one person of another, based on racial group membership, usually with an element of intent" (Loewen, 1994, p. 33 [glossary]). But most agreed there could *not* be institutional black racism defined as "unfavorable treatment by a social institution of a group of persons, based upon group membership, often with no element of intent" because blacks lacked sufficient control over significant institutions to carry this out. (Loewen, 1994, p. 33 [glossary]).

A main issue of which students were generally unaware was the "caste effect" of segregation on blacks, which, in effect, *declasses* them—consigning them to a life moving outside the class and status systems of the larger society. Thus, whereas European immigrant populations in America were treated individually as to their class (wealth) and status (prestige), and hence were able to rise or fall in these regards, a black person could become a millionaire and a leader in the black community and still be barred from downtown restaurants. He or she was fixed in a caste position outside the prevailing class system and so could neither rise nor fall in regard to it on the basis of money or prestige.

FORMS OF BLACK RELIGIOUS LIFE

Forms of black religious life are numerous and difficult to handle. In all, I see eight principal types, grouped under four headings. In rough chronological order, they are: the African "conjuration" mode of religious life; the older Calvinist puritanism of election, morality, and heaven; the newer Calvinist/Baptist/Methodist evangelical revivalism of individual conversion; natural rights deism; the prophetic social gospel of a New Jerusalem; Pentecostal sects; Islam; and, finally, positive thinking and "divine vessel" groups like Father Divine's movement.

I now find it simpler to classify black religious life into four fundamental forms. First, although it lends emotional vitality to all other forms, African conjuration stands by itself. It poses formidable problems of interpretation at the outset of any study of black religious history. Second, Puritan Calvinism and purists like the Nation of Islam form another type around discipline and strict community standards. Third, revivalism, Pentecostal sects, and divine leadership groups cohere around intense conversion experiences that go quite beyond the usual free emotional style, communal catharsis, and gratitude for making it through another week that generally characterize black prophetic, social gospel religions, and natural rights deism. Finally, the fourth form of black religious life is the articulation of the social gospel of deliverance from all earthly bondage. The black church both drew from and contributed to the evolving aspiration to create a liberal social order. This most important form of black religious life, based on the Declaration of Independence, the prophets, and Jesus' love of the oppressed, has been the principal resource for black liberation in American History. My thesis is that, although it succeeded in the past, it cannot serve the future well and must be supplemented by an approach of interior centered awareness, both in social action and in the teaching approach in multicultural education courses. But first, what is the "liberal vision"?

THE LIBERAL VISION

For a long time almost everything has been formulated in terms of the emerging liberal vision: Western culture since 1830, public education, developing nations, and multicultural education itself. To understand our present position and options, we must consider in some detail the core values of that tradition, milestones in its march, and questions concerning its future viability.

Think of liberalism and you think of such things as Western-style democracy; rationalism; objectivity; moderation; settling things by argument instead of force; the rule of law; tolerance; genial appreciation of the varieties of human experience; avoidance of fanatical clutching at some final "truth"; and the moral virtues of industry, sobriety, prudence, integrity, economy, punctuality, courage, and perseverance. These virtues are topped off with an instinctive dislike of scholasticism—and the certainty, mysticism, and claims to final truth contained within it.

Giving structure and coherence to this collection of values are four central elements of liberalism. The first, going back to the 1560s, is an attitude of independent *questioning* in two senses: (a) suspicious reexamination of all received truths, and (b) open-minded investigation into the unknown to discover new truths. The heart of liberalism is, thus, the "critical attitude": the attempt to find out what might be right or wrong with something. Rational doubt, it holds, is the best safeguard against the dark waters of religious superstition, emotional subjectivity, mob passions, fanaticism, and tyranny.

By the 20th century, liberalism had added three other core elements: from the *Philosophes*, the demand for the political right to criticize all sacred cows, including church, state, and scripture; from 19th-century humanitarianism, the doctrine of equality and the goodness of human nature; and from the natural and social sciences, the ideal of progress through education and the extension of rights to new groups in new areas of life through redistributing wealth and mental health, thus simultaneously ending oppression and suppression and banishing fear and misery from human history.

The Anglo-American wing of this liberal tradition is closely associated with the extension of rights: the struggle for the right of *habeas corpus* and protection from the king in the Magna Carta of 1215; the right to self-government in the revolutions of 1648, 1688, 1776, and 1789; the American Bill of Rights; the abolitionist movement and the Emancipation Proclamation of 1863; child labor laws in the 1880s; women's suffrage in 1920; Indian rights in 1934; labor's right to collective bargaining in the Wagner Labor Relations Act of 1935; the right to social security in 1936; and the right to a union shop and unemployment benefits. Since 1960, the struggle to extend rights as the necessary basis to fulfill aspirations, inspired anew by the black Civil Rights Movement, has successfully been expanded to include many groups. For women, such rights include access to new types of careers; equal pay and advancement for equal work; freedom from sexual harassment, patriarchal theology, and one-sided historical narration; reproductive freedom of choice; religious ordination; and so on.

Legislatively, the 1970s saw the enactment of the Environmental Protection Act, the Occupational Safety and Health Act, the Comprehensive Employment and Training Act, and the tying of social security raises to the cost of living index. The liberal impulse has been at work in creating Medicare and Medicaid, in securing the right of the accused to remain silent and to have a lawyer, in promoting gay rights and rights for disabled persons—and now in efforts to win the right to national health insurance, and securing multiethnic education for minority and third-world students. Our focus here is on how the liberal vision relates to multiethnic educational models and how it fits with our future.

Certainly it still has a role to play. Black Christian liberalism provided the class with several of the sharpest questions in the course. For example, "Do white people, whose experience has been dehumanization, have a real experiential basis that would enable them to raise the question of the essential humanity of man?" Again, "Is it that black folks have never been Christians in this country, or is it that blacks are the only Christians this country has ever had?" And, "Does the quiet, unemotional serenity of white worship services cover up spiritual emptiness, selfishness, and narrowness? Does it serve to perpetuate the status quo?" In the words of Caldwell (1974), does "A close up view of our white brothers inform us that they are the inheritors of a congenital sickness, and that God has placed the vaccine to cure them in our hands" (p. 32)? Most disturbing of all was the claim to reparations made by Williams (1974): "Blacks need to right the Christian ethic and demand that whites directly take on the burden for their past sins. Since it is the height of injustice to treat those who are unequal as equals, reparations are indispensible" (pp. 184–185). Each of these questions bears on the question of multicultural education in important ways.

MODELS OF MULTIETHNIC EDUCATION IN THE UNITED STATES

In what follows, I argue that we need to go beyond present liberal-based ways of conducting multicultural courses in public education. Banks (1984) described four models of multiethnic education: three somewhere in use and the fourth as an ideal. The first is simply education within a traditional Anglo-American perspective. It looks at subjects of interest to whites in the light of liberal values and works to propagate them. In the second model, ethnic perspectives are added to a basically Anglocentric course: "We" study "others" and what they think about us. But this, too, is all set in an aspic of liberal values.

With the third, multiethnic model, things apparently shift. Here, social or historical events in American history are at the center of the curriculum and are viewed from the standpoints of Mexican Americans, Native Americans, Asian Americans, Anglo Americans, African Americans, Jewish Americans, and Puerto Rican Americans. This is an apparently admirable departure. However, even though it is all-American it is all American—it is American nationals talking about nationalistic topics. Also, although the aspiration, de jure, is to have the Anglo perspective be only one of several ways of looking at Columbus or whatever, that is in no way inferior or superior to other ethnic perspectives, de facto the house rules and the house game are liberal—objectivity, reason, moderation, individualism, democratic discussion, equality of status, and so on. If a Native American wishes to extol tribal collectivism instead of individualism, chiefs instead of democracy, and spirit-magic instead of reason, he or she will have to express this in modalities partaking of individuality, democratic fairness, and rationality in order to accord with the liberal host setup of the symposium schema. By the very act of participation, one tends to end up more or less assimilated in advance to a growing Anglo-liberal hegemony of style and values. All that happens here is that the controlling virtues that constitute the heart of the Anglo perspective are taken from the controlling center and spread evenly throughout the group setting.

The ideal model, according to Banks, is the "multinational." In this, social or historical events are looked at from the standpoints of South American nations, North American nations, African nations, European nations, Asian nations, Australia, and so on. I have nothing against internationalizing American education, but I would point out that we still have education grounded in the divisive conditionings of religion, race, nationalism, or ideology now regionalized into giant power aggregates. It is one of the less-noticed features of the tolerant liberal vision that it leaves unchallenged divisive conditionings that now bedevil every attempt to solve global problems. Other liberal shortcomings I discuss later; at this point I introduce a fifth model and argue why liberalism cannot continue to be the main compass guiding us in multicultural education or on our voyage to a future that is rapidly taking on a shape unlike anything in our past.

Transcendental and Transnational Education: Beyond the Disrespect of Divisive Conditioning[2]

The center of the model I propose here is neither the Anglo perspective nor

---

[2]For many aspects of this model I am indebted to conversations with Dr. Vasant Joshi, Chancellor of Osho Multiversity in Poona, India.

selected historical and social events, but "you." It completes the other models by saying, in effect:

> All right, now you know what you as a conditioned ethnic and national identity think about controversial issues; let's look at your enculturated filters, the forces conditioning you to see things that way—the major historical, cultural, religious, spiritual, social, and political influences. Let's allow you to decondition yourself as much as you want and then, with some observant and purely human identity, transcending conditionings, look again more freely at all these national, ethnic, and religious things on the planet. First know what's working on you to pattern you and then, centered in your own deeper alertness, return to take a look at those patterning influences, themselves, in terms of their helping or harming human prospects on the planet. This, I think represents a potentially revolutionary advance.

The first two Anglocentric models of education are really stances of disrespect toward the "others" and toward the student, the person, because they fundamentally neglect him or her. Good as liberal values may be to inculcate, inculcation is still inculcation and it controls. It is not respectful. The third and fourth models I call models of respect. The word respect means "to look at again," and these models do take a second look at our heritages. Although they may lead to respectful, politically correct ways of addressing you, they still address you as an instance of a person in a group, still, that is, with stereotypical overtones. You are some ALANA person or a white, and so on.

The fifth model I call one of real respect, where we can meet each other not as persons who have been completely "had" by conditioning, but as freer, aware beings. I would argue that this fifth model is not hopelessly idealistic. It gives one a new and more global identity as a simple human being on a journey of inner and outer awakening to replace the older identities of nation, race, religion, ethnicity, or radical ideologue. In class, one need not be cast in some identity as victim or oppressor. The four main models, I believe, all act to create a subtle but deadly "cocktail of conflict" in students. The models make you aware of your minority identity and its history of injustice. They then empower you, as it were, to argue effectively why your ethnic group should now have a larger slice of the national or international "pie." They, in effect, set groups to seizing at the toppings of our "planetary," ripping competitively at it based on separate, incompatible, inflamed identities. This was not bad from 1750 to the present, when the age of exploration and of industrialism created an era of expansionist plenty.

But today, we do not need to vociferously create plural and conflicting identities with intense historical grievances against each other. We need to create a single, more integrative identity of aware, deconditioned persons on a journey of awakening, able to look squarely at modern planetary problems with eyes unclouded by past-conditioned identities. Liberal models "celebrate diversity" but this is simplistic, even inflammatory, without even more strongly celebrating our unity. We need new answers to the twin questions "Who are we?" and "How are we together?" That answer cannot be the old liberal one of "equally valuable but differently conditioned minds." That way lies chaos. That way we shall not overcome injustice. Only awareness replacing conditioned minds can move toward a future of workable harmony. Only that way, shall we overcome the modern crisis.

Student response to this awareness model has been grateful and warm. This model awaits fuller theoretical explication and experimental implementation. I would argue that it is urgently needed because of the growing obsolescence of the prevailing liberal models.

REFERENCES

Banks, J. (1984). Multiethnic education in the U.S.A. In T. Corner (ed.), *Education in multicultural societies* (pp. 68–95). New York: St. Martin's Press.

Blassingame, J. W. (1972). *The slave community: Plantation life in the Antebellum South.* New York: Oxford University Press.

Caldwell, G. (1974). Black folk in white churches. In C. E. Lincoln (Ed.), *The black experience in religion* (pp. 28–33). New York: Anchor/Doubleday.

Escott, P. D. (1979). *Slavery remembered: A record of the twentieth-century slave narratives* Chapel Hill: University of North Carolina Press.

Hacker, A. (1992). *Two nations: Black and white, separate, hostile, unequal.* New York: Scribner's.

Lincoln, C. E. (Ed.). (1974). *The black experience in religion.* New York: Anchor/Doubleday.

Loewen, J. W. (1992). *The difference race makes in the United States: An introduction to outcomes and causes.* Burlington, VT: UVM Printing and Graphics.

Nieman, D. (1991). *Promises to keep: African-Americans and the constitutional order, 1776 to the present.* New York: Oxford University Press.

Raboteau, A. J. (1978). *Slave religion: The "invisible institution" in the Antebellum South.* New York: Oxford University Press.

Sernett, M. (1985). *Afro-American religious history: A documentary approach.* Durham, NC: Duke University Press.

Williams, P. N. (1974). The problem of a black ethic. In C. E. Lincoln (Ed.), *The black experience in religion* (pp. 180–188). New York: Anchor/Doubleday.

Wood, F. S. (1990). *The arrogance of faith: Christianity and race in America from the colonial era to the twentieth century.* New York: Knopf.

9

Economic Inequality

Elaine McCrate
University of Vermont

Most undergraduates I have taught have fairly firm mental pictures about the long trajectory of racial economic inequality in the United States, and equally strong opinions about policy issues such as affirmative action, public assistance, and urban economic development. Usually, they believe that the long-run trend has been for racial inequalities to diminish gradually and fairly consistently. Accordingly, the students feel that the need for legal and other remedies against inequality has subsided. Yet, when I probe into the basis for their beliefs, I usually find lots of assumptions and little historical or theoretical foundation.

In my course on African Americans in the U.S. economy, I try to fundamentally shake up students' prior beliefs about race and economics, and then provide them with several alternative frameworks for thinking about these issues. The course has three parts. For about the first third of the semester, I saturate students with the institutional history of racial economic inequality. For the next third, I discuss economic theory: Under what conditions might racism be reproduced or undermined, and who benefits from it? Finally, once the historical and theoretical context has been developed, I raise several pressing contemporary issues. These vary from semester to semester, but always include equal opportunity and affirmative action, and the black "underclass."

THE INSTITUTIONAL HISTORY OF RACISM

In this section of the course, I develop five key claims that seriously challenge most students' implicit beliefs about U.S. racism. The claims are developed in the following sections.

Claim 1: The United States has not always been clearly racist in the sense in which it is today; rather, slavery and virulent organized racism emerged in a specific historical context. This is important because it suggests that racism is based in specific historical conditions, rather than in a seemingly natural propensity of one race to mistreat another. It is, therefore, possible that if we fully understand the institutional foundations of racism, we just might be able to eliminate it.

I make this case with Fredrickson's (1988a, pp. 189–205) paper, "Social Origins of American Racism." Fredrickson argued that for a very brief period of time, between the arrival of the first Africans in Virginia in 1619 and the introduction of cash crops around 1640, blacks had basically the same status as did white indentured servants. Clearly, the exploitation of Africans was tied up with longstanding European beliefs that Africans were un-Christian, bestial, associated with Satanism, and so on. But these beliefs did not initially seem to be associated with different treatment of black and white indentured servants. Indeed, on release, Africans seem to have been about as able as white former indentured servants to own land, vote, marry whites, have servants of their own, and in some cases become prosperous small farmers. And even after slavery appeared, for a brief while, the overwhelming problem of a labor shortage led Maryland lawmakers to declare that white women who married black slaves, and their children, would henceforth become slaves. The dominant issue in the Southern colonies was a labor shortage, and at first the most significant dimensions of inequality were class and religion, not race (Bennett, 1975).

The status of Africans changed dramatically starting around 1640, with the appearance of tobacco as a cash crop, soon to be followed by rice, sugar cane, and cotton. The profitability, scale, and labor demands of these crops were immense, but there were few available hands to do the work: Whites could by and large farm their own land, and thus would not work for someone else. Plantation owners sought permanently unfree labor. Africans were uniquely vulnerable (and many from the West coast of Africa had skills in rice cultivation) and, therefore, became enslaved. Soon the legal and ideological climate changed profoundly: Blacks were stripped of the right to vote, to own land, to marry whites, and so on; limits were placed on the ability of slaveowners to voluntarily free their slaves; and blacks became uniquely regarded as lazy and not likely to work without the type of compulsion slavery provided. Hence, slavery and racism emerged with the birth and consolidation of a lucrative system of production for profit under conditions of labor shortage (Wright, 1978).

Besides introducing the concept of the institutional foundations of racism, Fredrickson's paper generally provoked some lively discussion on the role of attitudes and social structures in establishing and perpetuating racism. He contended that Eurocentric, ethnophobic beliefs about Africans were not initially associated with legal and economic racism. Finally, I emphasize that U.S. racism initially developed in a situation of severe labor shortage in order to contrast it with what later developed: racism in conditions of labor surplus.

Claim 2: The Civil War was not about racial equality or multiracial democracy. Here I fast-forward the historical tape, not dwelling on slavery because most students have some passing familiarity with it and, consequently, have a greater need to learn about its aftermath. Students typically know next to nothing about the 100 years between the Emancipation Proclamation and the Civil Rights Movement, in which most Southern blacks labored under conditions not far removed from slavery.

We discuss the various arguments as to why the Civil War happened and why slavery was destroyed. These include the hypotheses that the Civil War was fundamentally a conflict over the slave versus free status of the frontier territories, that it was a struggle by Southern planters to maintain the value of their substantial investment in slaves, or that it was fueled by a movement of Northern smallholders to protect "free labor" (Foner, 1978). The main point, however, is that there is no carefully documented historical case that the North fought the Civil War out of a humanitarian commitment to racial justice. Indeed, there was a significant proslavery movement in Indiana, where grains were being grown as a cash crop. Lincoln as well as most of the other Republican Party leaders wished to expatriate blacks to Africa after the Civil War rather than integrate them into American society (Fredrickson, 1988b; Marable, 1984). This part of the course does a lot to unsettle most students' tendency to equate the end of slavery with the dawn of racial justice.

Claim 3: Progress toward racial equality has not been a rising linear trend of justice triumphing over ill-will and ignorance. Students often come into the course subscribing to a teleological view of racial history: The South used to have slavery, there used to be inequality and segregation, but now the barriers to racial equality have largely fallen; those that have not yet come down are likely to drop in the future as a result of more enlightened attitudes. In contrast to this view, I try to get students to see that, in some periods, African Americans have made huge strides against inequality, but subsequently lost much of what they had gained. In other periods, gains were very geographically circumscribed. A very important case is the Reconstruction era, which was ended by the withdrawal of Northern troops from the South in 1877. I also try to get students to see both the tremendous gains of the Civil Rights Movement and its equally important limitations. It marked the first time that racial equality and multiracial democracy achieved a prominent place in U.S. political discourse. The Civil Rights Movement was also of immense economic importance for blacks living in the south.

As James J. Heckman and his coauthors documented, however, the gap between the earnings of blacks and whites did not fall for more than a few years outside the South after 1965. In addition, black unemployment rates, especially those of youth, were increasing rapidly relative to white rates (Donohue & Heckman, 1991). Blacks were becoming surplus labor on a large scale.

Claim 4: The northern United States did not welcome the influx of millions of blacks who migrated out of the South during the world wars and in the 1950s; Rather, it responded with policies that isolated and impoverished them, and virtually ensured their status as surplus labor. Blacks were widely used as strikebreakers: For example, the importation of 60,000 black strikebreakers during 1919 destroyed industrial unionism in steel until the 1930s (Reich, 1981). Northern whites instigated race riots and other violent incidents against blacks over many years in several cities as black immigrants spilled outside black residential enclaves. Real estate agents manipulated panic-stricken white residents into selling their homes cheaply, then resold these same houses at much higher prices to blacks who were desperate for housing. Because of a severe housing shortage, landlords did not maintain their units, neighborhoods became overcrowded, and sanitation and fire prevention deteriorated. All this led to the growth of what Arnold Hirsch (1983) called the "first ghetto." The extraordinary response of business leaders and public officials was "urban renewal": the creation of a "second ghetto" by ejecting black residents from the first. Chicago was a pioneer in developing policies of land acquisition and clearance in which black residents were forced to move. The land was purchased and cleared at public expense, and resold to the private and nonprofit sectors for redevelopment, at a fraction of the cost to the public. In the process, the number of housing units fell, exacerbating the housing shortage faced by blacks, and the ghetto spread horizontally (to other neighborhoods) and vertically (in high-rise public housing that only partially restored some of the lost housing). This set of policies has been replicated over time, with minor variations, all over the country.

Information on the creation of the ghettos, and on the lack of black economic progress in the North during the Civil Rights Movement, leads to a discussion on the differences between Northern and Southern racism. Students begin to see that racism can thrive even without the overt "whites only" trappings of the Jim Crow laws.

Claim 5: Blacks do worse than whites in economic downturns, yet blacks have usually been convenient scapegoats for the loss of white economic security. When the economy is doing well and jobs are relatively abundant, white workers are more comfortable with black workers entering the mainstream. Such was the case in the economic expansion of the 1950s and 1960s. But when a boom ends, blacks who were last hired become the first workers to be fired. White workers are more easily persuaded that black gains threaten their own precarious economic position. In the 1970s and 1980s, as the economy went into a tailspin, many politicians including Ronald Reagan easily manipulated white fears of job loss into a growing racial backlash. Yet black workers were hurt more severely than white by the anemic growth of the 1980s, contributing to a swelling of the black surplus labor pool, and to a new widening of the racial earnings gap (Bound & Freeman, 1989; Marable, 1983; Reich, 1981).

THEORY

The theoretical section of the course presents different views on the economic basis for racism. I start with the provocative neoclassical view that discrimination must self-destruct in the long run because it is costly to employers. According to this argument, if a firm refuses to hire qualified black workers and insists on lower quality white workers, it produces its goods at higher cost, eventually driving itself out of the market. In the meantime, employers who are less averse to dealing with qualified blacks will compete to hire them, offering them higher pay and ultimately eroding the pay gap.

Students argue the pros and cons of this view. Those who support it explain the persistence of the pay gap (now apparently anomalous) in terms of the characteristics of black workers: less and lower quality education, less labor market experience, and so on. Students who do not subscribe to the view that racism self-destructs develop a list of reasons why such a simple scenario might not come to pass: Customer and coworker discrimination that makes it costly for an employer *not* to discriminate, monopoly situations in product markets that reduce the pressures for firms to produce at low cost, high rates of unemployment that keep qualified blacks from demanding the higher wages they deserve, and so on.

Other authors believe that these circumstances do not fully account for the virulence and persistence of the racial economic inequality that the United States has experienced since the Civil War. Reich (1981) was the first of several authors to argue that racism, far from becoming eroded over time, is reproduced as an intrinsic part of the U.S. economic system. He emphasized the importance of racism as a device that pits workers against each other and undermines their common struggle against exploitative employers. Marable (1983) continued this line of reasoning, and further argued that capitalism underdevelops black America. The problem is not that African Americans are not fully integrated within the capitalist system, but, rather, that they are all too fully enmeshed within that system, which impoverishes them at the same time that it enriches white elites. Harrison and Sum (1979) explained the theory of segmented labor markets and described the concentration of blacks in the secondary sector, which is characterized by job insecurity and low wages. Carmichael and Hamilton (1967) expanded on the theme of underdevelopment, arguing that wealth is extracted from the African American community just as it has been from colonized countries. This extraction is accomplished by low wages for blacks as well as high prices for essentials such as housing and food, where these revenues accrue to white establishments outside black neighborhoods.

Most of these authors agreed that, at least in some ways, whites are hurt by racism and helped by anti-racist policies. Shulman (1990) asked, then, whether this is the entire story behind racism. He contended that racism unifies white ethnics and enhances their bargaining power in relation to employers, and that whites successfully erect barriers to black job competition. Thus, there are two offsetting economic effects of racism for whites, and the net effect depends on the concrete historical situation.

CONTEMPORARY ISSUES

Perhaps the most hotly contested and personally felt racial issue for college students is affirmative action and equal employment policy. I review the major laws, executive orders, and court decisions in this area, making clear what they require and do not require. Affirmative action especially needs to be explained in detail, because it means different things in different contexts. Most students are astonished to learn that the law does not require companies to hire blacks or to establish quota programs. Rather, federally mandated affirmative action simply requires large federal contractors to document that they look for qualified women and persons from ethnic or racial groups historically discriminated against whenever they have job openings. In some cases, court opinions have gone beyond this, upholding the right of companies and unions voluntarily to establish set-aside programs in instances where blacks are severely underrepresented. Finally, in the large class-action discrimination suits of the 1970s, courts often required companies found in violation of Title VII of the Civil Rights Act to establish affirmative action programs in order to redress proven discrimination.

Once students have the factual information about what affirmative action and equal employment law do, they debate the effectiveness of such measures in reducing race discrimination, their consequences for productive efficiency, and implications for fairness.

The course also addresses the issue of the black "underclass." We examine the dimensions of underclass status: labor surplus, poverty, reproductive norms and trends, welfare dependence, crime, educational inadequacy, and so on. Here the question is how can we tell cause from effect: For example, do poor black women tend to become mothers as teenagers because they are poor, or do they become poor as a result of teenage motherhood (Geronimus, 1991)? Is welfare dependency the result of job scarcity, or do welfare dependency and the personal traits that are supposedly associated with it act as an employment barrier?

CONCLUSION

Throughout this course I try to get students to understand how racism operates in a systemic way, how their own beliefs developed in this context, and how their own actions have consequences for race relations whether they intend them and are aware of them or not. The point is to be able to understand personal responsibility for racism in a context of systemic racism, by developing some historical and theoretical clarity. I believe this approach works well because it probes the causes of racism while largely short-circuiting the response of white guilt, which simply enables whites to continue being racist, albeit in a more covert or bumbling way.

REFERENCES

Bennett, L., Jr. (1975). *The shaping of black America*. Chicago: Johnson.

Bound, J., & Freeman, R. (1989). Black economic progress: Erosion of the post-1965 gains in the 1980s? In S. Shulman & W. Darity (Eds.), *The question of discrimination: Racial inequality in the U.S. labor market* (pp. 32–49). Middletown, CT: Wesleyan University Press.

Carmichael, S., & Hamilton, C. V. (1967). *The politics of liberation in America*. New York: Random House.

Donohue, J. H. III, & Heckman, J. (1991). Continuous versus episodic change: The impact of civil rights policy on the economic status of blacks. *Journal of Economic Literature, 29*(4), 1603–1643.

Foner, E. (1978). *Free soil, free labor, free men: The ideology of the Republican Party before the Civil War.* New York: Oxford University Press.

Fredrickson, G. M. (1988a). *The arrogance of race: Historical perspectives on slavery, racism, and social inequality.* Middletown, CT: Wesleyan University Press.

Fredrickson, G. M. (1988b). Abraham Lincoln: A man but not a brother. In G. M. Fredrickson, *The arrogance of race: Historical perspectives on slavery, racism, and social inequality* (pp. 54–72). Middletown, CT: Wesleyan University Press.

Geronimus, A. (1991). Teenage childbearing and social and reproductive disadvantage: The evolution of complex questions and the demise of simple answers. *Family Relations, 40*(4), 463–471.

Harrison, B., & Sum, A. (1979). The theory of "dual" or segmented labor markets. *Journal of Economic Issues, 13* (3), 687–706.

Hirsch, A. R. (1983). *Making the second ghetto: Race and housing in Chicago, 1940–1960.* Cambridge, England: Cambridge University Press.

Marable, M. (1983). *How capitalism underdeveloped black America: Problems in race, political economy, and society.* Boston: South End Press.

Marable, M. (1984). *Race, reform and rebellion: The second Reconstruction in black America, 1945–1982.* Jackson: University Press of Mississippi.

Reich, M. (1981). *Racial inequality.* Princeton, NJ: Princeton University Press.

Shulman, S. (1990). Racial inequality and white employment: An interpretation and test of the bargaining power hypothesis. *Review of Black Political Economy, 18*(3), 5–20.

Wright, G. (1978). *The political economy of the cotton South.* New York: Norton.

10

Teaching Multiculturalism Anthropologically

Sarah J. Mahler
Florida International University

Anthropology is quintessentially multicultural. It has always been a discipline dedicated to the cross-cultural comprehension of human diversity. However, my own classroom experience has taught me that my ability to communicate cultural differences between peoples living in "exotic" places does not easily translate into the successful communication of ethnic and racial subcultural differences within the United States. Rather, in the highly politically charged debates on multiculturalism versus *E pluribus unum*, anthropologists have often been excluded and have had to prove that their voices are legitimate. As a white middle-class woman who was hired by the University of Vermont to teach courses on racial and ethnic diversity in the United States, I am often haunted by identity politics. Students and colleagues have raised this red flag repeatedly, despite my scholarly expertise in the area. Consequently, I have developed numerous approaches to teaching that draw on anthropological insights and methods. I discuss a few of them here.

In my introductory cultural anthropology course, I spend several days convincing students that all humans are enculturated—that we are taught the norms of our culture before becoming conscious of them. The hardest thing to do, I insist, is to bring to consciousness these expectations unless they are juxtaposed to another culture's. Anthropologists who do fieldwork are professional outsiders who experience constant culture shock by living in a foreign culture. Immersion and keen observation over time produce knowledge of the other culture; I explain this process to my students as going from being an outsider to being an insider.

Because ethnographic fieldwork not only teaches researchers about another culture but also tends to encourage empathy toward that culture, it is a requirement for my race and ethnicity courses. At times, the fieldwork assignments are simple, such as spending an afternoon in a working-class section of town and then one in a middle-class section. I ask my students to observe how space communicates cultural ideals. For instance, we remark on how the middle-class single-family home is generally separated from others by a lawn and a fence. I then suggest that this distance symbolizes the American ideal of economic independence. But I also require semester-long fieldwork in which students must find a willing informant(s) who is racially or ethnically different from themselves. After explaining the project and gaining their informants' permission, my students must meet with their subjects a minimum of five times and keep detailed fieldnotes on each meeting. After roughly two meetings, I review the fieldnotes and try to suggest how the research might be directed along a theme. At the end of the semester, students develop their fieldwork into a final paper and submit it to me along with all their fieldnotes and any other background information they can provide. The research is carefully monitored from start to finish in order to guarantee that it is as fruitful an experience as possible for both students and informants.

At the beginning of the semester, when I outline the fieldwork project to my students, I emphasize that it is a requirement designed to fulfill a goal of the course that I cannot fulfill personally. Most of my courses examine racism as it occurs in this society's institutions. Although I feel confident to teach about institutional racism, I do not feel comfortable teaching about how people perceive racism. It is critical to me, however, to put a human face on the problem of racism. Sometimes this void is filled by vocal students from groups that have been racially discriminated against who offer their testimonies. At other times I have few such students in class or I have students who feel uncomfortable teaching others about racism. Consequently, I include the fieldwork project to fulfill a goal of sensitivity: White students must interact with people from other racial backgrounds and gain insight into their experience as members of a "minority." Students of color can choose to research the experience of someone who is from a different minority group or can explore issues of race and ethnicity with white students. The latter approach is designed to help break up stereotypes of whites as a homogeneous group that shares "white privilege." On occasion, when students have requested it, I have permitted them to document their day-to-day experience as "others" within the university community. This type of information has been particularly useful in extending my own knowledge of how race and ethnicity are expressed on campus.

Over the past years of integrating the fieldwork component into my race and ethnicity classes, I have found my method to be very successful but not problem-free. It makes a profound impression on the majority of my students, white students in particular. Initially, many are shocked and scared, afraid to leave the comfort and security of the ivory tower. The greater Burlington community has been experiencing a growing influx of people of diverse racial and ethnic backgrounds, and I encourage my students to do their research off-campus to take advantage of this. From outside academia they find that their campus is far different from the "real world." I assist them by suggesting that they contact various organizations and groups that I know or with whom students have worked successfully in the past.

Nevertheless, they are extremely nervous making initial contacts and lining up their first meeting. This is humbling and, in my opinion, positive. Additionally, students face the anthropological quandary of developing mutual relations. "What can I do for them so they don't think I'm taking advantage of them?" many of my students ask me. We then work on finding ways in which they can contribute to their informants' lives. I find that the articulation of a concern for others marks a critical achievement, particularly because students are enculturated to be primarily passive recipients in the educational exchange.

Working with students so intensively on their projects helps me to learn about them, too—much more profoundly than in my large lecture courses. But there is no discounting the amount of work involved. I spend hours with each student, monitoring the research's progress and suggesting ways of interpreting information. Additionally, I spend many hours coordinating efforts with local organizations, often asking them for their time and cooperation. I put myself on the line along with my students. I have had failures: students who procrastinated or who failed to climb out of their shells, or student–informant relationships that had been interpreted as more than platonic. But I have had many more successes. In numerous cases the relationships started during my courses have continued long after these courses ended. They have matured as the level of trust has risen. But perhaps the most enduring rationale for expending so much energy on the fieldwork requirement is my confidence that, years from now, my students are more likely to recall this experience and its lessons of sensitivity and tolerance than any of the readings and intellectual debates that took place within the classroom.

Another point that I make in my introductory course but extend to my race and ethnicity courses is the contrast between nature and culture. Fledgling anthropology students learn early on that all people impose culture on nature. Nature tells us that we are hungry but it does not tell us that we should satisfy our hunger three times a day. Nature has endowed humans with the capacity for sex at any time, but culture tells us when, where, and with whom it is appropriate. Culture is a way of ordering nature, of controlling instincts. People who share a culture expect its members to conform to these norms.

In both my introductory anthropology and race and ethnicity courses, I teach students that all peoples utilize this nature/culture divide to their advantage in some way. A good example is how many peoples give themselves names that translate to "human beings" whereas they assign names to their adversaries that imply that the adversaries are subhuman. *Eskimo*, for instance, is derived from a French corruption of the Athabaskan word for "eaters of raw meat."[1] The term is insulting to the Eastern "Eskimos," however, who prefer to call themselves *Inuit* (meaning "the people"). For the Inuit, *Eskimo* implies that they are lower than human beings, and occupy the same status as animals who do not cook their food as humans do.

Americans are far from immune to such nature/culture distinctions. For instance, children who do not observe proper dining table manners are often admonished by

---

[1]In some translations, "one who eats raw," but controversial (see Damas, 1984).

their elders for acting like animals. We also speak of the importance of our legal system lest we devolve into "the law of the jungle." More important, I have found that the nature/culture paradigm is an extremely useful tool for analyzing the stereotyping of subordinate and dominant groups in American culture.

Dominant groups are inevitably portrayed as being more "civilized" than are subordinate groups, which are depicted as closer to nature. Instead of presenting this baldface to my students, however, I involve them in a pedagogical exercise designed to illuminate the contrasts. I break the class into small discussion groups and ask them to list ways in which "civilized" people behave with regard to several items such as work, sex, family, marriage, problem solving, emotions, and instincts. I write the groups' responses on the board and remark that the answers basically conform to expected or ideal behaviors in American culture. Responses tend to be that "civilized" people work hard, are not lazy, arrive on time, are discreet when having sex, have sex only with significant others (if not exclusively with spouses), are monogamous, are dedicated to family, are rational and scientific, show limited emotions, and are able to control most instinctual urges.

I then ask students a series of questions. I first ask them, "Which gender is considered closer to nature, male or female?" Students respond quickly to this question, given that metaphors tying women to nature, such as "Mother Earth," abound in U.S. culture. Then I suggest that they think about the way subordinate people are stereotyped in U.S. culture. "Are they portrayed as closer to nature or culture? To industriousness or laziness? To reason or passion? To intact or dysfunctional families?" I find that students are often more reluctant to speak up unless I lead them through the secondary questions. I also break down my question by asking about African Americans, Latinos, Native Americans, and Asian Americans separately, so that students must face the fact that in most cases they are characterized in similar ways. I intentionally begin the exercise with students' definitions of "civilized" people after we have discussed how all peoples subordinate nature to culture. In this way, I am able to get them to see how the nature/culture divide is used to stereotype subordinates without actually listing (and thereby perhaps reinforcing) the stereotypes themselves.

After the exercise is completed, I emphasize to my students that the attribution of culture to whites, men in particular, and nature to women and people of other racial groups is *not* new in American culture. In *Iron Cages: Race and Culture in 19th Century America*, Takaki (1990) documented how preeminent American leaders used similar comparisons. Ben Franklin remarked that "The proneness of human Nature to a life of ease, of freedom from care and labor appears strongly in the little success that has hitherto attended every attempt to civilize our American Indians ..." (Takaki, 1990, p. 13). Thomas Jefferson observed that "Never yet could I find that a black had uttered a thought above the level of plain narration; never saw even an elementary trait of painting or sculpture" (Takaki, 1990, p. 58). Horace Mann viewed educating the masses of turn-of-the century immigrants as a means to keep "a considerable portion" of the population from "falling back into the conditions of half-barbarous or of savage life" (Takaki, 1990, p. 116).

Newspapers and novels further advanced the cause. The poem "The Heathen Chinee" was published in the *Overland Monthly* in 1870 and fueled anti-Chinese attitudes. The poem depicted one Chinese immigrant as "childlike" (i.e., not fully enculturated) and faulted him for his "'peculiar' ways, his deceptiveness and slyness, his 'sin'-fulness and his threat to white labor" (Takaki, 1990, p. 224). At the same time, Latinas were "cast in the role of primitive sensualist," as Pike (1992) argued in *The United States and Latin America*:

> Many American men who settled in the Southwest, or who visited points south of the border, married Latinas. Perhaps they were lured in part by stereotypes of Latin women as docile and submissive—an image not necessarily compatible with that of the Latina as spitfire. ... For a Yankee man to marry a Latin woman did not upset the imperialist concepts about races meant to dominate and races destined for dependence. However, for an American woman to marry a Latin man did upset the natural balance. It meant that the woman of a race destined for dominance would be dependent (in line with sexist assumptions) on the man of a race naturally destined for submission. (p. 9)

I challenge my students to investigate whether this balance of nature versus culture is preserved even today in interracial marriages.

Then I ask students to contemplate what purpose is served by attributing "culture" to such a limited segment of the population. My question usually elicits a response from a female student, who suggests that it justifies power domination by the "civilized" group. "And who is in power?" I ask her. "White men," she adds. Then I exhort the class to think about this question on a much larger, global scale. "How do Americans see themselves vis-à-vis other peoples? Do we see ourselves as more 'civilized,' more 'developed,' in a state of higher progress than others?" When several students agree, I link the lesson to theories of progress and suggest that our culture conditions us to see progress as linear, while placing ourselves furthest along the continuum. I mention Lewis Henry Morgan's model in which cultures pass through stages of "savagery," "barbarism," and "civilization." As well, we discuss Darwinian evolutionism and its application to culture as Social Darwinism.

Finally, even if it takes me another day of class, I like to get students to think critically, to punch holes in paradigms no matter how seductive they may seem to be. "If culture is to predominate over nature," I ask them, "why did Adam and Eve start out in the Garden of Eden? And why did Moses and Jesus go into the wilderness ("wild"erness) to receive laws (culture) from God? And why, especially in Vermont, do we voluntarily hike and camp in the woods? Why do hundreds of thousands of people seek refuge in Central Park every week when they live in Manhattan's shrine to civilization? Why do we extol the virtue of nature? Ralph Waldo Emerson viewed nature as "'the ultimate restorer and purifier of a humanity corrupted by civilization'" (quoted in Pike, 1992, p. 16).

Do these views make our distinction between nature and culture problematic? Pike actually suggested that they do not. He intimated that nature is not completely pacified. Parts of it are preserved so that people can rejuvenate themselves in it and then turn those newfound energies toward the project of civilization. Thus, Americans of "epic proportions" like Davy Crockett, Daniel Boone, Teddy Roosevelt, and others "*passed through* the Indian stage and then returned to civilization better able to serve the cause of progress" (Pike, 1992, p. 18). Much like the program Outward Bound, the journey into the wilderness is a journey into yourself and, as you conquer your fears of nature, you also conquer your self-doubts.

I end the class by suggesting that students think about an even more challenging reinterpretation of the nature/culture paradigm, one developed by Sander L. Gilman in *Difference and Pathology: Stereotypes of Sexuality, Race, and Madness* (1985) and elaborated on by Pike and Takaki. They argued that whites have created stereotypes by projecting the undesirable traits in themselves onto subordinate groups. Through these opposite depictions, they defend the status quo and justify others' repression. White men, Takaki (1990) wrote, "tried to impute to peoples they called 'savages' the instinctual forces they had within themselves" (p. 12). This introspection, I argue, is not so different qualitatively from groups who deemed themselves "the people" and labeled their enemies as subhuman, but the quantitative impact is incomparably greater.

REFERENCES

Damas, D. (1984). Introduction. In *Handbook of North American Indians* (Vol. 5). Washington, DC: Smithsonian Institution.

Gilman, S. L. (1985). *Difference and pathology: Stereotypes of sexuality, race, and madness*. Ithaca, NY: Cornell University Press.

Pike, F. (1992). *The United States and Latin America: Myths and stereotypes of civilization and nature*. Austin: University of Texas Press.

Takaki, R. (1990). *Iron cages: Race and culture in 19th-century America*. New York: Oxford University Press.

11

Visual Arts

Cynthia Beth Rubin
Rhode Island School of Design

Teachers of art operate in two domains: They teach their craft, and they teach sensibility. Instruction of craft can be straightforward: Blue and yellow make green, no air bubbles in clay, and so on. The instruction of sensibility is not so clear. Masked by such terms as *aesthetics* and *design*, sensibility is always personal, and it is always culturally influenced.

My colleague at the University of Vermont, Stephen M. Carter, and I wanted to develop a course that would incorporate the latter as well as the former. "Working With Culturally Diverse Sources" was designed to help students understand that their visual vocabularies were limited by the sensibilities of their culture and their previous experiences, and then, in turn, to find a way to expand their own sensibilities. Our goal was to break the cycle of the teaching of art in which each generation passes on its own idea of high art to the next, a tradition that has inherent limitations for encompassing new ideas from other cultures, and that has left most American art instruction clearly in the legacy of the Western European Renaissance tradition.

"Working With Culturally Diverse Sources" was unusual in that the course focused on using research as the stimulus for studio production, and was not tied to the use of a specific media. It was a first step in opening studio art courses to respond to issues surrounding cultural equality. In developing this approach to teaching, it was wonderful to have the opportunity to collaborate with a colleague who shared my belief that we could develop a new approach to studio teaching.

The basic format of the course was simple: We asked students to look at art from specific traditions, and then respond by producing a work of their own. We did not ask for emulation or for mastery of technical problems. Rather, students were to find a way to bring a visual concept of the original object into their own way of thinking. We complemented the studio work with required readings that raised the issues of exclusion, cultural voyeurism, tourist art, and political art. We explored the cultures together. We also asked that students work in a medium in which they had already demonstrated proficiency.

On the surface, the goal of teaching students a method for the expansion of their own visual vocabularies to encompass the legacies of diverse cultures does not seem like a very radical objective. The influence of one culture on another, the transmission of ideas from one part of the world to another, is one of the primary ways in which cultures develop and grow. We have all long been painfully aware that the American educational system still fails to incorporate the non-European side of our culture. Furthermore, it is not difficult to understand that our sensibilities or our tastes are linked to our culture.

Experience with this course helped us to understand that the current failure of the university system to incorporate sources from other cultures may result from more than mere resistance to change, or even cultural elitism. Rather, we began to understand that the very tradition of how art is taught is a factor contributing to stagnation in visual repertoires. As Stephen Carter commented to me in assessing our teaching experience: "The predisposition of the academic world is to regard historians and social scientists as the experts in culture and artists as mere transmitters of technical knowledge" (S. M. Carter, personal communication, April 15, 1994).

Colleagues and students alike argued that students could not study other cultures in a studio setting without incorporating additional elements—as if no transmission of culture was taking place in a standard studio course. We rejected this argument because we both believe that as visual artists we are continually searching for sources that enrich our visual vocabularies. Standard studio courses inspire students with examples of works by accomplished artists without providing significant background information, even when the artist is not a contemporary. These classes rely on a traditional art history, which in turn assumes a basic knowledge of Western European Christian culture. Because such an assumption is increasing questionable, it seems perfectly logical to approach other cultural legacies with equal enthusiasm and without any preconceptions about the cultural knowledge that students may bring to the discourse. As Stephen Carter noted in our exchange:

> The very essence of being an artist is to communicate through a visual medium and, as viewers, to come to some understanding of the artist's intent through interaction with the creator's object. Cultural understanding takes many forms and mere mastery of facts ensures no more empathy with a culture than other forms of exchange, including visual interactions. (S. M. Carter, personal communication, April 15, 1994)

Assumptions about what a studio course should be deny the reality of the exchanges that take place between teacher and students in the usual studio setting, with possibly dangerous consequences. Many of us studied under the "hero" syndrome of art, in which our teachers—usually white males whose personal lifestyles reflected the stereotypical tormented artist—merely shared with us their life stories and their own aesthetic, without raising issues of context. The issues of content and aesthetic bias were inherent in these courses but not discussed. Fortunately, we have seen a great shift through the years, but the shifting is not yet complete. It is precisely for this reason that we believed that it was important to offer this course.

Our presumption that students who chose to take this course (which was, after all, an elective) would already have given some thought to the issues of cultural basis proved to be wrong. The truth is, we were operating in a time warp. Although we each had different ways of approaching the appropriation of art from other cultures—no doubt stemming from our very different experiences—we shared a sense that the cultural is inherently political. Furthermore, although we are sensitive to the potential problems involved in superficial appropriation, we believe that it is the responsibility of the individual artist to ensure that cultural retrieval is more than cultural colonialism.

Happily, the first time that we taught the course we experienced a wonderful beginning. Carefully structuring the first half of the term, we studied three broad cultural groups (Native American, focusing on the Southwest; Jewish art, focusing on Europe and North Africa; and West African and African American art), looking at visual art from each of the these cultures. We then asked students to produce work in response to what they saw, in the medium of their choice. The results were astounding! Students broke into new imagery, layering and combining as they had never dared before, using their newly expanded visual vocabularies.

The second part of the course, however, proved to be disappointing. We gave students the freedom to pursue their own interests in researching the visual legacy of a culture of their choosing, and asked them to produce both a class presentation and creative studio work. Left to their own, they wandered aimlessly. Many created work about the *history* of the cultures, but did not respond to the cultural traditions per se. We often got images of poverty created within a Western aesthetic.

It is important to note here that students' confusion on this issue is understandable, as it is reflected in both the literature and the composition of several curated exhibitions. Frequently, curators and critics combine race as subject matter with works in a particular visual tradition, as well as grouping works according to the race or ethnicity of the artists. Our own efforts to ensure that our students thought about the complex issues involved in using the art of diverse cultures for inspiration may further have contributed to the confusion, ultimately detracting from the actual experience of looking at the work. The first time that we offered this class, we held frequent discussions on issues of what constitutes art and how the mainstream art world defines art by artists of diverse backgrounds. As Stephen Carter and I reflected on what to do differently, he observed that:

> One aspect of the discussion that seemed to cause problems during this first offering were issues that dealt directly with the problems of

artists who were people of color and women. This topic more than any other may have diverted the students' attention away from the making of art that used the visual legacies of these groups as source material to making art that responded more or less to the plight of the peoples that they were studying. (S. M. Carter, personal communication, April 15, 1994)

In this course format, the confusion persisted despite the class discussions of important essays on the matters of race, culture, and marginalization (Clifford, 1990; Kagawa, 1976; Lippard, 1990; Thompson, 1989). This was one of the major problems that eventually led to the revamping of the entire course, so that in its current form philosophical discussions are held only after students have already developed a personal approach to working with cultural sources.

The second time that we taught "Working With Culturally Diverse Sources" we changed it by presenting the students with real objects rather than reproductions. By necessity we limited the number of sources. Working with Janie Cohen, assistant curator, and Ann Porter, curator, of the University of Vermont's Fleming Museum, we selected three pieces from five different cultures. Every 2 weeks, we went to the Museum (with the exception of the session at Ohavi Zedek Synagogue, where we went to examine Jewish art), where the students were given a chance to draw, photograph, and generally closely examine objects that were not in the glass cases of the museum or in books. We shot slides of the sources, and then discussed what we had seen in the subsequent class.

The limiting of the objects successfully ensured that every one in the class shared a common experience of looking and that we, as instructors, were some-what familiar with the sources that the students were using in their work. To our surprise, however, this did not eliminate the confusion that students had about the importance of becoming familiar with a variety of cultural legacies. This time, several students challenged the very premise of the course, raising very intelligent questions but ultimately showing that they came into the course with more preconceptions than we had anticipated. Stephen Carter summarized the wide range of difficulties that we faced:

> While some seemed open to new ideas concerning the nature of art, it soon became apparent in their discussions and writing that other students had a difficult time letting go of traditional notions of art and, more importantly, letting go of their notions regarding the proper place of art in society. These students wanted to hold on to traditional distinctions between art, craft, and artifact. While this may have been comfortable for them, this way of thinking, by its very nature, excluded consideration of numerous artifacts that fulfilled a utilitarian role ... more problematic situations were presented by students who came to the class with a set agenda. Many enrolled in this class with their own ideas of what a class dealing with issues of cultural diversity should be. While it is normal that they would have certain expectations, it did present some problems. The most troubling was the notion that they would be free to respond negatively against many of the Western

concepts of art, as opposed to responding positively to art presented in class from all streams. Because of this, some work done by the students would be better considered "protest art" rather than art based on sources outside the Western tradition. (S. M. Carter, personal communication, April 15, 1994)

Some students accused us of cultural voyeurism, charging that we wandered into uncommon territory just for the thrill of the new, without respecting the traditions. They contended that there can be no legitimate influence without full understanding of the culture, and that anything short of this is illegitimate appropriation.

What is troubling about this argument is that we can never fully place ourselves inside another culture. We can all only be influenced, and if we regard every step away from Renaissance dominance as illegitimate cultural appropriation, we are forever stuck with what we know. One is reminded of the opening passage of Jean Baudrillard's (1981) book *Simulacres et Simulations*, in which he describes the Borges story of the community that makes a map which is so like the original that it finally takes the form of the original. At what point do we stop and give ourselves permission to experience? An even more fascinating aspect of this discussion is that this standard seems to be applied more often to visual art than to other cultural forms. In a cooking class, for example, no one would have taken exception to adopting the use of peanut sauces or curries. In fact, our American cuisine has been more strongly influenced by Native American culture (popcorn, maple syrup, various squashes) than our art. What is it about visual art that is so exceptional?

Through team teaching, we learned how radical an experiment our course was, and together we were able to identify those approaches that worked and those that were too far from student expectations to be effective tools for teaching. We learned that students are still more comfortable in a media-specific studio, where shared technical concerns reassure them that they are not alone in their struggles to grow as artists. We also found that, contrary to our own impulses, it is imperative in a studio setting that students be equipped with the conceptual tools for establishing true respect for different cultural traditions before approaching the questions of social and economic inequity.

We also found confirmation of our initial belief that students can be taught how to expand their thinking to include art that is traditionally excluded. Given the right structure for working with visual sources across cultures and time, students can acquire the habit of thinking about the influences on their own creative work in a global framework. The key is to introduce students to the concepts gradually, without asking them to discard what they already know.

"Working With Culturally Diverse Sources" evolved first into a computer animation course, and then into a computer painting/collage course. "Cultural Transformations: Computer Animations," which I taught at the University of Vermont, and "Computer Transformations: Accessing Cultural Motifs," which I currently teach at the Rhode Island School of Design, both developed out of a complementary academic need to offer more computer-based courses to art students. Not all of the students enrolled because of an interest in cultural sources; some simply wanted to learn more about computer art. Nonetheless, these media specific courses have been more successful in accomplishing the goal of encouraging students to look carefully at the art from all visual traditions (Rubin, 1995).

Use of the computer as a medium may have contributed to the success of the subsequent courses. Inside the computer, the traces of the artist's hand are more difficult to discern; thus, students often feel more urgency in transforming scanned images than they might in working with nondigital images. This is true even when the scan is their own drawing of the original source rather than a photograph. Students are motivated to work long hours with their source material inside the computer, in a sense entering into a dialogue with the original artists as they construct new images out of the fragments of their inspirational sources.

In "Computer Transformations: Accessing Cultural Motifs," I begin the class with a common project: Every student works with an identical quilt square pattern, as an acknowledgment of our shared American tradition and forgotten women artists. Examples of contemporary artists such as Miriam Schapiro and Faith Ringold who produced quilt-influenced works show students how far the creative artist can go in adapting conventions to fit their own visual thought. From here, we move slowly into integrating sources from the Rhode Island School of Design Museum. First, students research cultural motifs in books and on the Web, and produce works based on this research. Then, they visit the Museum independently, make pencil drawings from original sources, and produce another work. Finally, we visit the Museum as a group for a photographing session, and the students move into producing the more independent work of the term. Comments from student evaluations and peer reaction to the work produced in this class both rate it a success on all levels.

Questions surrounding cultural equity, in terms of recognizing both the significant legacies of all cultures and the struggles of the individual artists of various cultural and ethnic groups, continue to be part of each version of this course. "Computer Transformations: Accessing Cultural Motifs" emphasizes the value of learning from all cultural traditions, and balances this with an in-depth class discussion on the dangers of cultural colonialism and appropriation. I distribute a long and varied bibliography from which the students choose their own reading. Thus, students come into the class with different perspectives, and the conversation remains open, with students sharing how they formed their personal approach to using art from various cultures. This discussion takes place in one or two long sessions near the end of the term, after several trips to the Rhode Island School of Design Museum, and after students become excited by the variety of images that they are able to create with their new inspirations. Concern for the lack of economic and political power of many cultural groups is not ignored, but it is closely tied to the deeper respect for these groups that students gain from exploring their artistic legacies.

The pivotal moment in the development of my teaching courses on culturally diverse sources came during the second offering of the course that I team taught with Stephen Carter at the University of Vermont. Just as we wondered how we would ever successfully communicate the joys of simply experiencing the legacy of culture to our students, we were saved by Rabbi Max B. Wall, the Emeritus Rabbi at Ohavi Zedek Synagogue in Burlington, who was called out of retirement to host our visit to the synagogue's art collection. The students, most of whom had never been in a synagogue before, were thrilled to have a knowledgeable representative of the culture before them, and bombarded him with questions of meaning. The rabbi, although happy to answer their questions, pointed out that the significance of art is more than just the meanings of symbols, but lies in the human need "to decorate the things we love." He was successful in communicating to the students what we could not: that merely studying the facts about objects without taking pleasure in their aesthetic qualities denies their true purpose.

Now, when I take students to the museum to look at work from diverse cultures, I quote Rabbi Wall. His words are magic, giving students permission to trust their eyes in taking pleasure in the beauty of art across time and cultures. Once students can enjoy looking at the visual legacies of all traditions, they can develop a sincere respect for other cultures. This is an essential step in building cultural equity in our society.

ACKNOWLEDGMENTS

Many of the ideas in this chapter were developed jointly through teaching and in correspondence with my co-teacher, Stephen M. Carter. I thank him for his contributions, and for the experience of developing a course together.

REFERENCES

Baudrillard, J. (1981). *Simulacres et simulation*. Paris: Galilee.

Clifford, J. (1990). On collecting art and culture. In R. Ferguson (Ed.), *Out there: Marginalization and contemporary cultures*. New York: New Museum of Contemporary Art. Cambridge, MA: MIT Press.

Kagawa, P. (1976). Third world art as a state of mind. In *Other sources: An American essay* [Exhibition catalog]. San Francisco: San Francisco Art Institute.

Lippard, L. R. (1990). *Mixed blessings: New art in a multicultural America*. New York: Pantheon.

Rubin, C. B. (1995). Morphing sensibility. *Computer Graphics, 29*(3), 21-22.

Thompson, R. (1989). The song that named the land: The visionary presence of African-American art. In *Black art ancestral legacy: The African impulse in African-American art* [Exhibition catalog]. Dallas: Dallas Museum of Art.

12

Music and Multiculturalism

Jane P. Ambrose
University of Vermont

The impetus behind the approach described here was my interest in teaching American music as part of the college's newly required interdisciplinary study of "Race and Ethnicity in the United States." Although my own training is in traditional Western musicology, I wanted to explore other forms and approaches that would broaden our understanding of American musical culture beyond the purely historical and artistic parameters that usually frame courses in music history.

Just as attitudes toward modern music have been slow to change, modern methods of teaching traditional subjects in music have also changed slowly. In the 1950s and 1960s, standard texts for courses in American music, such as Lowens' (1964) essay *Music and Musicians in Early America* and Chase's (1966) survey of *America's Music: From the Pilgrims to the Present*, began with the music of the Puritan psalm singers, as though there had been no music on the American continent before the publication of the *Bay Psalm Book* in 1640.[1] Howard's (1929) *Our American Music: Three Hundred Years of It* was the model for these texts. Later works, such as Chase's, extended Howard's coverage both chronologically and ethnically to include jazz and ragtime, but his chapters on "Our Folk Music" ("The Music of the North American Indian," "Negro Folk Music," and "Other Sources of Folk Songs") had disappeared.

Howard had made some interesting statements and asked some provocative questions. These became part of our early class discussions during the first semester the course was taught in the 1992–1993 academic year, because it included strong themes centered on changing attitudes toward ethnic music and the ways in which musical predilections are formed by family histories and backgrounds. These questions are particularly interesting to us in Vermont, because many students have French-Canadian and/or Native American (mainly Abenaki) ancestry. Howard asked: "Although the Indians inhabited America for centuries before our ancestors

---

[1]This is reputed to be the first book published in North America.

came here, who are the Americans today: the white men or the red men? A brutally asked question but pertinent. ... Can it then be said that primitive Indian music is American folk song?" (Howard, p. 614). The "Although" was not lost on the class. This comparison became the source of a most interesting discussion.

To his credit, Howard surveyed both musical and anthropological studies of indigenous music, but his credibility came into question when he baldly stated, in talking about the use of "Indian" themes by classical composers, that "To select Indian tunes because they are useful is one thing. To choose them for nationalistic purposes is a different matter entirely, for they are American in the geographic sense alone" (Howard, 1929, p. 622).

Hamm's (1983) *Music in the New World* is a good example of a second generation textbook. Hamm began with "The Music of the Native American." His coverage of music that is not derived from Europe is balanced, and his contextual remarks are consistent with revisionist history such as one might find in Zinn's (1980) *A People's History of the United States* rather than in classics such as Morison's (1942) *Admiral of the Ocean Sea; a Life of Christopher Columbus*. Another important text from the 1980s is the third edition of Hitchcock's (1974) *Music in the United States: A Historical Introduction*. Hamm and Hitchcock keyed their texts to the new major source of recorded material for all courses in American music, New World Records. Our class read portions of Zinn and, for primary source material, sections of Bartolome de las Casas' (1474–1566) *Personal Narrative of the First Voyage of Columbus to America: From a Manuscript Recently Discovered in Spain* (1827) and his better-known work, *The Devastation of the Indies* (1974).

The class read "Columbus at the Gates of Heaven: A Masque" from Parini's (1992) *Bay of Arrows*. The *dramatis personae*—God, St. Peter, Noam Chomsky, Samuel Eliot Morison, Bartholomé de las Casas, Dona Felipa Columbus, Don Diego Columbus, and Christopher Columbus—debate the appropriateness of Columbus' presence among the angels. "All down the centuries Columbus fell, then caught his footing, turned to climb; through many layers he was hauled aloft by strings of light, half self-propelled, half pulled by agents who would hear his case debated at the blazing gates of heaven" (Parini, 1992, pp. 371–383). Since our course was last taught, Robertson's (1992) superb *Musical Repercussions of 1492: Encounters in Text and Performance*, a collection of ethnomusicological essays, has been published. Her introduction, "The Dance of Conquest," and several other essays are excellent frames of reference for viewing early music on our continent. The class also read portions of Wilfrid Mellers' (1964) *Music in a New Found Land*, because its author is an ethnomusicologist and an always intriguing if frequently infuriating writer (known to some students for his book on the Beatles).

The other course offered in American music that semester was "History of Jazz." Our department also offers "Blues and Related Traditions" in alternate years. These two courses are, however, offered at the introductory level. The new course was taught at the intermediate level, and enrollment was fairly evenly divided between music majors and nonmajors. The course description read as follows:

> This course will examine the variety of "American" musical experiences in order to attempt to define American music and to examine the lives of American musicians from all ages and cultures. Readings, listening, performances and guest lecturers will supplement our regular classes. Papers, class writing exercises, and projects will be used to explore topics of interest to individuals and the class to help us further our understanding of the multiplicity of experiences that form our common musical heritage and to give us the opportunity to improve and enhance our ability to think, talk, and write about music. All music will be considered in the context of intellectual and chronological history. Folk, popular, and classical music will be considered, with the emphasis always on the place of music in its time and culture.

A theme for the semester for discussion and writing assignments was "American Originals" to be identified across the spectrum of American music—Charles Ives, William Billings, the Bay Psalm Book, Scott Joplin and ragtime, the gospel hymn, shape-note singing, Louis Moreau Gottschalk, William Grant Still, revivalism and the camp meeting, rock and its roots in country music and blues, James Weldon Johnson, "Ethiopian Song" and minstrelsy, the Harlem Renaissance, Stephen Sondheim and the "adult musical," Stephen Foster and the "parlor song," John Philip Sousa, John Cage, and so on. Other suggestions came from the class.

Required texts for the course were the second edition of Kingman's (1979) *American Music: A Panorama* and Johnson's (1965) classic *The Autobiography of an Ex-Colored Man*, a suggestion from one of my colleagues in our race and ethnicity cohort. A bonus in this Penguin edition is the reprinting of the introduction to the 1927 edition by Carl Van Vechten, a novelist and photographer who wrote for the *New York Times* from 1906 to 1913. I remembered my own reactions to reading about Johnson, a classically trained African American jazz musician who chose to "pass," when I was in high school, and I anticipated the spirited discussion that took place after the students finished this "novel," in reality Johnson's autobiography. On reserve were several articles and books including Epstein's (1983) "A White Origin for the Black Spiritual? An Invalid Theory and How It Grew"; Southern's (1971) groundbreaking study *The Music of Black Americans: A History;* Bennett's (1962) *Before the Mayflower: A History of Black America*; and Dennis' (1984) *Black History for Beginners*. Several students had Native Americans in their ancestry; there were no African American, Asian American, or Hispanic students.

Early assignments asked the students to trace their families to see what kinds of racial, ethnic, social, political, and economic considerations might shape musical tastes. A second assignment was to write an obituary for John Cage, one of our originals, who had died the preceding summer. The point was to find out why Cage had been so famous (infamous?). We then discussed Cage and counterculturalism in modern American music. The next assignment was based on a quotation from a student paper received for the first assignment: "All republicans listen to Wayne Newton, all hippies listen to psychedelic music." We talked again about musical genres and tastes, and the class read and wrote a response paper on Babbitt's (1958) "Who Cares if You Listen?", one of the most talked-about and reprinted articles of our time. Babbitt stated that the responsibility of the composer is to his art, that advanced musical concepts are not intended for the average person, and that communication with the lay listener is not the objective of the composer—obviously a controversial view.

While students were reading Johnson outside of class, in class we read some ballad texts, listened to the music, and considered what they taught us about history and social attitudes, particularly those relative to the relationships between men and women. We continued to read Kingman and talked about the contributions to the study of American music by Frances Densmore (an early ethnologist for the Smithsonian Institution) and other pioneers in field studies whose work began the serious study of the music of Native Americans. A later assignment—an "area" project—inspired several students to do studies of individual tribes.

During the second month of our course, the fine American pianist Alan Feinberg was invited to campus to play his "American Romantics." The class wrote program annotations in preparation for the concert, which they later reviewed. Creole composer Louis Moreau Gottschalk and several women ranging from Amy Beach (1867–1944) to Shulamit Ran (b. 1950) and a piece (commissioned in part by our concert series) by Laura Kaminsky were featured. Alan stayed on campus and spoke eloquently to us about his commitment to American music and how it has affected his concert career, and the very real problems of a young performer in today's concert world. Other concerts booked to accompany the course and the quincentennial were given by the Chilean folk group Inti-Illimani, also guests of our class, and the early music group Hesperus, who played a program entitled "Spain in the New World."

Timely newspaper and magazine articles were read and discussed. On July 31, Mike Royko had "pulled the chains" of rock fans with his "Rock music threatens as much as Twinkies," in which he talked about the absurdity of "warnings" ("This song contains the F word 23 times, the Mother word 5 times, and rape and female stomping"; Royko, 1992, p. 8a) and gratuitous censorship. On August 31, Richard Brookhiser's (1992) essay for *Time*, "We Can All Share American Culture," proclaimed "Happily—what with multicultural education and bilingualism—the very concept of a mainstream is being junked" (p. 74). On October 2, Gregory Cerio's "Japanese Orchestra Wows Salsa Crowd" appeared on the "Leisure & Arts" page of *The Wall Street Journal*. Next time I will add another article (Cerio, 1992). Erikson's (1989) book *Encounters* contains an essay by jazz hornist Willi Ruff (1989) about his class with Paul Hindemith, described to Ruff by Charlie Parker as "a little German cat," who taught him about the music of the spheres, shared his passion for the horn, and led him through an introduction to early music to a spiritual journey to Venice (1989).

Other written assignments included a final paper on a subject of the student's choice, preceded by a proposal submitted a month before the end of the semester, a definition of American music at both the beginning and end of the semester, and the area study mentioned earlier. Many special topics for research and discussion in the area of pluralism were suggested by our reading of Kingman. Some of these were studies of the "current state" of various kinds of music; studies of musical lives—female jazz singers in the 1920s; touring artists like Gottschalk and Jenny Lind, comparisons of historical and social events such as a Kentucky revival meeting with a contemporary rock festival; and a study of the phenomenon of "Kakewalk," the focus of the University of Vermont's winter weekend for many decades, and the social and political reasons for its removal. Videos illustrating the birth of jazz, the life and times of Charles Ives, and Gian Carlo Menotti's fascinating opera, "The Medium" (1984), were watched and discussed.

In a chapter of this length, one can only begin to suggest the excitement that this approach adds to the classroom. Students were free to elect to study and discuss topics that went far beyond their commitments to the traditional curriculum. As part of a faculty team, I found constant stimulation from colleagues preparing papers, grappling with their own prejudices and their efforts to overcome them, and accomplishing thereby a substantial change in the nature and degree of the college's assumption of responsibility for multicultural education.

REFERENCES

Babbitt, M. (1958). Who cares if you listen? *High Fidelity, 8*, 38–40, 126–127.

Bay Psalm Book. (1640). *The whole Booke of Psalms/faithfully translated into English metre; whereunto is prefixed a discourse declaring not only the lawfullness, but also the necessity of the heavenly ordinace of singing Scripture psalmes in the churches of God.* Cambridge, MA: Stephen Day.

Bennett, L. (1962). *Before the Mayflower: A history of black America, 1619–1962.* Chicago: Johnson Publishing.

Brookhiser, R. (1992, August 31). We can all share American culture. *Time,* p. 74.

Cerio, G. (1992, October 2). Japanese orchestra wows salsa crowd. *The Wall Street Journal,* p. A12.

Chase, G. (1966). *America's music: From the Pilgrims to the present* (2nd ed.). New York: McGraw-Hill.

de las Casas, B. (1827). *Personal narrative of the first voyage of Columbus to America: From a manuscript recently discovered in Spain.* Boston: T.B. Wait and Son.

de las Casas, B. (1974). *The devastation of the Indies: A brief account.* (Herma Briffault, Trans.). New York: Seabury.

Dennis, D. (1984). *Black history for beginners.* New York: Norton.

Epstein, D. (1983). A white origin for the black spiritual? An invalid theory and how it grew. *American Music, 1*(2), 52–59.

Erikson, K. (Ed.). (1989). *Encounters.* New Haven: Yale University Press.

Hamm, C. (1983). *Music in the New World.* New York: Norton.

Hitchcock, H. W. (1974). *Music in the United States; A historical introduction.* Englewood Cliffs, NJ: Prentice-Hall.

Howard, J. T. (1929). *Our American music: Three hundred years of it.* New York: Thomas Y. Crowell.

Johnson, J. W. (1965). The autobiography of an ex-colored man. In W. E. B. DuBois, J. W. Johnson, & B. T. Washington, *Three Negro classics: The souls of black folk, The autobiography of an ex-colored man, and up from slavery.* New York: Avon Books.

Kingman, D. (1979). *American music: A panorama.* New York: Schirmer.

Lowens, I. (1964). *Music and musicians in early America.* New York: Norton.

Mellers, W. H. (1964). *Music in a new found land.* London: Barrie and Rockliff.

Menotti, G. C. (1984). *The medium.* [Videocassette]. New York: Video Arts International.

Morison, S. E. (1942). *Admiral of the ocean sea; a life of Christopher Columbus.* Boston: Little, Brown.

Parini, J. (1992). *Bay of arrows*. New York: Henry Holt.

Robertson, C. E. (Ed.). (1992). *Musical repercussions of 1492: Encounters in text and performance*. Washington, DC: Smithsonian Institution Press.

Royko, M. (1992). Rock music threatens as much as Twinkies. *Burlington Free Press*, p. 8a.

Ruff, W. (1989). Three passions of Paul Hindemith. In K. Erikson (Ed.), *Encounters* (p. 99). New Haven: Yale University Press.

Southern, E. (1971). *The music of black Americans: A history*. New York: Norton.

Zinn, H. (1980). *A people's history of the United States*. New York: Harper & Row.

13

Conclusion: Toward a Transdisciplinary Conceptualization of Multicultural Studies

S. D. Berkowitz
University of Fort Hare
University of Vermont

Howard Ball
University of Vermont

Almost every day brings fresh evidence that the major social problems faced by American society today—homelessness, illiteracy, poor education, unemployment, drug use, the dissolution of families and neighborhoods, spousal abuse, and so on—are complex, multifaceted, and interdependent. Welfare reform, we are told, is stymied by our lack of a comprehensive and accessible health care system. Health care reform, we have heard, is being held back by the relatively high cost of care and by relatively low productivity in the workplace. Productivity is low, it has been asserted, because of a lack of basic skills on the part of workers. This lack of skills—what, in many cases, amounts to functional illiteracy—has, in turn, been attributed to a collapse of large parts of the public school system and to persistent teenage drug use. Poor access to health care suppresses productivity, low productivity helps to sustain unemployment, and so on—an almost endless series of vicious cycles. None of these problems, in effect, is simply social, nor economic, nor political, nor psychological. None is thoroughly individual and unrelated to the cultural forces shaping our perceptions and actions. None does not have roots in social structure.

The interconnectedness of these problems is not, however, mirrored in the ways in which universities go about studying them. If homelessness, adult illiteracy, unemployment, poor education, drug use, and so on are highly interrelated (and we have every reason to suspect they are), it follows that we must look at them from the perspectives offered by a variety of different fields. However, the ways in which universities typically divide up knowledge makes this difficult. Indeed, it is a rare undergraduate or graduate student who is able fit all the pieces together in more than a superficial way. To most, university curricula consist of bewildering arrays of apparently separate and unrelated subjects.[1]

The intellectual and practical consequences of the fragmentation of knowledge is nowhere more striking than in the study of race and ethnic relations in America. Race or ethnicity either underlies (if one accepts Willie's argument) or is related to (if one accepts Wilson's argument) most social problems present within American society today. Members of caste minorities are more often homeless, illiterate, and unemployed than are other Americans. They more often live in deteriorating neighborhoods, use drugs, and have high rates of crime and spousal abuse. They are more subject to diseases—such as tuberculosis—that spread through populations without the resources to maintain adequate health standards. In this sense, as Loewen has shown us, inequality is related to ethnic background and is, in some sense, indivisible.

Despite this, we have not even begun the process of creating the frameworks needed to understand the interplay of the factors that underlie race and ethnicity. For instance, anthropologists, sociologists, and those humanists influenced by literary theory each use the term *culture*, but in very different ways. Anthropologists are interested in the ways in which groups symbolically interpret and represent the ideas, customs, and material artifacts that they have created. Sociologists are interested in the structural sources of culture (the "sociology of knowledge") and in the specific relationship between particular structural conditions and the emergence of specialized or localized patterns within a culture (subcultures). Those humanists influenced by literary theory are primarily interested in how culture is "represented" through language and other symbolic media (e.g., music). As a result, each misses part of the point when considering a phenomenon like the Harlem Renaissance: As a rule, anthropologists miss the ties between the Harlem Rennaisance and the larger literary culture; sociologists miss not only its roots in folk idiom, but the interplay between subcultures and literary forms; and literary theorists miss the social structural sources of the *specific* culture of groups and subgroups. Each has an incomplete view of the phenomenon, but each can contribute to a larger interpretation of it.

It was part of our understanding of what we were doing in establishing the University of Vermont's approach to studying and teaching about multiculturalism that these kinds of larger perspectives would grow out of our shared teaching

---

[1]The organization of American universities into separate "disciplines" was modeled on the division of knowledge developed in Germany in the 19th century. Over time, areas of learning—especially in the social sciences and humanities—were broken down even further. "Political economy," for instance, became "political science," "economics," and "sociology." Departments of "language" or "literature" were abolished in favor of departments of English, French, German, and so on.

practice. We began by creating a faculty seminar that specifically examined issues such as the history of the biological notion of race, the current use of the idea, the state of scientific understanding of the term, and so on.

At this stage in our development of joint understandings about race and ethnicity, discussions were often lively and far ranging. We then began to examine, systematically, patterns of inequality by race and ethnic group in American society. The Berkowitz and Barrington and Loewen chapters in this volume grew out of this stage in the development of our common practice. After these were written, each was subjected to intense and lively criticism by the group and rewritten several times.

Almost a year had gone by since we had begun the process of developing our common, but diverse, approach to these issues. Some 22 courses had been approved as fulfilling the requirement. Copies of the Berkowitz and Barrington and Loewen chapters were made available to instructors. We began to get systematic feedback about how students were reacting to each of the courses and to the "plenary sessions" through which we had brought students in each of the classes together to hear a wide range of speakers—including figures such as Houston Baker and Andrew Hacker.

This feedback indicated that we had been largely successful in creating a common or "core" approach to the issue of multiculturalism, but that students in the humanities, as opposed to the social sciences, were still inclined to use terms such as *black* and *white* in commonsensical rather than scientific ways. Moreover, students who elected to fulfill their requirements through arts and humanities courses seemed less interested in the issue of, for instance, what "races" were as opposed to what kinds of cultural artifacts could be attributed to them (e.g., "Black Art in America").

This led to another lively round of debates among faculty on these questions and to a further discussion of an issue raised by African, Latino, Asian, and Native American (ALANA) students in some of our classes: Is it possible, in principle, for "white" instructors to convey pertinent and useful information to ALANA students, as well as "whites," about the life experiences and circumstances of "people of color?" This issue was, of course, never resolved, but it led to discussions, in a number of our classes, of "personal" as opposed to "systematic/scientific" forms of information.

After these debates, what began to emerge was the outline of a transdisciplinary course that capitalized on our experiences as an ALANA Studies cohort. There was general agreement that such a course has to "teach the conflicts" associated with race and ethnicity. Without a commitment to this—one that forces our students and ourselves into a more objective mode of thinking—a race and ethnicity course will fail. We decided that such a course should have four foci: the explication of theories of race and ethnicity, as distinct from racial ideology; explaining about the cultural basis of race and ethnicity; making clear the social, political, and economic consequences of race and ethnicity; and, finally, dealing with the future of a society that has, at last, come to grips with "America's dilemma": the dilemma of the "color line."

As Diouf argued in chap. 3, such a course must teach the conflicts. The "browning of America" leaves little room at this largely white university (and most other major universities and colleges in America) for us to do otherwise. Like Danigelis', our model course must also distinguish between theory and ideology in order to disentangle our students from their ideology.

As described by many of the contributors to this book, a model transdisciplinary course on race and ethnicity in America must also examine America's complex cultural, political, social, and economic foundations and how, specifically, they bear on an understanding of race and ethnicity in America. And, as Mzamane noted in chap. 4, to fully understand the nature of race and ethnicity, the American experience must be placed in comparative perspective.

The course must also incorporate techniques such as those described and illustrated by Danigelis (chap. 7), Dickerson (chap. 5), and Ball (chap. 6). Using these techniques and others created by students and faculty, students are drawn out of their own particular *Weltanschauungen*. Certainly, team teaching is very appropriate here.

At the very least, such a course should have guest discussants from a variety of disciplines who can provide insights and knowledge about the realities of race and ethnicity in America. Anthropologists and sociologists will enable students to understand the critical nature of enculturation and socialization processes in interpreting the ways in which ethnic relations are structured in a given society, whereas fine and performing arts faculty can provide students with a range of less specifiable but equally important experiences. Economists, political scientists, and historians can provide additional insights into the core aspects of politics and political economy as they impact on race and ethnicity.

One essential goal of a transdisciplinary course on race and ethnicity is to overcome the division of knowledge as it presently exists across all but the most experimental of institutions of higher learning in America. *Aufgehabuung*, Hegel's concept of transcending, is the appropriate path to an understanding of what we are urging all educators to do when teaching about race and ethnicity.

America's social problems are interrelated, and one must deal with understanding them in a manner that recognizes this. Our approach to teaching race and ethnicity, at its core, brings many different disciplines and approaches together to bear on multifaceted problems. Not addressing race and ethnicity in this way means, at the very least, perpetuating the problem of race, with all its attendant inequalities and consequences, well into the next century.

As we argued earlier, ending racism calls for a radically different, idealistic, pedagogical approach. Through a transdisciplinary course on race and ethnicity, we can take as our goal using all the tools available to us to build a multiracial, integrated community. After the verdict in the O. J. Simpson criminal trial was announced, African American scholar Henry Louis Gates, Jr. (1995) wrote about the almost categorical dissonance in the African American and white communities in America: "If we disagree about something so basic [as the "facts" presented in the O. J. Simpson trial]," he said, "how can we find agreement about far thornier matters?" How, indeed, can conversations take place between the races "when we disagree about reality?" (p. 59).

This book is an effort to try to agree about the reality of race in America and to encourage educators all across the university environment to teach and discuss it. In doing this, we must ourselves understand the serious challenge we face as a society. We found that this is not easy: It takes effort to encourage educators to rekindle their own idealism in order to assist in tackling one of America's chronic dilemmas.

REFERENCES

Gates, H. L., Jr. (1995, October 25). Thirteen ways of looking at a black man. *New Yorker,* 56–65.

About the Authors

Jane P. Ambrose is a graduate of Skidmore College (BS in music education) and the University of Vermont (MA in music literature). She has done additional graduate work at Harvard and the University of Michigan. She is professor of music and chair of the music department at the University of Vermont (UVM), where she also directs the George Bishop Lane Artist Series. She teaches music history at UVM, where she has been a member of the faculty since 1967. She is also involved in elder education. She performs on both baroque and modern flutes. Her academic specialties are baroque performance practice, women in music, and American music.

Howard Ball is professor of political science and former dean of the college of arts and sciences at UVM. He received his BA in history from CUNY–Hunter College, and his PhD in political science from Rutgers University. He has written 21 books and dozens of articles on the U.S. Supreme Court and on the judicial process, including, most recently, *Of Power and Right: Hugo Black, William O. Douglas, and America's Constitutional Revolution; Hugo Black: Cold Steel Warrior;* and *A Defiant Life: Thurgood Marshall and the Persistence of Racism in America.* Dr. Ball teaches courses on the U.S. Supreme Court and on civil rights in America.

David Barrington is professor and chair of the botany department at UVM. He received his BS from Bates College in 1970, and his PhD from Harvard University in 1975. His research centers on the nature of hybridization and speciation in tropical plants. He is the editor of a recent symposium on the biogeography of ferns. Currently, he is studying the distribution and relationships of species in high-altitude wet-forest belts of Central America, especially in Mexico and Costa Rica. He teaches courses on the diversity of flowering plants and ferns in temperate and tropical regions.

S. D. Berkowitz is professor of sociology and Canadian studies at UVM. He received his AB from the University of Michigan, and his PhD from Brandeis University. He is the author of *An Introduction to Structural Analysis*; (with Robert Logan) *Canada's Third Option*; *Models and Myths in Canadian Sociology*; (with Barry Wellman) *Social Structures: A Network Approach* (1st and 2nd editions); and approximately 60 articles, book chapters, monographs, technical reports, and reviews. He teaches courses on race and ethnicity in America, minority groups, research methods, medical sociology, organizations, and families.

Nicholas L. Danigelis received his BA from UVM, and his MA and PhD from Indiana University. He has been teaching courses on race and ethnic relations since 1972, at the University of Wisconsin–Madison and at UVM. He currently is professor of sociology and a member of the Center for the Study of Aging at UVM. His other teaching interests include social gerontology and research methods and statistics. His research on the African Americans has been published in the *American Sociological Review*, *Social Forces*, the *Journal of Gerontology: Social Sciences*, and *Research on Aging*. His present scholarly interests include an extension of his research on older black Americans' productivity to examine the differential meaning such activity has for older blacks and older whites; health screening initiatives among women of color, especially older women; and a sociohistorical theory of aging that emphasizes intergroup relations.

Mary Jane Dickerson is an associate professor of English at UVM. She was born in Sanford, North Carolina, and was educated at the University of North Carolina at Greensboro and Chapel Hill. She teaches courses in autobiography (Comparative American Identities, Women's Autobiography), and African American literature surveys and other related topics (The Color Line: Faulkner and Morrison). With Henry Steffens, she coauthored *Writer's Guide: History* (1987). She has published many articles on William Faulkner, most recently on women in *Go Down, Moses* for *Women's Studies* (1993), as well as articles on Jean Toomer's *Cane* and other American literary figures. Her poetry has appeared in such publications as *Harper's*. Currently she is writing a book on autobiography, *Writing Myself and Other(s)*.

Moustapha Diouf is an associate professor of sociology at UVM. He received a BA and an MA in sociology from the University of Paris, and an MS and a PhD in sociology from the University of Missouri, Columbia. He is the author of numerous articles on rural development, social change, and development in the Third World, including "State Formation and Legitimation Crisis in Senegal" (*Review of African Political Economy*), "Development Sociology in Transition: Recapturing the New Trends" (*Journal of Asian and African Studies*), and "Western Sociology and the Third World: Asymmetrical Forms of Understanding and the Inadequacy of Social Discourse," in T. R. Vaughn, G. Sjoberg, and L. T. Reynolds

(Eds.), *A Critique of Contemporary American Sociology*. His current work centers on African state formation and the legitimation crisis, and state–civil society relations. He is currently working on a book to be entitled *Democratization and Development in Africa: An Agenda for the Twenty-First Century*. He teaches courses on social change, development, political sociology, and race and ethnicity.

Robert Gussner is professor emeritus of religion at UVM. He earned his BA in history from Hamline University, an STB at Boston University, and a PhD at Harvard University in comparative religion. Prior to teaching, he worked for 5 years organizing peace action projects and nonviolent direct action for civil rights and, then, for another 5 years as a Unitarian-Universalist minister. He teaches and writes in the areas of theory and methods of developmental deep structuralism in religious studies, transpersonal psychologies, meditation, and religion. His courses deal with subjects such as the social problems of war, environmental issues, population, race relations, new religious movements, and neo-Gandhian social theory.

James W. Loewen is professor emeritus of sociology at UVM. He holds a BA in sociology from Carleton College, and an MA and a PhD in sociology from Harvard University. He taught for 7 years at predominantly black Tougaloo College in Mississippi before coming to the predominantly white UVM. His three-way study of race relations, *The Mississippi Chinese: Between Black and White*, in its second edition, is widely used in sociology courses. Loewen has also been an expert witness in more than 40 civil rights and voting rights cases involving African American, Hispanic, and Asian American plaintiffs. *Lies My Teacher Told Me*, his analysis of what we mislearn in American history, was published in 1994 by The New Press.

Sarah J. Mahler is an associate professor of sociology/anthropology at Florida International University. She holds a BA from Amherst College, and a PhD from Columbia University. She specializes in cultural anthropology, in particular, race and ethnicity in the United States and current immigration from Latin America and the Caribbean. Among her recent publications are *American Dreaming: Immigrant Life on the Margins* (1995) and *Salvadorans in Suburbia: Symbiosis and Conflict* (1995).

Elaine McCrate is an associate professor of economics and women's studies at UVM. She has a BA from Ohio State University, and a PhD from the University of Massachusetts. She teaches in the areas of labor, demography, and the economics of gender and race. She is currently doing research on teenage mothers, welfare, and gender and race wage differentials.

Mbulelo Mzamane is an associate professor of African/third world literature and African/international studies at UVM, and rector and vice chancellor of the University of Fort Hare (South Africa), where he is jointly appointed. He received a BA in English and philosophy, a concurrent certificate in education, and an MA in English literature/linguistics from the University of Botswana, Lesotho, and Swaziland (UBLS). He has a PhD in African/English literature from the University of Sheffield. He has held other academic posts at UBLS, the University of Sheffield, Ahmadu Bello University, Yale University, and the University of Georgia. He is the author of numerous articles and books, including *The Children of Soweto, My Cousin Comes to Jo'burg and Other Stories, Children of the Diaspora*, and *Mzala*. He has edited several books of poetry and fiction, including: *Selected Poems of Sipho Sepamla, Selected Poems of Mongane Serote*, and *Hungry Flames and Other Black South African Short Stories*. He is co-editor of several works, including *Images of the Voiceless: Essays on Popular Culture and Art, Global Voices: Non-Western World Literature*, and *Contemporary Writing From the Non-Western World*.

Cynthia Beth Rubin is an independent artist who occasionally teaches at the Rhode Island School of Design. She received her BA in art from Antioch College and her MFA in painting from the Maryland Institute of Art. Drawing on the legacy of Jewish culture, she uses the new technology of the computer as an instrument of cultural retrieval, incorporating traditional motifs in constructing both video works and fixed images. Her computer animations *Inherited Memories* (1997) and *Les affinités recouvrées* (1994) screened at festivals around the world, including France, the Netherlands, Israel, Canada, Poland, Russia, the United Kingdom, Brazil, and Morocco, as well as in the United States. Her computer painting/collages have also received international attention in exhibitions and publications in North America, Asia, and Europe.

Author Index

Subject Index

A

Affirmative Action programs, 62, 129–130
African American literature, 87 *ff.*
Allen, R., 116
America, 69 *ff.*, 83
  majority groups in, 70
  as meritocracy, 69
  minority groups in, 70–71
  multiracialism in, 35–37
  as open society, 69–70
  pluralism of, 109–110
  race relations in, 83–85, 105
  as racially segregated society, 56
  racism in, 70 *ff.*
  slavery in, 52–53
American Indian Movement (AIM), 36–37
American racism, 153 *ff.*
African American and economy in,
    125–126
  economic inequality and, 125
  institutional racism and, 125–128
  Native Americans victims of, 38 *ff.*
Anglocultural populations, 79 *ff.*
  bigotry of, 79
Assimilation, 21–25 passim
  accommodation and, 25
  cultural, 24–25

B

Baldwin, J., 88–89, 92
Binet, A., 9
Birmingham bus boycott, 99
Black Nationalism, 99
Black Panther Party, 100
Blumenbach, J. F., 7

Bolshevik Revolution, 81–82
*Brown v. Board of Education of Topeka,
    Kansas* (1954, 1955), 95, 99
Buffon, G., 7
Burt, Cyril, 10
Bush (R) Administration, 97–98

C

Cairnes, J. E., 8
Chamberlain, H. S., 7
Chesnutt, C. W., 88
Clinton (D) Administration, 98–99
Columbus, C., 36–37, 48–49
  as white supremacist hero, 48
Conflict, 67 *ff.*
  teaching, 67–74 passim
Congress of Racial Equality (CORE), 99
Jim Crow, Crowism, *see* Discrimination

D

Darwin, C., 7–8
  biological basis of, 7
  Herbert Spencer and, 8
Dash, J., 88
de Gobineau, A., 7
Discrimination, 26 *ff.*, 45 *ff.*, 109–110
  environmental pollution and, 56–57
  impact of, 45–47
  inferior local services and, 57
  institutionalized, 26–27
  integration and, 63–63
  psychology of, 53–54
  restrictive covenants and, 27n
  segregation as, 26–27
  social structure of, 55–56

167